PostgreSQL High Performance Cookbook

Mastering query optimization, database monitoring, and performance-tuning for PostgreSQL

Chitij Chauhan
Dinesh Kumar

Packt>

BIRMINGHAM - MUMBAI

PostgreSQL High Performance Cookbook

First published: March 2017

Production reference: 1240317

Published by Packt Publishing Ltd.
Livery Place
35 Livery Street
Birmingham
B3 2PB, UK.
ISBN 978-1-78528-433-5

www.packtpub.com

Credits

Authors

Chitij Chauhan
Dinesh Kumar

Reviewers

Baji Shaik
Feng Tan

Commissioning Editor

Dipika Gaonkar

Acquisition Editor

Nitin Dasan

Content Development Editor

Mayur Pawanikar

Technical Editor

Dinesh Pawar

Copy Editor

Safis Editing

Project Coordinator

Nidhi Joshi

Proofreader

Safis Editing

Indexer

Aishwarya Gangawane

Production Coordinator

Shraddha Falebhai

About the Authors

Chitij Chauhan currently works as a senior database administrator at an IT-based MNC in Chandigarh. He has over 10 years of work experience in the field of database and system administration, with specialization in MySQL clustering, PostgreSQL, Greenplum, Informix DB2, SQL Server 2008, Sybase, and Oracle. He is a leading expert in the area of database security, with expertise in database security products such as IBM InfoSphere Guardium, Oracle Database Vault, and Imperva.

Dinesh Kumar is an enthusiastic open source developer and has written several open source tools for PostgreSQL. He recently announced pgBucket, a brand new job scheduler for PostgreSQL. He is also a frequent blogger at `manojadinesh.blogpsot.com`, where he talks more about PostgreSQL. He is currently working as a senior database engineer in OpenSCG and building the PostgreSQL cloud operations. He has more than 6 years of experience as an Oracle and PostgreSQL database administrator and developer, and is currently focusing on PostgreSQL.

Thanks to my loving parents, Sreenivasulu and Vanamma, who raised me in a small village called Viruvuru, which is in the Nellore district of India. Thanks to my loving wife, Manoja, who enlightens my life with her wonderful support. Also, thanks to my friend Baji Shaik and coordinators, Mayur Pawanikar and Nitin Dasan, for their excellent support. Finally, thanks to every PostgreSQL contributor, author, and blogger.

About the Reviewers

Baji Shaik is a database administrator and developer. He is a co-author of *PostgreSQL Development Essentials* and has tech-reviewed *Troubleshooting PostgreSQL* by Packt Publishing. He is currently working as a database consultant at OpenSCG. He has an engineering degree in telecommunications, and had started his career as a C# and Java developer. Baji started working with databases in 2011, and over the years he has worked with Oracle, PostgreSQL, and Greenplum. His background spans a length and breadth of expertise and experience in SQL/NoSQL database technologies. He has good knowledge of automation, orchestration, and DevOps in a cloud environment. He likes to watch movies, read books, and write technical blogs. He also loves to spend time with family. Baji is a certified PostgreSQL professional.

Feng Tan is from China. His nickname is Francs. He was a PostgreSQL DBA at SkyMobi (NASDAQ: MOBI) for more than 5 years, where he was maintaining more than 100 PostgreSQL instances. He gave presentations at the China PostgreSQL conference on topics such as Oracle VS PostgreSQL and PostgreSQL 9.4 new features.

Feng Tan likes to share PostgreSQL technology in his blog at `http://francs3.blog.163.com/`. He is also one of the translators of PostgreSQL 9 Administration Cookbook Chinese Edition.

Currently, he serves as the open source database administrator at China Mobile Group Zhejiang Co. Ltd.

www.PacktPub.com

For support files and downloads related to your book, please visit www.PacktPub.com.

Did you know that Packt offers eBook versions of every book published, with PDF and ePub files available? You can upgrade to the eBook version at www.PacktPub.com and as a print book customer, you are entitled to a discount on the eBook copy. Get in touch with us at service@packtpub.com for more details.

At www.PacktPub.com, you can also read a collection of free technical articles, sign up for a range of free newsletters and receive exclusive discounts and offers on Packt books and eBooks.

 Mapt

https://www.packtpub.com/mapt

Get the most in-demand software skills with Mapt. Mapt gives you full access to all Packt books and video courses, as well as industry-leading tools to help you plan your personal development and advance your career.

Why subscribe?

- Fully searchable across every book published by Packt
- Copy and paste, print, and bookmark content
- On demand and accessible via a web browser

Customer Feedback

Thanks for purchasing this Packt book. At Packt, quality is at the heart of our editorial process. To help us improve, please leave us an honest review on this book's Amazon page at `https://www.amazon.com/dp/1785284339`.

If you'd like to join our team of regular reviewers, you can e-mail us at `customerreviews@packtpub.com`. We award our regular reviewers with free eBooks and videos in exchange for their valuable feedback. Help us be relentless in improving our products!

Table of Contents

Preface

PostgreSQL is one of the most powerful and easy-to-use database management systems. It has strong support from the community and is being actively developed with a new release every year. PostgreSQL supports the most advanced features included in SQL standards. It also provides NoSQL capabilities and very rich data types and extensions. All of this makes PostgreSQL a very attractive solution in software systems. If you run a database, you want it to perform well and you want to be able to secure it. As the world's most advanced open source database, PostgreSQL has unique built-in ways to achieve these goals. This book will show you a multitude of ways to enhance your database's performance and give you insights into measuring and optimizing a PostgreSQL database to achieve better performance.

What this book covers

Chapter 1, *Database Benchmarking*, deals with a few major system component benchmarkings such as CPU, disk, and IOPS, besides database benchmarking. In this chapter, we will discuss a benchmarking frame called phoronix, along with disk RAID levels.

Chapter 2, *Server Configuration and Control*, deals with how to control the PostgreSQL instance behavior with the help of a few major configuration parameter settings.

Chapter 3, *Device Optimization*, discusses CPU, disk, and memory-related parameters. Besides this, we will be discussing memory components of PostgreSQL along with how to analyze the buffer cache contents.

Chapter 4, *Monitoring Server Performance*, discuss, various Unix/Linux related operating system utilities that can help the DBA in performance analysis and troubleshooting issues.

Chapter 5, *Connection Pooling and Database Partitioning*, covers connection pooling methods such as pgpool and pgbouncer. Also, we will be discussing a few partitioning techniques that PostgreSQL offers.

Chapter 6, *High Availability and Replication*, is about various high availability and replication solutions, including some popular third-party replication tools such as Slony, Londiste, and Bucardo. Also, we will be discussing how to set up the PostgreSQL XL cluster.

Chapter 7, *Working with Third-Party Replication Management Utilities*, discusses different third-party replication management tools, such as repmgr. Also, this chapter covers a backup management tool called Barman, along with WAL management tools, such as walctl.

Chapter 8, *Database Monitoring and Performance*, shows different aspects of how and what to monitor in the PostgreSQL instance to achieve the better performance. Also, in this chapter, we will be discussing a few troubleshooting techniques that will help the DBA team.

Chapter 9, *Vacuum Internals*, is about MVCC and how to handle PostgreSQL's transaction wraparound issues. Also, we will see how to control the bloat using snapshot threshold settings.

Chapter 10, *Data Migration from Other Databases to PostgreSQL and Upgrading PostgreSQL Cluster*, covers heterogeneous replication between Oracle and PostgreSQL using Goldengate.

Chapter 11, *Query Optimization*, discusses the functionality of PostgreSQL query planner. Besides this, we will be discussing several query processing algorithms with examples.

Chapter 12, *Database Indexing*, covers various index loop techniques PostgreSQL follows. Besides, we will be discussing various index management methods, such as how to find unused or missing indexes from the database.

What you need for this book

In general, a modern Unix-compatible platform should be able to run PostgreSQL. To make the most out of this book, you also require CentOS 7. The minimum hardware required to install and run PostgreSQL is as follows:

- 1 GHz processor
- 1 GB of RAM
- 512 MB of HDD

Who this book is for

If you are a developer or administrator with limited PostgreSQL knowledge and want to develop your skills with this great open source database, then this book is ideal for you. Learning how to enhance the database performance is always an exciting topic to everyone, and this book will show you enough ways to enhance the database performance.

Sections

In this book, you will find several headings that appear frequently (Getting ready, How to do it, How it works, There's more, and See also).

To give clear instructions on how to complete a recipe, we use these sections as follows.

Getting ready

This section tells you what to expect in the recipe, and describes how to set up any software or any preliminary settings required for the recipe.

How to do it...

This section contains the steps required to follow the recipe.

How it works...

This section usually consists of a detailed explanation of what happened in the previous section.

There's more...

This section consists of additional information about the recipe in order to make the reader more knowledgeable about the recipe.

See also

This section provides helpful links to other useful information for the recipe.

Conventions

In this book, you will find a number of text styles that distinguish between different kinds of information. Here are some examples of these styles and an explanation of their meaning.

Code words in text, database table names, folder names, filenames, file extensions, pathnames, dummy URLs, user input, and Twitter handles are shown as follows: "In Linux, `tmpfs` is a temporary filesystem, which uses the RAM rather than the disk storage."

Any command-line input or output is written as follows:

```
$ phoronix-test-suite benchmark pts/memory
Phoronix Test Suite v6.8.0
Installed: pts/ramspeed-1.4.0
To Install: pts/stream-1.3.1
To Install: pts/cachebench-1.0.0
```

New terms and **important words** are shown in bold. Words that you see on the screen, for example, in menus or dialog boxes, appear in the text like this: "Select the product pack **Fusion Middleware** and the **Linux x86-64 platform**. Click on the **Go** button."

> Warnings or important notes appear in a box like this.

> Tips and tricks appear like this.

Reader feedback

Feedback from our readers is always welcome. Let us know what you think about this book-what you liked or disliked. Reader feedback is important for us as it helps us develop titles that you will really get the most out of.

To send us general feedback, simply e-mail feedback@packtpub.com, and mention the book's title in the subject of your message.

If there is a topic that you have expertise in and you are interested in either writing or contributing to a book, see our author guide at www.packtpub.com/authors.

Customer support

Now that you are the proud owner of a Packt book, we have a number of things to help you to get the most from your purchase.

Downloading the example code

You can download the example code files for this book from your account at http://www.p acktpub.com. If you purchased this book elsewhere, you can visit http://www.packtpub.c om/support and register to have the files e-mailed directly to you.

You can download the code files by following these steps:

1. Log in or register to our website using your e-mail address and password.
2. Hover the mouse pointer on the **SUPPORT** tab at the top.
3. Click on **Code Downloads & Errata**.
4. Enter the name of the book in the **Search** box.
5. Select the book for which you're looking to download the code files.
6. Choose from the drop-down menu where you purchased this book from.
7. Click on **Code Download**.

You can also download the code files by clicking on the **Code Files** button on the book's webpage at the Packt Publishing website. This page can be accessed by entering the book's name in the **Search** box. Please note that you need to be logged in to your Packt account.

Once the file is downloaded, please make sure that you unzip or extract the folder using the latest version of:

- WinRAR / 7-Zip for Windows
- Zipeg / iZip / UnRarX for Mac
- 7-Zip / PeaZip for Linux

The code bundle for the book is also hosted on GitHub at https://github.com/PacktPubl ishing/PostgreSQL-High-Performance-Cookbook. We also have other code bundles from our rich catalog of books and videos available at https://github.com/PacktPublishing/. Check them out!

Errata

Although we have taken every care to ensure the accuracy of our content, mistakes do happen. If you find a mistake in one of our books-maybe a mistake in the text or the code- we would be grateful if you could report this to us. By doing so, you can save other readers from frustration and help us improve subsequent versions of this book. If you find any errata, please report them by visiting `http://www.packtpub.com/submit-errata`, selecting your book, clicking on the **Errata Submission Form** link, and entering the details of your errata. Once your errata are verified, your submission will be accepted and the errata will be uploaded to our website or added to any list of existing errata under the Errata section of that title.

To view the previously submitted errata, go to `https://www.packtpub.com/books/content/support`and enter the name of the book in the search field. The required information will appear under the **Errata** section.

Piracy

Piracy of copyrighted material on the Internet is an ongoing problem across all media. At Packt, we take the protection of our copyright and licenses very seriously. If you come across any illegal copies of our works in any form on the Internet, please provide us with the location address or website name immediately so that we can pursue a remedy.

Please contact us at `copyright@packtpub.com` with a link to the suspected pirated material.

We appreciate your help in protecting our authors and our ability to bring you valuable content.

Questions

If you have a problem with any aspect of this book, you can contact us at `questions@packtpub.com`, and we will do our best to address the problem.

1
Database Benchmarking

In this chapter, we will cover the following recipes:

- CPU benchmarking
- Memory benchmarking
- Disk benchmarking
- Performing a seek rate test
- Working with the fysnc commit rate
- Checking IOPS
- Storage sizing
- Discussing RAID levels
- Configuring pgbench
- Running read/write pgbench tests

Introduction

PostgreSQL is renowned in the database management system world. With every PostgreSQL release, it's gaining in popularity due to its advanced features and performance. This cookbook is especially designed to give more information about most of the major features in PostgreSQL, and also how to achieve good performance with the help of proper hardware/software benchmarking tools. This cookbook is also designed to discuss, all the high availability options we can achieve with PostgreSQL, and also give some details about how to migrate your database from other commercial databases.

To benchmark the database server, we need to benchmark several hardware/software components. In this chapter, we will discuss major tools that are especially designed to benchmark a certain component.

I would like to say thanks to the Phoronix Test Suite team, for allowing me to discuss their benchmarking tool. Phoronix is an open source benchmarking framework, which, by default, provides test cases for several hardware/software components, thanks to its extensible architecture, where we can write our own test suite with the set of benchmarking test cases. Phoronix also supports to upload your benchmarking results to `http://openben chmarking.org/`, which is a public/private benchmark results repository, where we can compare our your benchmarking results with others.

> Go to the following URL for installation instructions for Phoronix Test Suite:
> `http://www.phoronix-test-suite.com/?k=downloads.`

CPU benchmarking

In this recipe, let's discuss how to benchmark the CPU speed using various open source benchmarking tools.

Getting ready

One of the ways to benchmark CPU power is by measuring the wall clock time for the submitted task. The task can be like calculating the factorial of the given number, or calculating the nth Fibonacci number, or some other CPU-intensive task.

How to do it...

Let us discuss about how to configure phoronix and sysbench tools to benchmark the CPU:

Phoronix

Phoronix supports a set of CPU tests in a test suite called CPU. This test suite covers multiple CPU-intensive tasks, which are mentioned at the following URL:
`https://openbenchmarking.org/suite/pts/CPU.`

If you want to run this CPU test suite, then you need to execute the Phoronix Test Suite benchmark CPU command as a root user. We can also run a specific test by mentioning its test name. For example, let's run a sample CPU benchmarking test as follows:

```
$ phoronix-test-suite benchmark pts/himeno
Phoronix Test Suite v6.8.0
    To Install: pts/himeno-1.2.0
    ...
    1 Test To Install
    pts/himeno-1.2.0:
        Test Installation 1 of 1
        1 File Needed
        Downloading: himenobmtxpa.tar.bz2
  Started Run 2 @ 05:53:40
  Started Run 3 @ 05:54:35  [Std. Dev: 1.66%]
Test Results:
  1503.636072
  1512.166077
  1550.985494
Average: 1522.26 MFLOPS
```

Phoronix also provides a way to observe the detailed test results via HTML file. Also, it supports the offline generation of PDF, JSON, CSV, and text format outputs. To open these test results in the browser, we need to execute the following command:

```
$ phoronix-test-suite show-result <Test Name>
```

The following is a sample screenshot of the results of the preceding command:

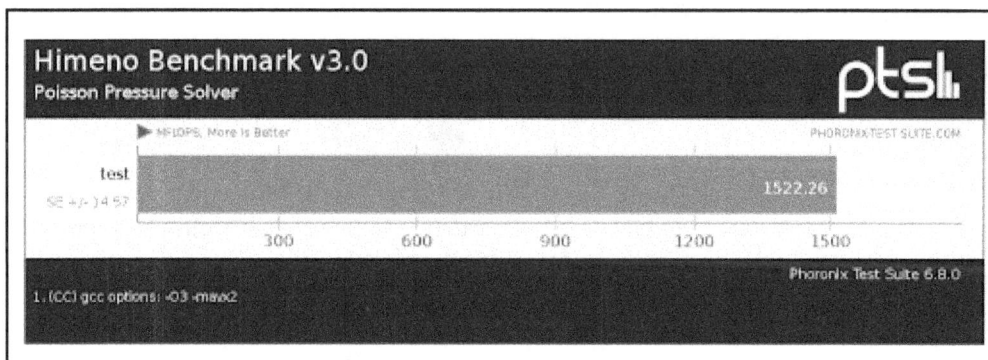

sysbench

The `sysbench` tool provides a CPU task, which calculates the number of prime numbers within a given range and provides the CPU-elapsed time. Let's execute the `sysbench` command as shown in the following screenshot, to retrieve the CPU measurements:

```
[root@localhost ~]# sysbench --test=CPU --CPU-max-prime=10000 --num-
threads=4 run
    Doing CPU performance benchmark
    Threads started!
    Done.
    Maximum prime number checked in CPU test: 10000
    Test execution summary:
        total time:                          3.2531s
        total number of events:              10000
        total time taken by event execution: 13.0040
        per-request statistics:
            min:                                 1.10ms
            avg:                                 1.30ms
            max:                                 8.60ms
            approx.  95 percentile:              1.43ms
    Threads fairness:
        events (avg/stddev):            2500.0000/8.46
        execution time (avg/stddev):    3.2510/0.00
```

How it works...

The preceding results are collected from CentOS 7, which was running virtually on a Windows 10 machine. The virtual machine has four processing units (CPU cores) of Intel Core i7-4510U of CPU family six.

Phoronix

The URL http://openbenchmarking.org/ provides a detailed description of each test detail along with its implementation, and would encourage you to read more information about the himeno test case.

sysbench

From the previous results, the system takes 3.2531 seconds to compute the 10,000 prime numbers, with the help of four background threads.

Memory benchmarking

In this recipe, we will be discussing how to benchmark the memory speed using open source tools.

Getting ready

As with the CPU test suite, phoronix supports one another memory test suite, which covers RAM benchmarking. Otherwise, we can also use a dedicated memtest86 benchmarking tool, which performs memory benchmarking during a server bootup phase. Another neat trick would be to create a tmpfs mount point in the RAM and then create a tablespace on it in PostgreSQL. Once we create the tablespace, we can then create in-memory tables, where we can benchmark the table read/write operations. We can also use the dd command to measure the memory read/write operations.

How to do it...

Let us discuss how to install phoronix and how to configure the tmpfs mount point in Linux:

Phoronix

Let's execute the following phoronix command, which will install the memory test suit and perform memory benchmarking. Once the benchmarking is completed, as aforementioned, observe the HTML report:

```
$ phoronix-test-suite benchmark pts/memory
Phoronix Test Suite v6.8.0
  Installed: pts/ramspeed-1.4.0
  To Install: pts/stream-1.3.1
  To Install: pts/cachebench-1.0.0
```

tmpfs

In Linux, tmpfs is a temporary filesystem, which uses the RAM rather than the disk storage. Anything we store in tmpfs will be cleared once we restart the system:

Refer to the URL for more information about tmpfs: `https://en.wikiped`
`ia.org/wiki/Tmpfs` and `https://www.jamescoyle.net/knowledge`
`/1659-what-is-tmpfs`.

Let's create a new mount point based on `tmpfs` using the following command:

```
# mkdir -p /memmount
# mount -t tmpfs -o size=1g tmpfs /memmount
# df -kh -t tmpfs
Filesystem       Size   Used  Avail  Use%  Mounted on
tmpfs            1.9G   96K   1.9G    1%   /dev/shm
tmpfs            1.9G  8.9M   1.9G    1%   /run
tmpfs            1.9G     0   1.9G    0%   /sys/fs/cgroup
tmpfs            1.0G     0   1.0G    0%   /memmount
```

Let's create a new folder in `memmount` and assign it to the tablespace.

```
# mkdir -p /memmount/memtabspace
# chown -R postgres:postgres /memmount/memtabspace/
postgres=# CREATE TABLESPACE memtbs LOCATION '/memmount/memtabspace';
CREATE TABLESPACE
postgres=# CREATE TABLE memtable(t INT) TABLESPACE memtbs;
CREATE TABLE
```

Write test

```
postgres=# INSERT INTO memtable VALUES(generate_series(1, 1000000));
INSERT 0 1000000
Time: 1372.763 ms

postgres=# SELECT
pg_size_pretty(pg_relation_size('memtable'::regclass));
 pg_size_pretty ----------------
 35 MB (1 row)
```

From the preceding results, to insert 1 million records it took approximately 1 second with a writing speed of 35 MB per second.

Read test

```
postgres=# SELECT COUNT(*) FROM memtable;
count
---------
1000000
(1 row)
Time: 87.333 ms
```

From the preceding results, to read the 1 million records it took approximately 90 milliseconds with a reading speed of 385 MB per second, which is pretty fast for the local system configuration. The preceding read test was performed after clearing the system cache and by restarting the PostgreQSL instance, which avoids the system buffers.

How it works...

In the preceding `tmpfs` example, we created an in-memory table, and all the system calls PostgreQSL tries to perform to read/write the data will be directly affecting the memory rather than the disk, which gives a major performance boost. Also, we need to consider to drop these in-memory tablespace, tables after testing, since these objects will physically vanish after system reboot.

Disk benchmarking

In this recipe, we will be discussing how to benchmark the disk speed using open source tools.

Getting ready

The well-known command to perform disk I/O benchmarking is dd. We all use the dd command to measure read/write operations by specifying the required block size, and we also measure the direct I/O by skipping the system write buffers. Similarly, phoronix supports a complete test suite for the disk as CPU and memory that perform different storage-related tests. Another famous disk benchmarking tool is bonnie++, which provides more flexibility in measuring the disk I/O.

How to do it...

Let us discuss how to run the disk benchmarking using phoronix and using bonnie++ testing tools:

Phoronix

To run the complete disk test suite on the system, run the following command:

```
$ phoronix-test-suite benchmark pts/disk
```

Phoronix also supports a quick I/O test case, where you can perform an instant disk performance test using the following command test, which is interactive and collects the input, and then runs the test cases:

```
$ phoronix-test-suite benchmark pts/iozone
Phoronix Test Suite v6.8.0
    Installed: pts/iozone-1.8.0
Disk Test Configuration
        1: 4Kb
        2: 64Kb
        3: 1MB
        4: Test All Options
        Record Size: 1
        1: 512MB
        2: 2GB
        3: 4GB
        4: 8GB
        5: Test All Options
        File Size: 1
        1: Write Performance
        2: Read Performance
        3: Test All Options
        Disk Test: 3
```

bonnie++

bonnie++ is a filesystem and disk-level benchmarking tool and can perform the same test multiple times. You can install this tool using either yum or apt-get install or installing it via the source code. Let's run the bulk I/O test case using the following arguments, where it tries to create 8 GB files:

```
$ /usr/local/sbin/bonnie++ -D -d /tmp/ -s 8G -b
Writing with putc()...done
```

```
Writing intelligently...done
...
localhost.localdomain,8G,68996,106,14151,53,46772,15,95343,93,123633,16,201
.0,7,16,795,58,+++++,+++,733,46,757,57,+++++,+++,592,38
```

How it works…

Let us discuss how the bonnie++ performs the benchmarking, and what are all the tools bonnie++ offers to understand the benchmarking results:

bonnie++

From the preceding test case, we provided the results the bonnie++ as to use only direct I/O using the -D option. Also, we asked to create 8 GB random files in the /tmp/ location to measure the disk speed. As the final output from bonnie++, we will get CSV values, which we need to feed to the bon_csv2html command, which provides some detailed information about the test results, as shown in the following screenshot:

```
$ echo
"localhost.localdomain,8G,68996,106,14151,53,46772,15,95343,93,123633,16,20
1.0,7,16,795,58,+++++,+++,733,46,757,57,+++++,+++,592,38"|bon_csv2html >
~/Desktop/bonresults.html
```

	Size:Chunk Size	Sequential Output					Sequential Input				Random Seeks		Num Files	Sequential Create						Random Create					
		Per Char		Block		Rewrite		Per Char		Block					Create		Read		Delete		Create		Read		Delete	
		K/sec	% CPU	K/sec	% CPU	K/sec	% CPU	K/sec	% CPU	K/sec	% CPU	/ sec	% CPU		/ sec	% CPU	/ sec	% CPU	/ sec	% CPU	/ sec	% CPU	/ sec	% CPU	/ sec	% CPU
localhost.localdomain	8G	68996	106	14151	53	46772	15	95343	93	123633	16	201.0	7	16	795	58	+++++	+++	733	46	757	57	+++++	+++	592	38

bonnie++ performs three different tests for disk benchmarking. They are read, write and then seek speed. We will be discussing the seek rate in the further topics. The bonnie++ do always recommend to have high number in /sec section in the preceding table, and lower % CPU values for better disk performance. Also, ++++ shows that the test was not performed accurately by bonnie++, as the test was incomplete with the provided arguments. To get the complete results, we need to rerun the same test multiple times using the -n option, where bonnie will get enough time/resources to complete the job.

Performing a seek rate test

In this recipe, we will be discussing how to benchmark the disk seek rate speed using open source tools.

Getting ready

A file can be read from the disk in two ways: sequentially and at random. Reading a file in sequential order requires less effort than reading a file in random order. In PostgreSQL and other database systems, a file needs to be scanned in random order as per the index scans. During the index scans, as per the index lookups, the relation file needs to fetch the data randomly, by moving its file pointer backward and forward, which needs an additional mechanical overhead in spinning the disk in the normal HDD. In SSD, this overhead is lower as it uses the flash memory. This is one of the reasons why we define that `random_page_cost` as always higher than `seq_page_cost` in `postgresql.conf`. In the previous bonnie++ example, we have random seeks, which were measured per second as 201.0 and used 7% of the CPU.

How to do it...

We can use the same bonnie++ utility command to measure the random seek rate, or we can also use another disk latency benchmarking tool called ioping:

```
# ioping -R /dev/sda3 -s 8k -w 30
--- /dev/sda3 (block device 65.8 GiB) ioping statistics ---
2.23 k requests completed in 29.2 s, 17.5 MiB read, 76 iops, 613.4
KiB/s
generated 2.24 k requests in 30.0 s, 17.5 MiB, 74 iops, 596.2 KiB/s
min/avg/max/mdev = 170.6 us / 13.0 ms / 73.5 ms / 5.76 ms
```

How it works...

Ioping is a disk latency benchmarking tool that produces an output similar to the network utility command ping. This tool also provides no cache or with cache disk benchmarking as bonnie++ and also includes synchronous and asynchronous I/O latency benchmarking. You can install this tool using yum or apt-get in the respective Linux distributions. The preceding results were generated based on PostgreSQL's default block size of 8 KB, which ran for 30 seconds. Ioping provides another useful feature called ping-pong mode for read/write. This mode displays the instant read/write speed of the disk as shown in the following screenshot:

```
$ ioping -G /tmp/ -D -s 8k
8 KiB >>> /tmp/ (xfs /dev/sda3): request=1 time=1.50 ms (warmup)
8 KiB <<< /tmp/ (xfs /dev/sda3): request=2 time=9.73 ms
8 KiB >>> /tmp/ (xfs /dev/sda3): request=3 time=2.00 ms
8 KiB <<< /tmp/ (xfs /dev/sda3): request=4 time=1.02 ms
8 KiB >>> /tmp/ (xfs /dev/sda3): request=5 time=1.95 ms
```

In the preceding example, we ran ioping in ping-pong mode (-G) and used the direct I/O (-D) with a block size of 8 KB. We can also run the same ping-pong mode in pure cache mode using the (-C) option.

Working with the fsync commit rate

In this recipe, we will be discussing how to benchmark the fsync speed using open source tools.

Getting ready

Fsync is a system call that flushes the data from system buffers into physical files. In PostgreSQL, whenever a CHECKPOINT operation occurs, it internally initiates the fsync, to flush all the modified system buffers into the respective files. The fsync benchmarking defines the transfer ratio of data from memory to the disk.

How to do it...

To perform `fsync` benchmarking, we can use a dedicated benchmark test called `fs-mark` from Phoronix. This `fs-mark` test was built based on a filesystem benchmarking tool called `fs_mark`, or `fio`, which supports several `fsync` test cases. We can run this `fs-mark` test case using the following command:

```
$ phoronix-test-suite benchmark fs-mark FS-Mark 3.3:
    pts/fs-mark-1.0.1
    Disk Test Configuration
        1: 1000 Files, 1MB Size
        2: 1000 Files, 1MB Size, No Sync/FSync
        3: 5000 Files, 1MB Size, 4 Threads
        4: 4000 Files, 32 Sub Dirs, 1MB Size
        5: Test All Options
        Test:
```

The preceding command failed to install while testing on the local machine. Once I installed `glibc-static` via `yum install`, then the test went smooth.

How it works...

Phoronix installs all the binaries on the local machine when we start benchmarking the corresponding test. In the preceding command, we are benchmarking the test `fs-mark`, where it installs the tool at `~/.phoronix-test-suite/installed-tests/pts/fs-mark-1.0.1/fs_mark-3.3`. Let's go to the location, and let's see what fsync tests it supports:

```
./fs_mark -help
Usage: fs_mark
        -S Sync Method (              0:No Sync,
        1:fsyncBeforeClose,
        2:sync/1_fsync,
        3:PostReverseFsync,
        4:syncPostReverseFsync,
        5:PostFsync,
        6:syncPostFsync)
```

I would encourage you to read the readme file, which exists in the same location, for detailed information about the sync methods. Let's run a simple `fs_mark` benchmarking by choosing one sync method as shown in the following here:

```
./fs_mark -w 8096 -S 1 -s 102400 -d /tmp/ -L 3 -n 500
#   ./fs_mark  -w  8096  -S  1  -s  102400  -d  /tmp/  -L  3  -n  500
#       Version 3.3, 1 thread(s) starting at Fri Dec 30 04:26:28 2016
#       Sync method: INBAND FSYNC: fsync() per file in write loop.
#       Directories:  no subdirectories used
#       File names: 40 bytes long, (16 initial bytes of time stamp with 24
random bytes at end of name)
#       Files info: size 102400 bytes, written with an IO size of 8096
bytes per write
#       App overhead is time in microseconds spent in the test not doing
file writing related system calls.
FSUse%        Count        Size     Files/sec     App Overhead
    39          500       102400       156.4           17903
    39         1000       102400        78.9           22906
    39         1500       102400       116.2           24269
```

We ran the preceding test with write files of size 102,400 and block size of 8,096. The number of files it needs to create is 500 and it needs to repeat the test three times by choosing sync method 1, which closes the file after writing the content to disk.

Checking IOPS

In this recipe, we will be discussing how to benchmark the disk IOPS using open source tools.

Getting ready

As mentioned previously, a disk can be read in either sequential or random orders. To measure the disk accurately, we need to perform more random read/write operations, which gives more stress to the disk. To calculate the **IOPS (Input/Output Per Second)** of a disk, we can either use fio or bonnie++ tools, which do sequential/random operations over the disk. In this chapter, let's use the **fio (Flexible I/O)** tool to calculate the IOPS for the disk.

How to do it...

Let's download the latest version of the `fio` module from `http://brick.kernel.dk/snaps /`, also download `libaio-devel`, which would be the `ioengine` we will be using for the IOPS. This `ioengine` defines, how the `fio` module needs to submit the I/O requests to the kernel. There are multiple ioengines you can specify for the I/O requests such as `sync`, `mmap`, and so on. You can refer to the main page of fio for all the supported ioengines. After downloading the fio module, let's follow the regular Linux source installation method as `configure`, `make`, and `make install`.

Sequential mixed read and write

Let's run a sample sequential mixed read/write, as shown here:

```
$ ./fio --ioengine=libaio --direct=1 --name=test_seq_mix_rw --
filename=test_seq --bs=8k --iodepth=32 --size=1G --readwrite=rw --
rwmixread=50
    test_seq_mix_rw: (g=0): rw=rw, bs=8K-8K/8K-8K/8K-8K, ioengine=libaio,
iodepth=32
    ...
    ...
    test_seq_mix_rw: (groupid=0, jobs=1): err= 0: pid=43596: Fri Dec 30
23:31:11 2016
       read : io=525088KB, bw=1948.1KB/s, iops=243 , runt=269430msec
    ...
        bw (KB/s)  : min=    15, max= 6183, per=100.00%, avg=2002.59,
```

```
stdev=1253.68
    write: io=523488KB, bw=1942.1KB/s, iops=242 , runt=269430msec
  ...
      bw (KB/s)  : min=  192, max= 5888, per=100.00%, avg=2001.74,
stdev=1246.19
  ...
    Run status group 0 (all jobs):
      READ: io=525088KB, aggrb=1948KB/s, minb=1948KB/s, maxb=1948KB/s,
mint=269430msec, maxt=269430msec
      WRITE: io=523488KB, aggrb=1942KB/s, minb=1942KB/s, maxb=1942KB/s,
mint=269430msec, maxt=269430msec
    Disk stats (read/write):
      sda: ios=65608/65423, merge=0/5, ticks=869519/853644,
in_queue=1723445, util=99.85%
```

Random mixed read and write

Let's run a sample random mixed read/write, as shown here:

```
$ ./fio --ioengine=libaio --direct=1 --name=test_rand_mix_rw --
filename=test_rand --bs=8k --iodepth=32 --size=1G --readwrite=randrw --
rwmixread=50
    test_rand_mix_rw: (g=0): rw=randrw, bs=8K-8K/8K-8K/8K-8K,
ioengine=libaio, iodepth=32
  ...
  ...
    test_rand_mix_rw: (groupid=0, jobs=1): err= 0: pid=43893: Fri Dec 30
23:49:19 2016
    read : io=525088KB, bw=1018.9KB/s, iops=127 , runt=515375msec
  ...
      bw (KB/s)  : min=    8, max= 6720, per=100.00%, avg=1124.47,
stdev=964.38
    write: io=523488KB, bw=1015.8KB/s, iops=126 , runt=515375msec
  ...
      bw (KB/s)  : min=    8, max= 6904, per=100.00%, avg=1125.46,
stdev=975.04
  ...
    Run status group 0 (all jobs):
      READ: io=525088KB, aggrb=1018KB/s, minb=1018KB/s, maxb=1018KB/s,
mint=515375msec, maxt=515375msec
      WRITE: io=523488KB, aggrb=1015KB/s, minb=1015KB/s, maxb=1015KB/s,
mint=515375msec, maxt=515375msec
    Disk stats (read/write):
      sda: ios=65609/65456, merge=0/4, ticks=7382037/5520238,
in_queue=12902772, util=100.00%
```

How it works...

We ran the preceding test cases to work on 1 GB (`--size`) file without any cache (`--direct`), by doing 32 concurrent I/O requests (`--iodepth`), with a block size of 8 KB (`--bs`) as 50% read and 50% write operations (`--rwmixread`). From the preceding sequential test results, the `bw` (bandwidth), IOPS values are pretty high when compared with random test results. That is, in sequential test cases, we gain approximately 50% more IOPS (`read=243`, `read=242`) than with the random IOPS (`read=127`, `write=126`).

Fio also provides more information such, as I/O submission latency and complete latency, along with CPU usage on the conducted test cases. I would encourage you to read more useful information about fio's features from its man pages.

Storage sizing

In this recipe, we will be discussing how to estimate disk growth using the pgbench tool.

Getting ready

One of the best practices to predict the database disk storage capacity is by loading a set of sample data into the application's database, and simulating production kind of actions using pgbench over a long period. For a period of time (every 1 hour), let's collect the database size using `pg_database_size()` or any native command, which returns the disk usage information. Once we get the periodic intervals for at least 24 hours, then we can find an average disk growth ratio by calculating the average of delta among each interval value.

How to do it...

Prepare the SQL script as follows, which simulates the live application behavior in the database:

```
Create connection;              --- Create/Use pool connection.
INSERT operation                --- Initial write operation.
SELECT pg_sleep(0.01);          --- Some application code runs here, and
waiting for the next query.
UPDATE operation                --- Update other tables for the newly
inserted records.
SELECT pg_sleep(0.1);           --- Updating other services which shows the
live graphs on the updated records.
DELETE operation                --- Delete or purge any unnecessary data.
SELECT pg_sleep(0.01);          --- Some application code overhead.
```

Let's run the following `pgbench` test case, with the preceding test file for 24 hours:

```
$ pgbench -T 86400 -f <script location> -c <number of concurrent
connections>
```

In parallel, let's schedule a job that collects the database size every hour using the `pg_database_size()` function, also schedule another job to run for every 10 minutes, which run the VACUUM on the database. This VACUUM job takes care of reclaiming the dead tuples logically at database level. However, in production servers, we will not deploy the VACUUM job to run for every 10 minutes, as the autovacuum process takes care of the dead tuples. As this test is not for database performance benchmarking, we can also make autovacuum more aggressive on the database side as well.

How it works...

Once we find the average disk growth per day, we can predict the database growth for the next 1 or 2 years. However, the database write rate also increases with the business growth. So, we need to deploy the database growth script or we need to analyze any disk storage trends from the monitoring tool to make a better prediction of the storage size.

Discussing RAID levels

In this recipe, we will be discussing about various RAID levels and their unique usage.

Getting ready

In this recipe, we will be discussing several RAID levels, which we configure for database requirements. **RAID (Redundant Array of Interdependent Disks)** has a dedicated hardware controller to deal with multiple disks, including a separate processor along with a battery backup cache, where data can be flushed to disk properly when a power failure occurs.

How to do it...

RAID levels can be differentiated as per their configurations. RAID supports configuration techniques such as striping, mirroring, and parity to improve the disk storage performance, or high availability. The most popular RAID levels are zero to six, and each level provides its own kind of disk storage capacity, read/write performance and high availability. The common RAID levels we configure for DBMS are 0, 1, 5, 6, or 10 (1 and 0).

How it works...

Let us discuss about how the mostly used RAID level works:

RAID 0

This configuration only focuses on read/write performance by striping the data across multiple devices. With this configuration, we can allocate the complete disk storage for the applications data. The major drawback in this configuration is no high availability. In the case of any single disk failure, it will cause the remaining disks to be useless as they are missing the chunks from the failed disk. This is a not recommended RAID configuration for real-time database systems, but it is a recommended configuration for storing non-critical business data such as historical application logs, database logs, and so on.

RAID 1

This configuration is only to focus on high availability rather than on performance, by broadcasting the data among two disk drives. That is, a single copy of the data will be kept on two disks. If one disk is corrupted, then we can still use the other one for read/write operations. This is also not a recommended configuration for real-time database systems, as it is lacking the write performance. Also, in this configuration, we will be utilizing 50% of the disk to store the actual data, and the rest to keep its duplicated information for high availability. This is a recommended configuration where the durability of data matters when compared with write performance.

RAID 5

This configuration provides more storage and high availability on the disk, by storing the parity blocks across the disks. Unlike RAID 1, it offers more disk space to keep the actual data, as parity blocks are spread among the disks. In any case, if one disk is corrupted, then we can use the parity blocks from the other disk, to fetch the missing data. However, this is also not a recommended configuration, since every read/write operation on the disk needs to process the parity blocks, to get the actual data out of it.

RAID 6

This configuration provides more redundancy than RAID 5 by storing the two parity blocks information for each write operation. That is, if both disks become corrupted, RAID 6 can still get the data from the parity blocks, unlike RAID 5. This configuration is also not recommended for the database systems, as write performance is less as compared than previous RAID levels.

RAID 10

This configuration is the combination of RAID levels 0 and 1. That is, the data will be striped to multiple disks and will be replicated to another disk storage. It is the most recommended RAID level for real-time business applications, where we achieve a better performance than with RAID 1, and higher availability than RAID 0.

For more information about RAID levels, refer to the following URLs:

- http://www.slashroot.in/raid-levels-raid0-raid1-raid 10-raid5-raid6-complete-tutorial
- https://en.wikipedia.org/wiki/Standard_RAID_levels

Configuring pgbench

In this recipe, we will be discussing how to configure the pgbench to perform various test cases.

Getting ready

By default, PostgreSQL provides a tool, pgbench, which performs a default test suite based on TPC-B, which simulates the live database load on the servers. Using this tool, we can estimate the tps (transactions per second) capacity of the server, by conducting a dedicated read or read/write test cases. Before performing the pgbench test cases on the server, we need to fine-tune the PostgreSQL parameters and make them ready to fully utilize the server resources. Also, it's good practice to run pgbench from a remote machine, where the network latency is trivial among the nodes.

How to do it…

As aforementioned, pgbench simulates a TPC-B-like workload on the servers, by executing three update statements, followed by SELECT and INSERT statements into different pre-defined pgbench tables, and if we want to use those pre-defined tables, then we would need to initiate pgbench using the -i or --initialize options. Otherwise, we can write a customized SQL script.

To get effective results from pgbench, we need to fine-tune the PostgreSQL server with the following parameters:

Parameter	Description
shared_buffers	This is the amount of memory for database operations
huge_pages	This improves the OS-level memory management
work_mem	This is the amount of memory for each backend for data operations such as sort, join, and so on
autovacuum_work_mem	This is the amount of memory for postgres internal process autovacuum
max_worker_processes	This is the maximum number of worker processes for the database

`max_parallel_workers_per_gather`	This is the number of worker processes to consider for a gather node type
`max_connections`	This is the number of database connections
`backend_flush_after`	Do fsync, after this many bytes have been flushed to disk by each user process
`checkpoint_completion_target`	This is used to set I/O usage ratio during the checkpoint
`archive_mode`	This is used to determine whether the database should run in the archive mode
`log_lock_waits`	This is used to log useful information about concurrent database locks
`log_temp_files`	This is used to log information about the database's temporary files
`random_page_cost`	This is used to set random page cost value for the index scans

> You can also find other parameters at the following URL, which are also important before conducting any benchmarking on the database server: `ht tps://www.postgresql.org/docs/9.6/static/runtime-config.html`.

Another good practice to get good performance is to keep the transaction logs (`pg_xlog`) in another mount point, and also have unique tablespaces for tables and indexes. While performing the pgbench testing with predefined tables, we can specify these unique tablespaces using the `--index-tablespace` and `--tablespace` options.

How it works...

As we discussed earlier, pgbench is a TPC-B benchmarking tool for PostgreSQL, which simulates the live transactions load on the database server by collecting the required metrics such as `tps`, `latency`, and so on. Using pgbench, we can also increase the database size by choosing the test scale factor while using predefined tables. If you wanted to test multiple concurrent connections to the database and wanted to use the pooling mechanism, then it's good practice to configure the pgbouner/pgpool on the local database node to reuse the connections.

For more features and options with the pgbench tool, visit `https://www.p ostgresql.org/docs/9.6/static/pgbench.html`.

Running read/write pgbench test cases

In this recipe, we will be discussing how to perform various tests using the pgbench tool.

Getting ready

Using pgbench options, we can benchmark the database for read/write operations. Using these measurements, we can estimate the disk read-write speed by including the system buffers. To perform a read-write-only test, then either we can go with pgbench arguments, or create a custom SQL script with the required `SELECT`, `INSERT`, `UPDATE`, or `DELETE` statements, then execute them with the required number of concurrent connections.

How to do it…

Let us discuss about read-only and write-only in brief:

Read-only

To perform read-only benchmarking with pgbench predefined tables, we need to use the `-S` option. Otherwise, as we discussed earlier, we need to prepare a SQL file with the required `SELECT` statements.

Write-only

To perform write-only benchmarking with pgbench predefined tables, we need to use the `-N` or `-b simple-update` options. Otherwise, as we discussed earlier, we have to prepare a SQL file with the required `UPDATE`, `DELETE`, and `INSERT` statements.

How it works...

While running read-only test cases, it's good practice to measure the database cache hit ratio, which defines the reduction in I/O usage. You can get the database hit ratio using the following SQL command:

```
postgres=# SELECT TRUNC(((blks_hit)/(blks_read+blks_hit)::numeric)*100, 2)
hit_ratio FROM pg_stat_database WHERE datname = 'postgres';
hit_ratio
-----------
99.69
(1 row)
```

Also, if we enable `track_io_timing` in `postgresql.conf`, it will provide some information about disk blocks read/write operations by each backend process. We can get these disk I/O timing values from the `pg_stat_database` catalog view.

> Refer to the following URL, where pgbench supports various test suites, such as disk, CPU, memory, and so on: `https://wiki.postgresql.org/wiki/Pgbenchtesting`.

2
Server Configuration and Control

In this chapter, we will cover the following:

- Starting the database server manually
- Stopping the server quickly
- Stopping the server in an emergency
- Reloading server configuration
- Restarting the database server quickly
- Tuning connection-related parameters
- Tuning query-planning parameters
- Tuning logging-related parameters

Introduction

This chapter basically deals with the server architecture and server control. Initially, we will discuss the different options available to start and stop the PostgreSQL server. As an administrator, one should be aware of the different methods available in order to use the appropriate option in emergency situations or during maintenance operations. We then move onto discussing different server parameters and the tuning aspects related to them. Some important server parameters that help improve the overall server throughput and performance are discussed here from an optimization perspective.

Starting the server manually

Normally, a PostgreSQL server will start automatically when the system boots up. If an automatic start is not enabled for a server, we would need to start the server manually. This may be required even for operational reasons.

Getting ready

Before we talk about how to start the database server, first we need to understand the difference between server and service. The term server refers to the database server and its processes, whereas the term service essentially indicates the operating system wrapper through which the server gets called.

How to do it...

On a majority of platforms, that is, Linux and Unix distributions, we can start the server using the `pg_ctl` command-line utility as shown here:

```
pg_ctl -D <location of data directory> start
```

Consider the following example:

```
pg_ctl -D /var/lib/pgsql/9.6/data start
```

The `-D` switch of the `pg_ctl` command indicates the data directory of the PostgreSQL server. In the preceding command, the data directory is defined at the location `/var/lib/pgsql/9.6/data`.

On Linux and Unix platforms such as Red Hat, the service can be started as mentioned here:

```
service <postgresql-version> start
```

For instance, to start the PostgreSQL server version 9.6 as a service, we can use the following command:

```
service postgresql-9.6 start
```

How it works...

Using the start mode of the `pg_ctl` command, the PostgreSQL server is started in the background and its background processes are initiated.

You can use the following command to check whether the PostgreSQL server background processes have started:

```
ps aux | grep "postgres" | grep -v "grep"

postgres  1289  0.0  0.3  51676  7900 ?   S    11:31   0:01
/usr/lib/postgresql/9.6/bin/postgres -D /var/lib/postgresql/9.6/main -c
config_file=/etc/postgresql/9.6/main/postgresql.conf
postgres  1303  0.0  0.0  21828  1148 ?   Ss   11:31   0:00 postgres:
logger process
postgres  1305  0.0  0.0  51676  1568 ?   Ss   11:31   0:02 postgres:
writer process
postgres  1306  0.0  0.0  51676  1324 ?   Ss   11:31   0:02 postgres: wal
writer process
postgres  1307  0.0  0.1  52228  2452 ?   Ss   11:31   0:00 postgres:
autovacuum launcher process
postgres  1308  0.0  0.0  22016  1432 ?   Ss   11:31   0:00 postgres: stats
collector process
```

When we execute the `pg_ctl` command, it internally performs various validations such as checking that the data directory that we mentioned is equal to the `data_directory` setting in `postgresql.conf`. If the `data_directory` parameter points to some other directory location, then PostgreSQL will instantiate to that directory location. After the validations have been completed, the `pg_ctl` binary internally invokes another process called `postgres`, which is the main process for the PostgreSQL cluster.

Stopping the server quickly

There are different modes available to stop the PostgreSQL server. Here we will talk about the mode in which we can stop the server quickly.

Getting ready

The `pg_ctl` command is used in combination with the stop option in order to stop the PostgreSQL server.

How to do it...

We can use the following command to stop the server quickly on Red Hat-based Linux distributions and other Unix-based systems:

```
pg_ctl -D /var/lib/pgsql/9.6/data -m fast stop
```

Here, /var/lib/pgsql/9.6/data is the location of the data directory.

How it works...

The -m fast option must be used in order to shut down as quickly as possible. In case of a normal shutdown, PostgreSQL will wait for all users to finish their transactions before halting and on a busy system this can sometimes take a very long time.

While initiating a fast stop with the -m fast option of the pg_ctl command, all the users will have their transactions aborted and all connections are disconnected. However, this is a clean shutdown because all the active transactions are aborted followed, by a system checkpoint before the server closes.

Also, it will verify various checks, such as whether PostgreSQL has started in a single user mode or whether the cluster is running in backup mode while shutting down the database, and will interact with the user by throwing the required notification messages.

Stopping the server in an emergency

In this recipe, we will show you the command that can be used to stop the server in an emergency situation.

How to do it...

We can use the following command to stop the PostgreSQL server in an emergency:

```
pg_ctl -D /var/lib/pgsql/9.6/data stop -m immediate
```

Here, the data directory location is defined at /var/lib/pgsql/9.6/data.

How it works...

The moment the immediate stop mode is used with the `pg_ctl` command, all the users have their transactions aborted and the existing connections are terminated. There is no system checkpoint either and the database basically requires crash recovery at the time of database restart.

In this shutdown mode, the PostgresSQL process will issue a direct `SIGQUIT` signal to each of the child processes, by including the backend processes such as bgwriter, autovacuum, and recovery processes. However, in smart shutdown mode, the PostgreSQL process will wait until these processes are terminated and then shut down the postmaster process.

Reloading server configuration

In this recipe, we will talk about the command that can be used to reload the server configuration and its parameters.

Getting ready

If any of the server parameters come into effect after reloading the server configuration files, such as `postgresql.conf`, then we need to reload the server configuration using the reload option of the `pg_ctl` command.

How to do it...

We can use the following command to reload the server configuration on Red Hat-based Linux and Unix distributions:

```
pg_ctl -D /var/lib/pgsql/9.6/data reload
```

You can also reload the configuration using the `pg_reload_conf` function while still being connected to PostgreSQL .The usage of the `pg_reload_conf` function is mentioned as follows:

```
postgres=# select pg_reload_conf();
```

How it works...

The reload mode of the `pg_ctl` command is used to send the postgres process a `SIGHUP` signal, which in turn causes it to reload its configuration files such as `postgresql.conf` and `pg_hba.conf`. The benefit of this mode is that it allows the configuration changes to be reloaded without requiring a complete restart of the PostgreSQL server to come into effect.

In this mode, PostgreSQL will send a `SIGHUP` signal to each child process, including the utility processes such as autovacuum, bgwriter, stats collector, and so on, to get the new settings from the latest configuration settings.

Restarting the database server quickly

Sometimes there are situations where you need a database bounce. This is most likely for the database parameters that require a server restart to come into effect. This is different from the reload option of the server configuration, which only reloads the configuration files without requiring a server bounce.

How to do it...

We can use the following command to restart the database server:

```
pg_ctl -D /var/lib/pgsql/9.6/data restart
```

Here, `/var/lig/pgsql/9.6/data` is the location of the data directory of the PostgreSQL server.

How it works...

Using the restart mode of the `pg_ctl` command first stops the running databases on the PostgreSQL server and then starts the server. It is in effect a two-way process, where the running server is first stopped and then started again. A database restart is needed in many situations. It could be likely that some of the server parameters require a server restart to enable the changes made to these parameters to come into effects or it can also be that some of the server processes have hung and a restart is needed.

In this mode, by default, the PostgreSQL process will terminate using SIGINT, which is a fast shutdown mode. However, we can also specify the restart mode using the -m argument.

Tuning connection-related parameters

In this recipe, we will talk about tuning the connection-related server parameters.

How to do it...

The following are the connection-related parameters that usually require tuning:

- `listen_addresses`
- `port`
- `max_connections`
- `superuser_reserved_connections`
- `unix_socket_directory`
- `unix_socket_permissions`

These parameters can be set to appropriate values in the `postgresql.conf` file and these parameter can be set at server start. The changes made to these parameters will only come into effect once the PostgreSQL server is restarted, either using the restart mode of the `pg_ctl` command or using the stop mode and then followed by the start mode of the `pg_ctl` command. This can be done as follows:

```
pg_ctl -D $PGDATA restart
```

Here, `$PGDATA` refers to the environment variable that refers to the data directory location of the PostgreSQL server.

How it works...

Here, we will talk about the connection-related parameters discussed in the preceding section:

- `listen_addresses`: The standard behavior of PostgreSQL is to respond to connections from localhost. This default behavior usually needs alterations to allow the PostgreSQL server to be accessed via the standard TCP/IP protocol widely used in client-server communications. The de facto practice is to set this value to * to allow the PostgreSQL server to listen to all incoming connections. Otherwise, we need to mention a comma-separated list of IP addresses where PostgreSQL needs to be responded. This gives an additional security control over reaching the database instance directly from any IP address.

- `port`: This parameter defines the port on which the PostgreSQL server will listen for incoming client connection requests. The default value of this parameter is set to `5432`. If there are multiple PostgreSQL instances running on the same server, the value of the port parameter for every PostgreSQL instance needs to be altered to avoid port conflicts.

- `max_connections`: This parameter governs the maximum number of concurrent client connections that the server can support. This is a very important parameter setting to other parameters such as `work_mem` that are dependent on this because memory resources can be allocated on a per-client basis, so the maximum number of clients in effect suggests the maximum possible memory use. The default value of this parameter is 100. If the requirement is to support thousands of client connections, connection pooling software should be used to reduce the connection overhead. On a Linux server with 8 GB of RAM, a value of 140 is a good start. Increasing the value of this parameter will cause the PostgreSQL server to request more shared memory from the operating system.

- `superuser_reserved_connections`: This parameter governs the number of connection slots reserved for superusers. The default value of this parameter is set to `3`. This parameter can only be set at server restart.

- `unix_socket_directory`: This parameter defines the directory to be used for the Unix socket connections to the server. The default location is `/tmp`, but it can be changed at build time. This parameter comes into effect during server start. This parameter is irrelevant on Windows, which does not have socket connections.

- `unix_socket_permissions`: This parameter defines the access permissions of the Unix domain socket. The default value is `0777`, which means anyone can connect using socket connections. This parameter value can be set only at server start.

Tuning query-related parameters

In this recipe, we will talk about the query planning related parameters and the associated tuning aspects.

How to do it...

The following are the query planning related parameters that usually require tuning:

- `random_page_cost`
- `seq_page_cost`
- `effective_cache_size`
- `work_mem`
- `constraint_exclusion`

These parameters can be set in the `postgresql.conf` configuration file.

How it works...

`random_page_cost`: This parameter is basically used to estimate the cost of a random page fetch in abstract cost units. The default value of this parameter is 4.0. Random page cost is basically used to represent the coefficient between the cost of looking up one row via sequential scans against the cost of looking up a single row individually using random access, that is, disk seeks. This factor influences the query planner's decision to use indexes instead of a table scan while executing queries. Reducing this value relative to the `seq_page_cost` parameter will cause the system to prefer index scans. If, however, this value is increased, it would make index scans appear expensive from a cost perspective.

`seq_page_cost`: This parameter is used to estimate the cost of a sequential page fetch in abstract cost units. The default value of this parameter is `1.0` and this may need to be lowered for caching effects. For situations where the database is cached entirely in RAM, this value needs to be lowered. Always set `random_page_cost` to be greater than or equal to `seq_page_cost`.

`effective_cache_size`: This parameter setting is used to provide an estimate of how much memory is available for disk caching by the operating system and within the database itself after considering and accounting for what is being used by the OS itself and other applications. This parameter does not allocate any memory, rather it serves as a guideline as to how much memory you expect to be available in the RAM, as well as in the PostgreSQL shared buffer. This helps the PostgreSQL query planner to figure out whether the query plans it is considering for query execution would fit in the system memory or not. If this is set too low, indexes may not be used for executing queries the way you would expect.

Let us assume that there is around 1.5 GB of system RAM on your Linux machine, the value of `shared_buffers` is set to 32 MB, and `effective_cache_size` is set to 850 MB. Now, if a running query needs around 700 MB of a dataset, PostgreSQL would estimate that all the data required should be available in memory and would hence opt for an aggressive plan from the context of optimization, involving heavier index usage and merge joins. But if the effective cache size is set to around 300 MB, the query planner will opt for the sequential scan. The rule of thumb is that if `shared_buffers` is set to a quarter of the total RAM, setting `effective_cache_size` to one half of the available RAM would be a conservative setting and setting it to around 75% of the total RAM would be an aggressive setting, but still reasonable.

`work_mem`: This parameter defines the amount of memory to be used by internal sort operations and hash tables before switching to temporary disk files. When a running query needs to sort data, an estimate is provided by the database as to how much data is involved and it will compare it to the `work_mem` parameter. If it is larger, it will write out all the data and use a disk-based sort mechanism instead of reverting to in-memory sort, which would be much slower than the memory-based sort. If there are a lot of complex sorts involved, and if you have good memory available, then increasing the value of the `work_mem` parameter would allow PostgreSQL to do in-memory sorts, which will be faster than disk-based ones. The amount of memory as specified by the value of the `work_mem` parameter gets applied for each sort operation done by each database session and complex queries can use multiple working memory-based sort buffers. For instance, if the value of `work_mem` is set to 100 MB, and if there are around 40 database sessions submitting queries, one would end up using around 4 GB of real system memory. The catch is that one cannot predict the number of sorts one client session may end up doing and thereby theoretically `work_mem` is a per sort parameter instead of being a per client one effectively indicating that the memory available from the use of `work_mem` is unbound, where there are a number of clients doing a large number of sorts concurrently. From the point of view of optimization to arrive at the optimum setting for the `work_mem` parameter, we must first consider how much free system memory is available after the allocation of `shared_buffers` further divided by the value of `max_connections` and then considering a fraction of that figure albeit half of that would be an assertive value for the `work_mem` parameter. One needs to set this value explicitly as the default value is too low for in-memory sorts.

constraint_exclusion: If in PostgreSQL you are using partitioned tables that utilize constraints, then enabling the constraint_exclusion parameter allows the query planner to ignore partitions that cannot have the data being searched for when that can be proven. In earlier PostgreSQL versions before 8.4, this value was set to off, which meant that unless toggled on partitioned tables, this will not work as expected. The new default value since version 8.4 has been to set this value to partition, in which case the query planner will examine constraints for inheritance child subtables and UNION ALL queries. If this value is turned on, it will examine constraints on all tables and this will impose extra planning overhead even for simple queries and thus there will be a performance overhead.

Tuning logging-related parameters

In this recipe, we will talk about tuning logging-related parameters.

How to do it...

The following are the logging-related parameters that usually require tuning:

- log_line_prefix
- log_statement
- log_min_duration_statement

How it works...

log_line_prefix: Usually the default value related to this parameter is empty and it is not desirable. A good way to put this in context would be to use the following format:

```
log_line_prefix='%t:%r:%u@%d:[%p]: '
```

Once this format is used, every line in the log will follow this format. The following is a description of the entries:

- %t: This is the timestamp
- %u: This is the database username
- %r: This is where the remote host connection is from
- %d: This is where the database connection is to
- %p: This is the process ID of the connection

Not all of these values will be required initially; however, at a later stage as you drill down further, they will be useful. For instance, the significance of `processID` becomes apparent when you are troubleshooting performance issues.

`log_statement`: This parameter defines which statements are logged. Statement logging is a powerful technique to find performance issues. The options for the `log_statement` values are as follows:

- `None`: At this setting, no statement-level logging is captured.
- `DDL`: When this setting is enabled, DDL statements such as `CREATE`, `ALTER`, and `DROP` statements are captured. This is a handy setting to find out whether there were any major changes introduced accidentally by developers or administrators alike.
- `MOD`: When this setting is enabled, all the statements that modify a value will be logged. From the point of view of auditing changes, this is a handy feature. This setting is not required if your workload includes running `SELECT` statements or for reporting purposes.
- `ALL`: When this setting is enabled, all the statements are logged. This should generally be avoided to counter the logging overhead on the server when all statements are being logged.

`log_min_duration_statement`: This parameter setting causes the duration of each statement to be logged if a given statement ran for at least a certain number of milliseconds. It is basically like setting a threshold and if any statement exceeds the defined thresholds, the duration of that statement is logged.

3
Device Optimization

In this chapter, we will cover the following recipes:

- Understanding memory units in PostgreSQL
- Handling Linux/Unix memory parameters
- CPU scheduling parameters
- Device tuning parameters
- Identifying checkpoint overhead
- Analyzing buffer cache contents

Introduction

Tuning only PostgreSQL-related parameters will not be sufficient to achieve good performance from any hardware. It is also required to tune specific device-related parameters, which will greatly improve the performance of any database server. In this chapter, we will be discussing various device configurations such as CPU, memory, and disk. Most of the content in this topic will be discussing Linux-related parameters, which you may need to refer for alternative configuration section in different operating systems.

Understanding memory units in PostgreSQL

In this recipe, we will be discussing the memory components of PostgreSQL instances.

Getting ready

PostgreSQL uses several memory components for each unique usage. That is, it uses dedicated memory areas for transactions, sort/join operations, maintenance operations, and so on. If the configured memory component doesn't fit the usage of the live application, then we may hit a performance issue, where PostgreSQL tries for more I/O.

How to do it…

Let us discuss about, how to tune the major PostgreSQL memory components:

shared_buffers

This is the major memory area that PostgreSQL uses for executing the transactions. On most Linux operating systems, it is recommended to allocate at least 25% of RAM as shared buffers, by leaving 75% of RAM to OS, OS cache, and for other PostgreSQL memory components. PostgreSQL provide multiple ways to create these shared buffers. The supported shared memory creation techniques are POSIX shared memory, System V shared memory, memory mapped files, and windows, in which we specify one method as an argument to the `default_shared_memory_type`.

temp_buffers

PostgreSQL utilizes this memory area for holding the temporary tables of each session, which will be cleared when the connection is closed.

work_mem

This is the memory area that PostgreSQL tries to allocate for each session when the query requires any joining, sorting, or hashing operations. We need to be a bit cautious while tuning this parameter, as this memory will be allocated for each connection whenever it is needed.

maintenance_work_mem

PostgreSQL utilizes this memory area for performing maintenance operations such as `VACUUM`, `ALTER TABLE`, `CREATE INDEX`, and so on. Autovacuum worker processes also utilize this memory area, if the `autovacuum_work_mem` parameter is set to `-1`.

wal_buffers

PostgreSQL utilizes this memory area for holding incoming transactions, which will be flushed immediately to disk (`pg_xlog` files) on every commit operation. By default, this parameter is configured to utilize 3% of the `shared_buffers` memory to hold incoming transactions. This setting may not be sufficient for busy databases, where multiple concurrent commits happen frequently.

max_stack_depth

PostgreSQL utilizes this memory area for function call/expression execution stacks. By default, it's configured to use 2 MB, which we can increase up to the kernel's configured stack size (ulimit -s).

effective_cache_size

This is a logical setting for PostgreSQL instances, which gives a hint about how much cache (`shared_buffers` and OS cache) is available at this moment. Based on this cache setting, the optimizer will generate a better plan for the SQL. It is recommended to set the 75% of RAM as a value for this parameter.

How it works...

In the preceding memory components, not all will get instantiated during PostgreSQL startup. Only `shared_buffers` and `wal_buffers` will be initialized, and the remaining memory components will be initialized whenever their presence is needed.

> For more information about these parameters, refer to the following
> URL: `https://www.postgresql.org/docs/9.6/static/runtime-config`
> `-resource.html`.

Handling Linux/Unix memory parameters

In this topic, let's discuss various kernel memory settings, and see the recommended configuration values.

Getting ready

The kernel provides various memory settings based on its distribution. Using these parameters, we can control the kernel behavior, which provides the necessary resources to the applications. PostgreSQL is a database software application, which needs to communicate to kernel with its system calls, to get its required resources.

How to do it…

Let us discuss about, how to tune few major kernel memory components in Linux:

kernel.shmmax

This setting defines the maximum size limit of a shared memory segment, which limits the processes required segment size. We need to specify the maximum allowed segment size in bytes. It is recommended to set this value as half of the RAM size in the form of bytes.

kernel.shmall

This setting defines the limit on the available shared memory in the system. In general, we need to set this parameter in the form of pages. While the PostgreSQL server is starting, it will calculate the amount of shared memory that is required based on `postgresql.conf` settings such as `max_connections`, `autovacuum_max_workers`, and so on. It is generally recommended to set this value as half of the RAM size in the form of pages.

kernel.shmmni

This setting defines the limit of the number of segments, which the kernel needs to allow in the system. The default value of 4096 is sufficient for a standalone PostgreSQL server. We can also get the number of shared memory segments in the system, by using the `ipcs` Linux utility command.

vm.swappiness

This setting defines the aggressiveness of kernel, in clearing the system cache. If we define this value as 100, then kernel will be in busy paging out the application into the swap file, and it also drops the cached data. Once the kernel drops the cache then it's a major performance hit to the database server, and also a major performance problem for the applications, where it needs to load its content from swap into the memory. The recommended value for this parameter is any value that is less than 10. In general, the kswapd Linux OS daemon process will start dumping all the pages into swap, if we have less free memory available.

vm.overcommit_memory

This setting defines the overcommit behavior, which will try to control the system stability by preventing **OOM (Out Of Memory)** issues. The suggested values for this parameter are either 0 or 2 (recommended). The setting value 2 will control the memory allocation, and will try to allocate the memory for the processes, by using swap size, and a percentage of the overcommit_ratio from the RAM size. The setting value 0 follows a heuristic approach, which allocates more address space (virtual memory) than the physical memory, which does not guarantee system stability.

vm.overcommit_ratio

This setting defines how much physical memory kernel needs to allocate for the processes. The suggested value for this parameter is 80. That is, 80% of the physical memory will be considered to allocate the memory for the requested processes. This parameter plays a major role in utilizing the memory to the full extent.

vm.dirty_background_ratio

This setting defines what percentage of the system memory can be dirtied before flushing it to disk. The suggested value for this parameter is less than 5, based on RAM size. Once the system memory fills with dirty data, then kernel will push all the modified content into the disk storage, by blocking the incoming I/O requests to system memory.

vm.dirty_ratio

This setting defines what percentage of the system memory can be dirtied before flushing it to disk. The suggested value for this parameter is 10 to 15 percent based on RAM size, and the configured RAID levels. When the system memory fills with dirty data, then the process that generated the dirty data is responsible for flushing the contents to disk, by blocking incoming I/O requests to the user memory space.

How it works...

These kernel parameters play a vital role for all the Linux applications, including the database server. Based on these configuration settings, we can indirectly control the PostgreSQL behavior, by controlling the operating system kernel.

> For more information about kernel parameters, check out the following URL: https://www.kernel.org/doc/Documentation/sysctl/.

CPU scheduling parameters

In this topic, let's discuss a few CPU scheduling parameters, which will fine tune the scheduling policy.

Getting ready

In the previous recipe, we discussed memory-related parameters, which are not sufficient for better performance. Much like memory, kernel also supports various CPU-related tuning parameters, which will drive the processes scheduling.

How to do it...

Let us discuss about, few major CPU kernel scheduling parameters in Linux:

kernel.sched_autogroup_enabled

This parameter groups all the processes that belong to the same kernel session ID, which are further processed as a single process scheduling entity rather than multiple entities. That is, the CPU will indirectly spend a contiguous amount of time on a group of processes that belong to the same session rather than switching to multiple processes. Using the `ps xa -o`, `sid`, `pid`, and `comm` command, where we can get the session ID of the processes. It is always recommended to set this value to 0 for the PostgreSQL standalone server, as each process belongs to a unique session ID.

kernel.sched_min_granularity_ns

This parameter defines the minimum time slice of the process that it needs to spend in the allocated CPU before its preemption. The recommended value for this parameter is 2,000,000 ns, and it can be tuned further by doing proper benchmarking with multiple settings.

kernel.sched_latency_ns

This parameter defines the kind of maximum time slice for each process that runs in CPU core. However, this process time slice will be calculated based on the load at that time in the server; it also includes the process's nice values along with the `sched_min_granularity_ns` parameter. The recommended value for this parameter is 10,000,000 ns, which gives better performance for the moderated number of process. If the database server is dealing with more processes, this setting may lead to more processes preemption and may reduce the performance of the CPU-bound tasks.

kernel.sched_wakeup_granularity_ns

This parameter defines whether the current running process needs to be preempted from the CPU, when it compares its vruntime (virtual run time of the process, that is, the actual time the process spends in CPU) with the woken process vruntime. If the delta of vruntime between these two processes is greater than this granularity setting, then it will cause the current process to preempt from the CPU. The recommended value for this parameter should always be less than half of the `sched_latency_ns`.

kernel.sched_migration_cost_ns

This parameter defines the amount of time in which the process is ready for the CPU migration. That is, after spending this much amount of time, a process is eligible to migrate to another CPU core, which is less busy. By reducing this value, the scheduler makes more task migrations among the CPU, which will effectively utilize all the cores. But migrating a task from one CPU to another requires additional efforts, which may reduce the performance of the process. The recommended value for this parameter is 500,000.

How it works...

In the Linux kernel, each process is called a **kernel scheduling entity** (**KSE**), which will be processed based on different scheduling policies. Using the preceding parameters, we can control the process scheduling and migration of the process among CPUs, which will improve the execution speed of a process. We can also process a set of processes as a single KSE by using the `sched_autogroup_enabled` option, where a set of processes will get more CPU resources than the others.

Disk tuning parameters

In this recipe, we will be discussing a few disk I/O related schedulers that are designed for a specific need.

Getting ready

The Linux kernel provides various device-specific algorithms, which give more flexibility in fine tuning the hardware devices. The Linux kernel by default provides several I/O scheduling algorithms, which have their own unique usages. Kernel also provides a way to change different I/O scheduling policies for different disk devices. The major disk I/O schedulers are **CFQ** (**Completely Fair Queuing**), noop, and deadline.

How to do it...

Let us discuss about, the Linux disk scheduling algorithms:

CFQ

This is the default I/O scheduler that we get for the disk devices. This scheduler provides I/O time slices, like the CPU scheduler. This algorithm also considers the I/O priorities by reading the process's `ionice` values, and also allots scheduling classes such as real time, best effort, and idle classes. An advantage of this scheduler is it tries to analyze the historical data of the I/O requests and will predict the process near future I/O requirements. If it is expected that a process will issue more I/O than it waits for it, rather processing the other waiting I/O process. Sometimes this I/O prediction may go bad, which leads to a bad disk throughput. However, CFQ provides a tunable parameter, `slice_idle`, which controls the amount of waiting time for the predicted I/O requests. It is always recommended to set this value to 0 for the RAID disk devices, and any positive integer setting for non-RAID devices.

noop

This I/O scheduler is pretty neat, as it doesn't include any restrictions such as time slices in CFQ and sends the request to the disk in FIFO order. This I/O scheduler works much more and gives more performance when the underlying disk devices are of a RAID or SSD type. This is because devices such as RAID or SSD follow their own unique techniques while reordering I/O requests.

Deadline

This I/O scheduler is widely used for all database servers, since it enforces the latency limits over all I/O requests. By using this scheduler, we can achieve good performance for the database server, which has more read operations than write operations. This algorithm dispatches the I/O tasks as batches. A single batch contains a set of read/write operations along with their expire timings. We can tune the batch size and expire timings of each read, write using the following parameters:

Parameter	Description
`fifo_batch`	This defines the batch size of the read/write requests. By increasing this parameter, we can get better disk throughput as we are increasing the I/O latency.

read_expire	The deadline for the read request to get serviced. Default is 500ms.
write_expire	The deadline for the write request to get serviced. Default is 5,000 ms.
writes_starved	This defines how many read batches need to be dispatched before dispatching the single write batch.

How it works...

As we discussed previously, each I/O request will be processed based on a unique I/O scheduler, which will try to rearrange the requests in a physical order to reduce the mechanical overhead while reading the data from the disk.

Identifying checkpoint overhead

In this recipe, we will be discussing the checkpoint process, which may cause more I/O usage while flushing the dirty buffers into the disk.

Getting ready

In PostgreSQL, the checkpoint is an activity that flushes all the dirty buffers from the shared buffers into the persistent storage, which is followed by updating the consistent transaction log sequence number in the data, WAL files. That means this checkpoint guarantees that all the information up to this checkpoint number is stored in a persistent disk storage. PostgreSQL internally issues the checkpoint as per the checkpoint_timeout and max_wal_size settings, which keep the data in a consistent storage as configured. In case the configured shared_buffers are huge in size, then the probability of holding dirty buffers will also be greater in size, which leads to more I/O usage for the next checkpoint process. It is also not recommended to tune the checkpoint_timeout and max_wal_size settings to be aggressive, as it will lead to frequent I/O load spikes on the server and may cause system instability.

How to do it...

To identify the overhead of the checkpoint process, we need to monitor the disk usage by using some native tools such as `iostat`, `iotop`, and so on, while the checkpoint process is in progress. To identify this checkpoint process status, we have to either query the `pg_stat_activity` view as follows, or otherwise we have to consider enabling the `log_checkpoints` parameter, which will log an implicit checkpoint begin status as checkpoint starting: `xlog` and for the explicit requests as checkpoint starting: immediate force wait `xlog`:

```
SELECT * FROM pg_stat_activity WHERE wait_event = 'CheckpointLock';
```

How it works...

Once we find that the I/O usage is high enough when the checkpoint process is running, then we have to consider tuning the `checkpoint_completion_target` parameter, which will limit the transfer rate between the memory and disk. This parameter accepts real numbers between 0 and 1, which will smooth the I/O transfer rate if the parameter value gets close to 1. PostgreSQL version 9.6 introduced a new parameter called `checkpoint_flush_after`, which will guarantee flushing the buffers from the kernel page cache at certain operating systems.

> For more information about the checkpoint process and its behavior, refer to the following URL: `https://www.postgresql.org/docs/9.6/static/wal-configuration.html`.

Analyzing buffer cache contents

In this recipe, we will be discussing how to analyze the content that resides in PostgreSQL shared buffers.

Getting ready

To analyze the shared buffer contents, PostgreSQL provides an extension called `pg_buffercache`, and we also use the `CREATE EXTENSION` command. This extension reports the buffer details such as which relation holds the number of buffers in the memory, what buffers are dirty at this moment, and what is a specific buffer's usage count.

In PostgreSQL, shared buffers are not specific to any database as they are managed at cluster level. Hence, while querying the pg_buffercache we may get relation details that are from other databases too. Also, it is not recommended to query the pg_buffercache too frequently as it needs to handle buffer management locks, to get the buffer's current status.

How to do it...

Let's install the pg_buffercache extension and then query the view as follows:

```
postgres=# CREATE EXTENSION pg_buffercache;
CREATE EXTENSION
postgres=# SELECT * FROM pg_buffercache LIMIT 1;
-[ RECORD 1 ]----+------
bufferid          | 1
relfilenode       | 1262
reltablespace     | 1664
reldatabase       | 0
relforknumber     | 0
relblocknumber    | 0
isdirty           | f
usagecount        | 5
pinning_backends  | 0
```

From the preceding output, the reldatabase is 0, which indicates that the bufferid 1 belongs to a table/view of the shared system catalogs, such as pg_database. Also, it displays the usagecount of that buffer as 5, which will be helpful during the buffer cache eviction policy.

How it works…

PostgreSQL has a built-in buffer manager that maintains the shared buffers for the cluster. Whenever a backend requests to read a block from the disk, then the buffer manager allocates a block for it from the available shared buffer memory. If the shared buffers don't have any available buffers, then the buffer manager needs to choose a certain number of blocks to evict from the shared buffers for the newly requested blocks.

PostgreSQL's buffer manager follows an approach called clock sweep for the buffer eviction policy. When a block is loaded from disk into the shared buffers, then its usage count will begin with 1. Whenever this buffer hits from the other backend processes, its usage count will be increased and its value will stay as 5 when its usage count exceeds 5. This usage count value is reduced by 1 during the eviction policy. When the buffer manager needs to evict the buffers for the incoming requests, then it scans all the buffers including dirty buffers, and will reduce all the buffer usage counts by 1. After the end of the scan, if it finds the buffers whose usage count is 0, then it treats those buffers as if they should be evicted from the shared buffers. If the chosen buffer is a dirty buffer, then the backend process request will be in waiting state, until that dirty buffer is flushed to the respective physical file storage. From the preceding output, the usage count of the bufferid is 5, which defines that it is not much closer to the eviction policy.

4

Monitoring Server Performance

In this chapter, we will cover the following:

- Monitoring CPU usage
- Monitoring paging and swapping
- Tracking CPU consuming processes
- Monitoring CPU load
- Identifying CPU bottlenecks
- Identifying disk I/O bottlenecks
- Monitoring system load
- Tracking historical CPU usage
- Tracking historical memory usage
- Monitoring disk space
- Monitoring network status

Introduction

In order to be able to solve performance problems we should be able to effectively use operating system utilities. We should be able to use the right operating system tools and commands in order to identify performance problems that may be due to CPU, memory, or disk I/O issues. Many times a DBA's duties often overlap with certain system administration-related functions and it is important for a DBA to be effective in using the related operating system utilities in order to correctly identify where the underlying issue on the server could be. In this chapter, we are going to discuss various Unix/Linux related operating system utilities that can help the DBA in performance analysis and troubleshooting issues.

Monitoring CPU usage

In this recipe, we are going to use the `sar` command to monitor CPU usage on the system.

Getting ready

The commands used in this recipe have been performed on a Sun Solaris machine. Hence the command output may vary in different Unix and Linux-related systems.

How to do it...

We can use the `sar` command with the -u switch to monitor CPU utilization:

```
bash-3.2$ sar -u 10 8
SunOS usstlz-pinfsi09 5.10 Generic_150400-04 sun4u     08/06/2014

23:32:17     %usr     %sys     %wio     %idle
23:32:27       80       14        3        3
23:32:37       70       14       12        4
23:32:47       72       13       21        4
23:32:57       76       14        6        3
23:33:07       73       10       13        4
23:33:17       71        8       17        4
23:33:27       67        9       20        4
23:33:37       69       10       17        4

Average        73       11       13        4
```

In the preceding command with the -u switch, two values are passed as input. The first value used here, that is 10, displays the number of seconds between `sar` readings and the second value used here, that is 8, indicates the number of times you want `sar` to run.

How it works...

The sar command provides a quick snapshot of how much the CPU is bogged down or utilized. The sar output reports the following four columns:

- `%usr`: This indicates percentage of CPU running in user mode
- `%sys`: This indicates percentage of CPU running in system mode

- `%wio`: This indicates percentage of CPU running idle with a process waiting for block I/O
- `%idle`: This indicates percentage of CPU that is idle

Often a low percentage of idle time points to a CPU intensive job or an underpowered CPU. You could use the `ps` command or `prstat` command in Solaris to find a CPU intensive job.

The following are general indicators of performance problems:

- If you see an abnormally high value in the `%usr` column, this would mean that applications are not being tuned properly or are over utilizing the CPU.
- If you see a high value in the `%sys` column, it probably indicates a bottleneck that could be due to swapping or paging and that needs to be investigated further. Also, this is the amount of CPU usage by the system calls, when applications makes several calls in background.

Monitoring paging and swapping

In this recipe, we are going to use the `sar` and `vmstat` commands with options to monitor paging and swapping operations.

Getting ready

It is necessary to monitor the amount of paging and swapping happening on the operating system. Paging occurs when a part of the operating system process gets transferred from physical memory to disk, or is read back from physical memory to disk. Swapping occurs when an entire process gets transferred to disk, from physical memory to disk, or is read back into physical memory from disk. Depending on the system, either paging or swapping could be an issue. If paging is occurring normally, and if you see a trend of heavy swapping, then the issue could be related to insufficient memory or sometimes the issue could be related to disk as well. If the system is heavily paging and not swapping, the issue could be related to either CPU or memory.

How to do it...

We could use the vmstat and sar command with the following to monitor the paging and swapping operations:

1. The `vmstat` command can be used with the `-S` switch to monitor swapping and paging operations:

```
bash$ vmstat -S
kthr        memory                         page          disk
 faults        cpu
 r b w    swap        free      si so   pi po fr de sr s0 s2 s3 s4
   in    sy                cs us sy id
 6 14 0 453537392 170151696 0   0    2444 186 183 0 0 1 1 1 1
    77696 687853            72596 13 4 83
```

   In the preceding snippet, the columns `si` and `so` represent swap in and swap out operations.

   Similarly, `pi` and `po` represent page in and page out operations, respectively. However, when the `sar` command is used with the required options, it provides more in depth analysis of paging and swapping operations.

2. We can also use the `sar` command with the `-p` switch to report paging operations:

```
bash-3.2$   sar -p 5 4

SunOS usmtnz-sinfsi17 5.10 Generic_150400-04 sun4u     08/08/2014

05:45:18  atch/s  pgin/s ppgin/s  pflt/s  vflt/s slock/s
05:45:23 4391.18    0.80    2.20 12019.44 30956.92    0.60
05:45:28 2172.26    1.80    2.40 5417.76 15499.80    0.20
05:45:33 2765.60    0.20    0.20 9893.20 20556.60    0.00
05:45:38 2194.80    2.00    2.00 7494.80 19018.60    0.00

Average  2879.85    1.20    1.70 8703.00 21500.25    0.20
```

   The preceding output reports the following columns:

   atch/s: Page faults per second that are satisfied by reclaiming a page currently in memory per second.

   pgin/s: The number of times per second that the filesystem receives page in requests.

`ppgin/s`: Pages paged in per second.

`pflt/s`: The number of page faults from protection errors.

`vflt/s`: Address translation page faults per second. This happens when a valid page is not found in memory.

`slock/s`: Faults per second caused by software lock requests requiring physical I/O.

Similarly, for swapping we can use the `sar` command with the `-w` switch to indicate whether there are any performance problems with swap.

3. Similarly, we can use the `sar` command with the `-w` switch to report swapping activities and identify whether there are any swap-related issues:

```
bash-3.2$ sar -w 5 4

SunOS usmtnz-sinfsi17 5.10 Generic_150400-04 sun4u     08/08/2014

06:20:55 swpin/s bswin/s swpot/s bswot/s pswch/s
06:21:00    0.00     0.0    0.00     0.0   53143
06:21:05    0.00     0.0    0.00     0.0   60949
06:21:10    0.00     0.0    0.00     0.0   55149
06:21:15    0.00     0.0    0.00     0.0   64075

Average     0.00     0.0    0.00     0.0   58349
```

The preceding output reports the following columns:

`swpin/s`: This indicates the number of LWP transfers in memory per second.

`bswin/s`: This indicates the number of blocks transferred for swap-ins per second.

`swpot/s`: This reports the average number of processes that are swapped out of memory per second.

`bswot/s`: This reports the number of blocks that are transferred for swap-outs per second.

`pswch/s`: This indicates the number of kernel thread switches per second.

How it works...

If the `si` and `so` columns of the `vmstat -S` output have non-zero values, then it serves as a good indicator of a possible performance issue related to swapping. This must be further investigated using the more detailed analysis provided by the `sar` command with the `-p` and `-w` switch, respectively.

For paging the key is to look for an inordinate amount of page faults of any kind. This would indicate a high degree of paging. The concern is not with paging, but with swapping because as paging increases it would be followed by swapping. We can look at the values in the `atch/s`, `pflt/s`, `vflt/s`, and `slock/s` columns of the `sar -p` command output to review the amount of page faults of any type and see the paging statistics to observe whether the paging activity remains steady or increases during a specific timeframe.

For the output of the `sar -w` command, the key column to observe is the `swpot/s` column. This column indicates the average number of processes that are swapped out of memory per second. If the value in this column is greater than 1, it is an indicator of memory deficiency and to correct this you would have to increase memory.

Tracking CPU consuming processes

In this recipe, we are going to use the top command to find the processes that are using a lot of CPU resources.

Getting ready

The top command is a Linux-based utility and it does not work in Unix-based systems. If you are using Solaris then use the `prstat` command instead to find CPU intensive processes.

How to do it...

The usage of the top command is shown in the following snippet:

```
bash-3.2$top

Cpu states: 0.0% idle, 82.0% user, 18.7% kernel, 0.8% wait, 0.5% swap
Memory: 795M real, 12M free, 318M swap, 1586M free swap
PID USERNAME PRI NICE SIZE RES STATE TIME WCPU CPU COMMAND
```

```
23624 postgres -25 2 208M 4980K cpu 1:20 22.47% 94.43% postgres
15811 root -15 4 2372K 716K sleep 22:19 0.61% 3.81% java
20435 admin 33 0 207M 2340K sleep 2:47 0.23% 1.14% postgres
20440 admin 33 0 93M 2300K sleep 2:28 0.23% 1.14% postgres
23698 root 33 0 2052K 1584K cpu 0:00 0.23% 0.95% top
23621 admin 27 2 5080K 3420K sleep 0:17 1.59% 0.38% postgres
23544 root 27 2 2288K 1500K sleep 0:01 0.06% 0.38% br2.1.adm
15855 root 21 4 6160K 2416K sleep 2:05 0.04% 0.19% proctool
897 root 34 0 8140K 1620K sleep 55:46 0.00% 0.00% Xsun
20855 admin -9 2 7856K 2748K sleep 7:14 0.67% 0.00% PSRUN
208534 admin -8 2 208M 4664K sleep 4:21 0.52% 0.00% postgres
755 admin 23 0 3844K 1756K sleep 2:56 0.00% 0.00% postgres
2788 root 28 0 1512K 736K sleep 1:03 0.00% 0.00% lpNet
18598 root 14 10 2232K 1136K sleep 0:56 0.00% 0.00% xlock
1 root 33 0 412K 100K sleep 0:55 0.00% 0.00% ini
```

The starting lines in the preceding output give general system information, whereas the rest of the display is arranged in order of decreasing current CPU usage.

How it works...

The top command provides statistics on CPU activity. It displays a list of CPU intensive tasks on the system and also provides an interface for manipulating processes.

In the preceding output, we can see that the top user is postgres with a process ID of 23624. We can see the CPU consumption of this user to be at 94.43%, which is way too high and it needs to be investigated or the corresponding operating system process needs to be killed if it is causing performance issues on the system.

Monitoring CPU load

In this recipe, we are going to use the uptime command to monitor overall CPU load.

How to do it...

The uptime command tells us the following information:

- Current system time
- How long the system has been running
- Number of currently logged on users in the system
- System load average for the past 1, 5, and 15 minutes

The uptime command can be used as follows:

```
bash-3.2$ uptime
11:44pm  up 20 day(s), 20 hr(s),  10 users,  load average: 27.80, 30.46,
33.77
```

Here in the preceding output we can see the current system time, 11.44pm GMT, and the system has been up and running for the last 20 days and 20 hrs without requiring a reboot. The output also tells us there are around 10 concurrently logged on users in the system. Finally, we also get the load average during the past 1, 5, and 15 minutes as 27.80, 30.46, and 33.77 respectively.

How it works...

The basic purpose of running the uptime command is to have a quick look at the current CPU load in the system. This provides a sneak peek of current system performance. System load can be defined as the average number of processes that are either in a runnable or uninterruptable state. A process is known to be in a running state when it is using the CPU resources or else is waiting for its turn to acquire CPU resources. A process is known to be in an uninterruptable state when it is waiting for some I/O operation, such as waiting on disk. Load average is then taken over the three time intervals, that is, 1, 5, and 15 minute periods. Load averages are not normalized for the number of CPUs in the system, that is, for a system with a single CPU, a load average of 1 would mean that the CPU was heavily loaded all the time with no idle time period, whereas for a system with five CPUs, a load average of 1 would indicate an idle time of 80% and a busy time period of only 20%.

Identifying CPU bottlenecks

In this recipe, we are going to use the mpstat command to identify CPU bottlenecks.

How to do it...

The mpstat command is used to report per processor statistics in a tabular format.

We are now going to show the usage of the mpstat command:

```
bash-3.2$ mpstat 1 1
```

CPU idl	minf	mjf	xcal	intr	ithr	csw	icsw	migr	smtx	srw	syscl	usr	sys	wt
0 73	672	0	2457	681	12	539	17	57	119	0	4303	18	10	0
1 79	90	0	1551	368	22	344	6	37	104	0	3775	17	4	0
2 86	68	0	1026	274	14	217	4	24	83	0	2393	11	3	0
3 92	50	0	568	218	9	128	3	17	56	0	1319	7	2	0
4 88	27	0	907	340	12	233	3	22	72	0	2034	9	2	0
5 74	75	0	1777	426	25	370	5	33	111	0	4820	22	4	0

How it works...

In the preceding output of the mpstat command, each row of the table represents the activity of one processor. The first table shows the summary of activity since boot time. The important column that is relevant from a DBA's perspective is the value in the smtx column. The smtx measurement indicates the number of times CPU failed to obtain the mutual exclusion lock or mutex. Mutex stalls waste CPU time and degrade multiprocessor scaling.

A general rule of thumb is if the values in the smtx column are greater than 200, then it is a symptom and indication of CPU bottleneck issues that need to be investigated.

Identifying disk I/O bottlenecks

In this recipe, we are going to use the iostat command to identify disk-related bottlenecks.

How to do it...

There are various options, that is, switches, available with the `iostat` command. The following are the most important switches used with `iostat`:

1. `-d`: This switch reports the number of kilobytes transferred per second for specific disks, the number of transfers per second, and the average service time in milliseconds. The following is the usage of the `iostat -d` command:

```
bash-3.2$iostat -d 5   5

sd0              sd2           sd3           sd4
Kps tps serv  Kps tps serv Kps tps serv Kps tps serv
1   0   53    57  5   145   19 1   89   0   0   14
140 14  16    0   0   0     785 31  21   0   0   0
8   1   15    0   0   0     814 36  18   0   0   0
11  1   82    0   0   26    818 36  19   0   0   0
0   0   0     1   0   22    856 37  20   0   0   0
```

2. `-D`: This switch lists the reads per second, writes per second, and percentage of disk utilization:

```
bash-3.2$ iostat -D 5 5

sd0              sd2           sd3           sd4
rps wps util rps wps util  rps wps util  rps wps util
0    0 0.3    4   0   6.2   1   1   1.8   0   0  0.0
0    0 0.0    0   35  90.6  237 0   97.8  0   0  0.0
0    0 0.0    0   34  84.7  218 0   98.2  0   0  0.0
0    0 0.0    0   34  88.3  230 0   98.2  0   0  0.0
0    2 4.4    0   37  91.3  225 0   97.7  0   0  0.0
```

3. `-x`: This switch will report extended disk statistics for all disks:

```
bash-3.2$ iostat -x
                    extended device statistics
device      r/s    w/s    kr/s    kw/s wait actv   svc_t  %w   %b
fd0         0.0    0.0    0.0     0.0  0.0  0.0     0.0    0    0
sd0         0.0    0.0    0.4     0.4  0.0  0.0     49.5   0    0
sd2         0.0    0.0    0.0     0.0  0.0  0.0     0.0    0    0
sd3         0.0    4.6    0.0   257.6  0.0  0.1     26.4   0    12
sd4         69.3   3.6    996.9 180.5  0.0  7.6     102.4  0    100
nfs10       0.0    0.0    0.4     0.0  0.0  0.0     24.5   0    0
nfs14       0.0    0.0    0.0     0.0  0.0  0.0     6.3    0    0
nfs16       0.0    0.0    0.0     0.0  0.0  0.0     4.9    0    0
```

How it works...

The iostat command reports statistics about disk input and output operations and to produce measurements of throughput, utilization, queue lengths, transaction rates, and service time. The first line of the iostat output is for everything since booting the system, whereas each subsequent line shows only the prior interval specified.

If we observe the preceding output of the `iostat -d` command in the How to do it section, we can clearly see that disk drive sd3 is heavily overloaded. The values for the kps column (kilobytes transferred per second), tps (number of transfers per second), and serv (average service time in milliseconds) for disk drive sd3 is consistently high over the specified interval. This leads us to the conclusion that moving information from sd3 to any other drive might be a good idea if this information is representative of disk I/O on a consistent basis. This would reduce the load on disk drive sd3.

Also, if you observe the output of the `iostat -D` command in the How to do it section, we can conclude that disk drive sd3 has high read activity as indicated by the high values in the rps column (reads per second). Similarly, we can see that disk drive sd2 has a high write activity, as indicated by the high values in the wps column (writes per second). Both the disk drives sd2 and sd3 are at a peak level of utilization, as can be seen from the high percentage in the util column (utilization). The high values in the util column are an indication of I/0 problems and this should be investigated by the system administrator.

Similarly, if we have a look at the preceding output of the `iostat -x` command in the How to do it section, we can easily come to the conclusion that disk drive sd4 is experiencing I/O problems, as can be seen from the %b column, which indicates the percentage of time that the disk is busy. For disk drive sd4, the disk utilization is at 100%, which in this case would need a system administrator's immediate attention.

Monitoring system load

Many a times there are situations when the application users start complaining about the database performance being slow and as a DBA you need to determine whether there are system resource bottlenecks on the PostgreSQL server. Running the vmstat command can help us to quickly locate and identify the bottlenecks on the server.

How to do it...

The vmstat command is used to report real-time performance statistics about processes, memory, paging, disk I/O, and CPU consumption. The following is the usage of the `vmstat` command:

```
$ vmstat
procs -----------memory---------- ---swap-- -----io---- --system-- ----cpu-
---
r b swpd free buff cache si so bi bo in cs us sy id wa
14 0 52340 25272 3068 1662704 0 0 63 76 9 31 15 1 84 0
```

In the preceding output, the first line divides the columns on the second line into six different categories, which are discussed in the following list:

- The first category is the process (procs) and it contains the following columns:
  - r: This column indicates the total number of processes waiting for runtime
  - b: This column reports the total number of processes in uninterruptible sleep
- The second category is memory and it contains the following columns:
  - swpd: This column indicates the total amount of virtual memory in use
  - free: This column reports the amount of idle memory available for use
  - buff: This column indicates the amount of memory used for buffers
  - cache: This column indicates the amount of memory used as page cache
- The third category is swap and it contains the following columns:
  - si: This column reports the amount of memory swapped in from disk
  - so: This column indicates the amount of memory swapped out from disk
- The fourth category is I/O (io) and it contains the following columns:
  - bi: This column indicates the blocks that are read in from a block device
  - bo: This column reports the blocks that are written out to a block device

- The fifth category is system and this category contains the following columns:
  - `in`: This column reports the number of interrupts per second
  - `cs`: This column reports the number of context switches per second
- The final category is the CPU and it contains the following columns:
  - `us`: This column reports the percentage of the time CPU ran user level code
  - `sy`: This column reports the percentage of the time the CPU ran system level code
  - `id`: This column reports the percentage of time the CPU was idle
  - `wa`: This column reports the amount of time spent waiting for I/O to complete

How it works...

The following are the general rules of thumb that are used while interpreting the `vmstat` command output:

- If the value in the `wa` column is high, it is an indication that the storage system is probably overloaded and necessary action needs to be taken to address that issue
- If the value in the `b` column is greater than zero consistently, then it is an indication that the system does not have enough processing power to service the currently running and scheduled jobs
- If the values in the `so` and the `si` column are greater than zero when monitored for a period of time, then it is an indication and a symptom of a memory bottleneck

Tracking historical CPU usage

In this recipe, we are going to show how to use the `sar` command in combination with various switches to analyze historical CPU load during some time in the past.

Getting ready

The commands used in this recipe have been performed on a CentOS Linux machine. The command output may vary in other Linux and Unix-based operating systems.

How to do it...

The sar command when used with the −u switch is used to display CPU statistics. When used this way, the sar command will report on the current day's activities.

If we are looking to analyze the CPU statistic over some time period in the past we would need to use the -f switch in conjunction with the −u switch of the sar command. The −f option is followed by the files that sar uses to report on statistics for different days of the month, and these files are usually located in the /var/log/sa directory and usually have a naming convention of sadd, where dd represents the numeric day of the month whose values are in a range from 01 to 31.

The following snippet shows the usage of the sar command to view CPU statistics for the eighth day of the month:

```
$ sar -u -f /var/log/sa/sa08
03:50:10 PM CPU %user %nice %system  %iowait  %idle
04:00:10 PM all 0.42  0.00   0.24     0.00    96.41
04:10:10 PM all 0.22  0.00   1.96     0.00    95.53
04:20:10 PM all 0.22  0.00   1.22     0.01    99.55
04:30:10 PM all 0.22  0.00   0.24     2.11    99.54
04:40:10 PM all 0.24  0.00   0.23     0.00    92.54
Average:        all 0.19  0.00   0.19     0.07    99.55
```

How it works...

Generally, the rule of thumb is that if the %idle is low, it serves as an indication that either the CPUs are underpowered or the application load is high. Similarly, if we see non-zero values in the iowait time column, it serves as a reminder that the I/O subsystem could be a potential bottleneck.

If we observe the preceding output of the sar command, we can clearly see that the %idle time is high, which clearly indicates that CPU is probably not overburdened and we don't see many non-zero values in the %iowait column, which tells us that there is not much contention for disk I/O either.

There's more...

When the sysstat package is installed, a few cron jobs are scheduled to create files used by the sar utility to report on historical server statistics. We can observe these cron jobs by taking a look at the /etc/cron.d/sysstat file.

Tracking historical memory usage

In this recipe, we are going to see how to analyze the memory load for a previous day in the week.

Getting ready

The commands used in this recipe have been performed on a CentOS Linux machine. The command output may vary in other Linux and Unix-based operating systems.

How to do it...

When it comes to analyzing memory statistics, we need to check for both paging statistics as well as swapping statistics.

We can use the sar command in conjunction with the −B switch to report on paging statistics, along with the −f switch to report on statistics for different days of the month. As mentioned in the previous recipe, the files that the sar command uses to report statistics for different days of the month are located in the /var/log/sa directory, where the files have a naming convention of sadd, where dd represent the numeric date of the month, and where these values are in the range from 01 to 31.

For instance, to report on the paging statistics for the fifth of the month, we can use the sar command as follows:

```
$ sar -B -f /var/log/sa/sa05

06:10:05 AM pgpgin/s   pgpgout/s   fault/s   majflt/s
06:20:05 AM 0.02          18.17      19.37     0.00
06:30:05 AM 4.49          26.68      76.15     0.05
06:40:05 AM 4512.43      419.24     380.14     0.65
06:50:06 AM 4850.03     1055.79    4364.73     0.51
07:00:06 PM 4172.68     1096.96    6650.51     0.16
```

Similarly, to report on the swapping statistics we can use the sar command in conjunction with the −W switch to report on swapping statistics, along with the −f switch to report on statistics for different days of the month.

For instance, to report on the swapping statistics for the fifth day of the month we can use the sar command as follows:

```
$ sar -W -f /var/log/sa/sa05

06:10:05 AM  pswpin/s pswpout/s
06:20:05 AM   0.00     0.00
06:30:05 AM   0.02     0.00
06:40:05 AM   1.15     1.45
06:50:06 AM   0.94     2.99
07:00:06 PM   0.67     6.95
```

How it works...

In the preceding output of the sar -B -f /var/log/sa/sa05 command, we can clearly see that around 6.40 am there was a substantial increase in paging from disk (pgpgin/s), pages paged out to disk (pgpgout/s), and page faults per second (fault/s).

Similarly, when swapping statistics are being reported with the sar -W -f /var/log/sa/sa05 command, we can clearly see that the swapping started around 06.40 am as can be seen from the values in the pswpin/s column and pswpout/s column. If we see high values in the pswpin/s column (pages swapped into memory per second) and in the pgpgout/s column (pages swapped out per second), it is an indication that current memory is inadequate and it needs to be either increased or for certain application components the existing memory needs to be optimally resized.

Monitoring disk space

In this recipe, we are going to show the commands that are used to monitor disk space.

How to do it...

We can use the df command with various switches to monitor disk space. To make the output more understandable, we often use the -h switch with the df command as follows:

```
bash-3.2$ df -h

Filesystem                                    size    used   avail
capacity  Mounted on
                                              132G    80G    50G
62%    /
```

```
/devices                                        0K      0K      0K
0%      /devices
ctfs                                            0K      0K      0K
0%      /system/contract
proc                                            0K      0K      0K
0%      /proc
mnttab                                          0K      0K      0K
0%      /etc/mnttab
swap                                          418G    488K    418G
1%      /etc/svc/volatile
swap                                          418G     38M    418G
1%      /tmp
swap                                          418G    152K    418G
1%      /var/run
/dev/dsk/c20t60000970000192602156533030374242d0s0  236G  240M  234G
1%      /peterdata/cm_new
/dev/dsk/c20t60000970000192602156533032353441d0s0   30G   30M   29G
1%      /peterdata/native
/dev/dsk/c20t60000970000192602156533033313441d0s0  236G   60G  174G
26%     /peterdata/db_new
/dev/dsk/c20t60000970000195701036533032454646d0s0   30G  6.9G   22G
24%     /peterdata/native
/dev/dsk/c20t60000970000195701036533032444137d0s0  236G  224G   12G
95%     /peterdata/db
/dev/dsk/c20t60000970000192602156533032333232d0s2  709G  316G  386G
45%     /peterdata/cm
usmtnnas4106-epmnfs.emrsn.org:/peterblap_2156   276G   239G    36G    87%
/peterblap
usmtnnas4106-epmnfs.emrsn.org:/peterdata_data_2156    98G    53G    45G
54%     /peterdata/data
usmtnnas4106-epmnfs.emrsn.org:/peterdata_uc4appmgr   9.8G   3.6G   6.3G
37%     /peterdata/uc4/
```

How it works...

If we observe the preceding output, we can see that the mountpoint `/peterdata/db` is nearing its full capacity as the mountpoint has reached a capacity of 95% and only another 12 GB of free disk space is available on the device. This is an indication that either the administrator needs to clean up some old files on the existing mountpoint to release more free space, or allocate more additional space to the given mount point before it reaches its full capacity.

Monitoring network status

In this recipe, we are going to show how to monitor the status of network interfaces.

Getting ready

The commands used in this recipe have been performed on a CentOS Linux machine. The command output may vary in other Linux and Unix-based operating systems.

How to do it...

We are going to use the `netstat` command with the `-i` switch to display the status of network interfaces that are configured on the system. The following is the usage of the `netstat` command:

```
bash-3.2$ netstat -i
Name    Mtu  Net/Dest       Address        Ipkts     Ierrs Opkts   Oerrs Collis Queue
lo0     8232 loopback       localhost      187358785 0     187358785 0     0      0
nxge909000 1500 usmtnz-sinfsi17.emrsn.com usmtnz-sinfsi17.emrsn.com 619320037 0     915300941 0       0      0
nxge909002 0    default        0.0.0.0        146274    0     0       0     0      0
nxge2761000 1500 0.0.0.0        0.0.0.0        619320058 0     915301069 0     0      0
nxge2761002 0    default        0.0.0.0        146274    0     0       0     0      0
sppp0   1500 192.168.224.1  192.168.224.3  13421     0     13489   0     0      0
```

How it works...

In the preceding output of the `netstat -i` command, we can determine the number of packets a system transmits and receives on each network interface. The `Ipkts` column determines the input packet count and the `Okpts` column determines the output packet count. If the input packet count (value in the `Ipkts` column) remains steady over a period of time, it means that the machine is not receiving network packets at all and the outcome suggests that it could possibly be a hardware failure on the network interface. If the output packet count (value in the `Okpts` column) remains steady over a period of time, then it could possibly point towards problems that may be caused due to an incorrect address entry in the hosts or the `ethers` database.

5
Connection Pooling and Database Partitioning

In this chapter, we will cover the following:

- Installing pgpool-II
- Configuring pgpool-II and testing the setup
- Installing PgBouncer
- Connection pooling using PgBouncer
- Managing Pgbouncer
- Implementing partitioning
- Managing artitions
- Installing PL/Proxy
- Partitioning with PL/Proxy

Introduction

pgpool-II is basically a middleware solution that works as an interface between a PostgreSQL server and a PostgreSQL client application. pgpool-II talks about the PostgreSQL's backend and frontend protocol and relays a connection between the two. pgpool-II caches incoming connections to PostgreSQL servers and reuses them whenever a new connection with the same properties comes in. This way it reduces connection overhead and improves overall throughput.

pgpool-II in fact offers a lot more features than connection pooling. pgpool-II offers the load balancing and replication modes along with the parallel query feature. However, since this chapter is dedicated to connection pooling, we are going to focus only on the connection pooling feature.

Pgbouncer is also a lightweight connection pooler for PostgreSQL. Applications connect to the Pgbouncer port just like the way it would connect to a Postgresql database on the database port. By using pgbouncer we can lower the connection overload impact on PostgreSQL servers. Pgbouncer provides for connection pooling by reusing existing connections.

The difference between PgBouncer and pgpool-II is that pgbouncer is lightweight and is only dedicated for connection pooling purposes, whereas pgpool-II offers a lot more features such as replication, load balancing, and parallel query features in addition to connection pooling.

Partitioning is defined as splitting up a large table into smaller chunks. PostgreSQL supports basic table partitioning. Partitioning is entirely transparent to applications. Partitioning has a lot of benefits, which are discussed in the following list:

- Query performance can be improved significantly for certain types of queries.
- Partitioning can lead to an improved update performance. Whenever queries update a big chunk of a single partition, performance can be improved by performing a sequential scan for that partition instead of using random reads and writes, which are dispersed across the entire table.
- Bulk deletes can be accomplished by simply removing one of the partitions.
- Infrequently used data can be shipped to cheaper and slower media.

For this chapter, we will be referring to pgpool-II as pgpool for the purpose of simplicity.

Installing pgpool-II

In this recipe, we are going to install pgpool.

Getting Ready

Installing pgpool from source requires GCC 2.9 or higher and GNU Make. Since pgpool links with the `libpq` library, the `libpq` library and its development headers must be installed prior to installing pgpool. Also the OpenSSL library and its development headers must be present in order to enable OpenSSL support in pgpool.

How to do it...

To install pgpool in a Debian or Ubuntu-based distribution we can execute the following command:

```
apt-get install pgpool2
```

On Red Hat, Fedora, CentOS, or any other RHEL-based Linux distributions, use the following command:

```
yum install pgpool*
```

If you are building from source, then follow these steps:

1. Download the latest tarball of pgpool from the following website: `http://www.pg pool.net/mediawiki/index.php/Downloads`.

2. The next step is to extract the pgpool tarball and enter the source directory:

   ```
   tar -xzf pgpool-II-3.4.0.tar.gz
   cd pgpool-II-3.4.0
   ```

3. The next step is to build, compile, and install pgpool software:

   ```
   ./configure --prefix=/usr --sysconfdir=/etc/pgpool/
   make
   make install
   ```

4. The next step is to create the location where pgpool can maintain activity logs:

   ```
   mkdir /var/log/pgpool
   chown postgres:postgres /var/log/pgpool
   ```

5. The next step is to create a directory where pgpool can store its service lock files:

   ```
   mkdir /var/run/pgpool
   chown postgres:postgres  /var/run/pgpool
   ```

How it works...

If you are using an operating system specific package manager to install pgpool then the respective configuration files and log files required by pgpool are automatically created. However, if you are proceeding with a full source-based pgpool installation then there are some additional steps required. The first step is required to run the configure script and then build and compile pgpool. After pgpool is installed you will be required to create the directories where pgpool can maintain activity logs and service lock files. All these steps need to be performed manually, as can be seen in steps 3, 4, and 5 respectively in the previous section.

Configuring pgpool and testing the setup

In this recipe, we are going to configure pgpool and show how to make connections using pgpool.

Getting ready

Before running pgpool if you are downloading from the tarball source then the pgpool software needs to be built and compiled. These steps are shown in the first recipe of this chapter.

How to do it...

We are going to follow these steps to configure pgpool and run the setup:

1. After pgpool is installed as shown in the first recipe of this chapter, the next step is to copy the configuration files from the sample directory with some default settings, which will be later edited as per our requirements:

```
cd /etc/pgpool/
cp pgpool.conf.sample-stream pgpool.conf
cp pcp.conf.sample etc/pcp.conf
```

2. The next step is to define a username and password in the `pcp.conf` file, which is an authentication file for pgpool. Basically, to use PCP commands user authentication is required. This mechanism is different from PostgreSQL 's user authentication. Passwords are encrypted in the md5 hash format. To obtain the md5 hash for a user we have to use the `pg_md5` utility, as shown in the following snippet. Once the `md5` hash is generated it can then be used to store the md5 password in the `pcp.conf` file:

```
/usr/bin/pg_md5 postgres
e8a48653851e28c69d0506508fb27fc5

vi /etc/pcp.conf
postgres:e8a48653851e28c69d0506508fb27fc5
```

3. The next step is to configure the `pgpool.conf` configuration file for pgpool settings to take effect:

```
listen_addresses = '*'
port = 9999
backend_hostname0 = 'localhost'
backend_port0 = 5432
backend_weight0 = 1
backend_data_directory0 = '/var/lib/pgsql/9.6/data'
 connection_cache = on
 max_pool = 10
 num_init_children = 20
```

4. Once the preceding parameters have been configured and saved in the `pgpool.conf` file, the next step is to launch pgpool and start accepting connections to the PostgreSQL cluster using pgpool:

```
pgpool -f  /etc/pgpool.conf -F /etc/pcp.conf

psql -p 9999 postgres postgres
```

How it works...

Let's now discuss some of the parameters that were configured in the earlier section:

- `listen_addresses`: We configure `listen_addresses` to * because we want to listen on all TCP connections and not specifically to a particular IP address.
- `port`: This defines the pgpool port on which the system will listen when accepting database connections.

- `backend_hostname0`: This refers to the hostname of the first database in our setup.
- `backend_port0`: The TCP port of the system, that is, the system identified by the value `backend_hostname0` on which the database is hosted.
- `backend_weight0`: The weight assigned to the node identified by the hostname obtained from the `backend_hostname0`. Basically, in pgpool weights are assigned to individual nodes. More requests will be dispatched to the node with a higher weight value.
- `backend_data_directory0`: This represents the data directory, that is, PGDATA for the host identified by the `backend_hostname0` value.
- `connection_cache`: To enable the connection pool mode we need to turn on `connection_cache`.
- `max_pool`: This value determines the maximum size of the pool per child. The number of connections from pgpool to the backend may reach a limit at `num_init_children*max_pool`.

In our case we configured `max_pool` to 10 and `num_init_children` to 20. So in sum, the total number of connections from pgpool to the backend may reach a limit of 200. Remember that the `max_pool * num_init_children` value should always be less than the `max_connections` parameter value.

Finally, once the parameters are configured it is time to launch pgpool and make connections on the pgpool port 9999.

> Please refer to the following web links for more details:
> `http://www.pgpool.net/mediawiki/index.php/Relationship_between _max_pool,_num_init_children,_and_max_connections` and `http://www.pgpool.net/docs/latest/en/html/`.

There's more...

Here we are going to show the commands that can be used to start/stop pgpool.

pgpool can be started in two ways:

1. By starting the `pgpool` service at the command line as the root user:

   ```
   service pgpool start
   ```

2. By firing the `pgpool` command on the terminal:

   pgpool

Similarly, pgpool can be stopped in two ways:

1. By stopping the `pgpool` service at the command line as the root user:

   service pgpool stop

2. By firing the pgpool command with the stop option:

   pgpool stop

Starting and stopping pgpool is relatively simple as was seen in the preceding section. However, pgpool comes with a lot of options and the following is the partial and most used syntax for starting pgpool:

pgpool [-f config_file] [-a hba_file] [-F pcp_config_file]

These options are discussed in the following list:

- `-c`: When the `-c` switch is used it is used to clear the query cache
- `-f config_file`: This option specifies the `pgpool.conf` configuration file and pgpool obtains its configuration from this file while starting itself
- `-a hba_file`: This option specifies the authentication file that is used when starting pgpool
- `-F pcp_config_file`: This option specifies the password file `pcp.conf` to be used when starting pgpool

> For full syntax of pgpool, refer to the following link: `http://www.pgpool.net/docs/latest/en/html/pgpool.html`.

For stopping pgpool the same options that were used earlier while starting pgpool can be used. However, along with these switches we can also specify the mode that needs to be used while stopping pgpool.

There are two modes in which pgpool can be stopped:

- **Smart Mode**: This option is specified by using the −m smart option. In this mode, we first wait for the clients to disconnect and then shutdown pgpool.
- **Fast Mode**: This mode can be set by specifying the −m fast option. In this mode, pgpool does not wait for clients to disconnect and it shuts down pgpool immediately.

The complete syntax of the `pgpool` stop command is as follows:

```
pgpool [-f config_file][-F pcp_config_file] [-m {s[mart]|f[ast]|]}] stop
```

> The pgpool tool is also helpful in doing the automatic failover and failback, which will reduce the database availability downtime. For more information about this, please check out the following URL: http://manoj adinesh.blogspot.in/2013/12/pgpool-configuration-failback.html.

Installing PgBouncer

In this recipe, we are going to show the steps that are required to install PgBouncer.

Getting ready

We can either do a full source-based installation or use the operating system-specific package manager to install PgBouncer.

How to do it...

On an Ubuntu/Debian based system, we need to execute the following command to install PgBouncer:

```
apt-get install pgbouncer
```

On CentOS, Fedora, or Red Hat-based Linux distributions, we can execute the following command:

```
yum install pgbouncer
```

If you are doing a full source based installation, then the sequence of commands are mentioned here:

1. Download the archive installation file from the given link:
   http://pgfoundry.org/projects/pgbouncer

2. Extract the downloaded archive and enter the source directory:

   ```
   tar -xzf pgbouncer-1.5.4.tar.gz
   cd pgbouncer-1.5.4
   ```

3. The next step is to build and proceed with the software installation:

   ```
   ./configure --prefix=/usr
   make & make install
   ```

4. After PgBouncer is installed, the next step is to create the directory where PgBouncer can maintain activity logs:

   ```
   mkdir /var/log/pgbouncer
   cd /var/log/pgbouncer
   chown postgres:postgres pgbouncer
   ```

5. The next step is to create a directory where PgBouncer can keep its service lock files:

   ```
   mkdir /var/run/pgbouncer
   chown postgres:postgres /var/run/pgbouncer
   ```

6. The final step is to create a configuration directory to hold a sample PgBouncer configuration file that can be used later on to make parameter changes:

   ```
   mkdir /etc/pgbouncer
   cp etc/pgbouncer.ini /etc/pgbouncer
   chown -R postgres:psgtes /etc/pgbouncer
   ```

How it works...

If you are using an operating system specific package manager to install PgBouncer then the respective configuration files and log files required by PgBouncer are automatically created. However, if you are proceeding with a full source based PgBouncer installation then there are some additional steps required. You will be required to create the directories where PgBouncer can maintain activity logs and service lock files. You will also be required to create the configuration directory where the configuration file for PgBouncer will be stored. All these steps need to be performed manually as seen in steps 4, 5, and 6 respectively in the preceding section.

Connection pooling using PgBouncer

Here in this recipe we are going to implement PgBouncer and benchmark the results for database connections made to the database via PgBouncer against normal database connections.

Getting ready

Before we configure and implement connection pooling, the PgBouncer utility must be installed prior to performing the steps mentioned in this recipe. Installing PgBouncer is covered in the previous recipe.

How to do it...

1. First we are going to tweak some of the configuration settings in the `pgbouncer.ini` configuration file, as shown in the following snippet. The first two entries are for the databases that will be passed through PgBouncer. Next we configure the `listen_addr` parameter to `*`, which means that it is going to listen on all IP addresses. Finally, we set the last two parameters, which are `auth_file`, that is, the location of the authentication file, and `auth_type`, which indicates the type of authentication used. We use plain as the authentication type, which indicates that we are using the password-based mechanism here for authentication:

   ```
   vi  /etc/pgbouncer/pgbouncer.ini

   postgres = host=localhost dbname=postgres
   ```

```
pgtest = host=localhost dbname=pgtest
listen_addr = *
auth_file = /etc/pgbouncer/userlist.txt
auth_type = md5
```

2. The next step is to create a user list that contains a list of users who would be allowed to access the databases through PgBouncer. Format of the entries in the user list would be supplied as username followed by the user's password, as shown in the following snippet where the first entry is for username whose value is author and the second entry is for password whose value is password. Since we are using the authentication type as md5 we have to use the md5 password entry in the user list. Had we been using the authentication type as plain then the actual password would have been supplied in the user list:

```
postgres=# CREATE role author LOGIN PASSWORD 'author' SUPERUSER;
CREATE ROLE

postgres=# select rolname ,rolpassword from pg_authid where
rolname='author';
rolname |              rolpassword
---------+------------------------------------
 author  | md5d50afb6ec7b2501164b80a0480596ded
(1 row)
```

The md5 password obtained can then be defined in the userlist file for the corresponding user:

```
vi /etc/pgbouncer/userlist.txt
"author" "md5d50afb6ec7b2501164b80a0480596ded"
```

3. Once we have configured the pgbouncer.ini configuration file and created the user list the next step is to start the pgbouncer service by using one of the following approaches:

```
service pgbouncer start
```

Alternatively:

```
pgbouncer -d /etc/pgbouncer/pgbouncer.ini
```

4. Once the pgbouncer service is up and running, the next step is to make connections to it. By default, the pgbouncer service runs on port 6432 so any connections made to the pgbouncer service need to be made on port 6432:

```
psql -h localhost -p 6432 -d postgres -U author  -W
```

5. Now that we have made connections using PgBouncer, the next logical step is to find out if there are any performance improvements using PgBouncer. For this purpose we are going to create a temporary database, the one that was initially defined in the `pgbouncer.ini` file, and then we are going to insert records into it and do benchmarking for connections made against this database:

```
createdb pgtest
pgbench -i -s 10 pgtest
```

6. The next step is to benchmark the results against the `pgtest` database:

```
bash-3.2$ pgbench -t 1000 -c 20 -S  pgtest
starting vacuum...end.
transaction type: SELECT only
scaling factor: 10
number of clients: 20
number of transactions per client: 1000
number of transactions actually processed: 20000/20000
tps = 415.134776 (including connections establishing)
tps = 416.464707 (excluding connections establishing)
```

7. The final step is to benchmark the results against the `pgbench` database on PgBouncer port `6432`:

```
bash-3.2$ pgbench -t 1000 -c 20 -S  -p 6432 -U author -P author
pgtest
starting vacuum...end.
transaction type: SELECT only
scaling factor: 10
number of clients: 20
number of transactions per client: 1000
number of transactions actually processed: 20000/20000
tps = 2256.161662 (including connections establishing)
tps = 410.006262 (excluding connections establishing)
```

How it works...

Here we can see a couple of things. Initially, we have to configure the `pgbouncer.ini` configuration file along with the user list that will be used for accessing databases via PgBouncer. Effectiveness of PgBouncer can be seen in steps 6 and 7 in the preceding section. We can see that the throughput increases to 2,256.15 transactions per second while using PgBouncer, whereas when PgBouncer is not being used the throughput decreases to 415.13 transactions per second. In effect, when using PgBouncer the throughput increases by five times approximately.

PgBouncer offers connection pooling in different modes such as transaction mode, statement mode, and session mode. The session mode of PgBouncer is the mostly preferred pooling mode, where a connection will be pooled back to the resource queue whenever the application closes the connection. The same session will be reused later for other transactions.

There's more...

In the How It Works section we configured a couple of parameters in the `pgbouncer.ini` configuration file. However, there are a lot more parameters that can be configured and if they are not configured they will take the default settings. Please refer to the following link for more details on PgBouncer parameters `https://pgbouncer.github.io/config.html`.

These days it is more common to include PgBouncer modules in application business logic to achieve better high availability. Refer to the following diagram, which shows how we need to manage PgBouncer to do failover to the slave node when the master is not available:

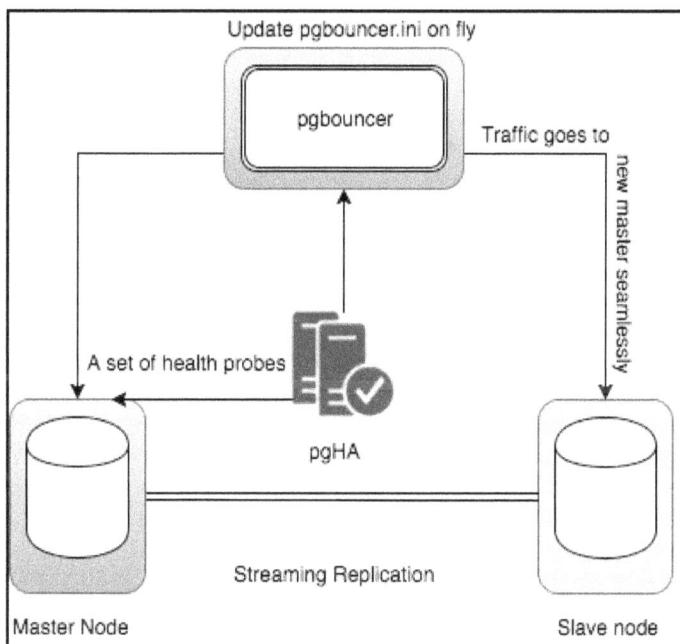

To achieve the preceding kind of setup in your business logic, we have to use a dedicated tool called pgHA, which is implemented by the OpenSCG team.

Please find more information about pgHA at the following URL:
`https://www.openscg.com/products/postgres-high-availability/`.

Managing PgBouncer

PgBouncer provides an administrative console to view pool status and client connections. In this recipe we are going to see information regarding PgBouncer connections, client connections, view pool status, and obtaining connection pooling statistics.

Getting ready

Before we issue any commands we first need to connect to the PgBouncer's administrative console. For this purpose we need to set the `admin_users` parameter in the `pgbouncer.ini` configuration file:

```
vi /etc/pgbouncer/pgbouncer.ini

admin_users = author
```

Once the preceding changes are saved in the `pgbouncer.ini` configuration file the PgBouncer service needs to be restarted in order to ensure that the parameter changes come into effect:

```
service pgbouncer restart
```

Once this is done we can then make connections to the PgBouncer administration console with the following command:

```
psql -p 6432 -U author pgbouncer
```

How to do it…

With the help of the PgBouncer administration console we can get information regarding the clients, servers, and the pool health:

1. To get information regarding the clients, issue the `show clients` command on the PgBouncer admin interface:

```
pgbouncer=# show clients;
type |  user  | database  | state  | addr | port | local_addr | local_port |   connect_time      |    request_time     |   ptr    |   link
-----+--------+-----------+--------+------+------+------------+------------+---------------------+---------------------+----------+----------
 C   | author | pgbouncer | active | unix | 6432 | unix       |       6432 | 2014-11-21 18:05:43 | 2014-11-21 18:06:44 | 0x9e1ca50 |
 C   | author | pgtest    | active | unix | 6432 | unix       |       6432 | 2014-11-21 18:06:42 | 2014-11-21 18:06:42 | 0x9e1d8d0 | 0x9e00518
 C   | author | pgtest    | active | unix | 6432 | unix       |       6432 | 2014-11-21 18:06:42 | 2014-11-21 18:06:42 | 0x9e1d448 | 0x9e00090
 C   | author | pgtest    | active | unix | 6432 | unix       |       6432 | 2014-11-21 18:06:42 | 2014-11-21 18:06:42 | 0x9e1d9b8 | 0x9e006e8
 C   | author | pgtest    | active | unix | 6432 | unix       |       6432 | 2014-11-21 18:06:42 | 2014-11-21 18:06:42 | 0x9e1daa0 | 0x9e007d0
 C   | author | pgtest    | active | unix | 6432 | unix       |       6432 | 2014-11-21 18:06:42 | 2014-11-21 18:06:42 | 0x9e1d7e8 | 0x9dfffa8
 C   | author | pgtest    | active | unix | 6432 | unix       |       6432 | 2014-11-21 18:06:42 | 2014-11-21 18:06:42 | 0x9e1cd08 | 0x9e00430
 C   | author | pgtest    | active | unix | 6432 | unix       |       6432 | 2014-11-21 18:06:42 | 2014-11-21 18:06:42 | 0x9e1db88 | 0x9dff868
 C   | author | pgtest    | active | unix | 6432 | unix       |       6432 | 2014-11-21 18:06:42 | 2014-11-21 18:06:42 | 0x9e1d530 | 0x9e00178
 C   | author | pgtest    | active | unix | 6432 | unix       |       6432 | 2014-11-21 18:06:42 | 2014-11-21 18:06:42 | 0x9e1d618 | 0x9e00260
 C   | author | pgtest    | active | unix | 6432 | unix       |       6432 | 2014-11-21 18:06:42 | 2014-11-21 18:06:42 | 0x9e1dc70 | 0x9e00348
 C   | author | pgtest    | active | unix | 6432 | unix       |       6432 | 2014-11-21 18:06:42 | 2014-11-21 18:06:42 | 0x9e1d700 | 0x9e009a0
 C   | author | pgtest    | active | unix | 6432 | unix       |       6432 | 2014-11-21 18:06:42 | 2014-11-21 18:06:42 | 0x9e1d190 | 0x9e008b8
```

2. To get information regarding server connections, issue the `show servers` command on the PgBouncer administrative console:

```
pgbouncer=# show servers;
type |  user  | database | state  |   addr    | port | local_addr | local_port |   connect_time      |    request_time     |    ptr    |   link
-----+--------+----------+--------+-----------+------+------------+------------+---------------------+---------------------+-----------+----------
 S   | author | pgtest   | active | 127.0.0.1 | 5432 | 127.0.0.1  |      56002 | 2014-11-21 18:05:57 | 2014-11-21 18:06:42 | 0x9e00518 | 0x9e1d8d0
 S   | author | pgtest   | active | 127.0.0.1 | 5432 | 127.0.0.1  |      55997 | 2014-11-21 18:05:57 | 2014-11-21 18:06:42 | 0x9e00090 | 0x9e1d448
 S   | author | pgtest   | active | 127.0.0.1 | 5432 | 127.0.0.1  |      56004 | 2014-11-21 18:05:57 | 2014-11-21 18:06:42 | 0x9e006e8 | 0x9e1d9b8
 S   | author | pgtest   | active | 127.0.0.1 | 5432 | 127.0.0.1  |      56005 | 2014-11-21 18:05:57 | 2014-11-21 18:06:42 | 0x9e007d0 | 0x9e1daa0
 S   | author | pgtest   | active | 127.0.0.1 | 5432 | 127.0.0.1  |      55996 | 2014-11-21 18:05:57 | 2014-11-21 18:06:42 | 0x9dfffa8 | 0x9e1d7e8
 S   | author | pgtest   | active | 127.0.0.1 | 5432 | 127.0.0.1  |      56001 | 2014-11-21 18:05:57 | 2014-11-21 18:06:42 | 0x9e00430 | 0x9e1cd08
 S   | author | pgtest   | active | 127.0.0.1 | 5432 | 127.0.0.1  |      55988 | 2014-11-21 18:05:57 | 2014-11-21 18:06:42 | 0x9dff868 | 0x9e1db88
 S   | author | pgtest   | active | 127.0.0.1 | 5432 | 127.0.0.1  |      55998 | 2014-11-21 18:05:57 | 2014-11-21 18:06:42 | 0x9e00178 | 0x9e1d530
 S   | author | pgtest   | active | 127.0.0.1 | 5432 | 127.0.0.1  |      55999 | 2014-11-21 18:05:57 | 2014-11-21 18:06:42 | 0x9e00260 | 0x9e1d618
 S   | author | pgtest   | active | 127.0.0.1 | 5432 | 127.0.0.1  |      56000 | 2014-11-21 18:05:57 | 2014-11-21 18:06:42 | 0x9e00348 | 0x9e1dc70
 S   | author | pgtest   | active | 127.0.0.1 | 5432 | 127.0.0.1  |      56007 | 2014-11-21 18:05:57 | 2014-11-21 18:06:42 | 0x9e009a0 | 0x9e1d700
```

3. Similarly, to get information regarding pool health you can issue the commands `show pools` and `show stats` to get information regarding pool status and pool statistics:

```
pgbouncer=# show pools;
 database  |   user    | cl_active | cl_waiting | sv_active | sv_idle | sv_used | sv_tested | sv_login | maxwait
-----------+-----------+-----------+------------+-----------+---------+---------+-----------+----------+---------
 pgbouncer | pgbouncer |         1 |          0 |         0 |       0 |       0 |         0 |        0 |       0
 pgtest    | author    |        20 |          1 |        20 |       0 |       0 |         0 |        0 |      85
(2 rows)

pgbouncer=# show stats;
 database  | total_requests | total_received | total_sent | total_query_time | avg_req | avg_recv | avg_sent | avg_query
-----------+----------------+----------------+------------+------------------+---------+----------+----------+----------
 pgbouncer |              1 |              0 |          0 |                0 |       0 |        0 |        0 |         0
 pgtest    |           8131 |         442818 |     536895 |         16433811 |       0 |        0 |        0 |         0
(2 rows)
```

How it works...

As we can see in the previous section, we can get information regarding the clients, servers, and pool health and statistics. We will first begin with discussing clients, then servers, and then finally pool health and statistics.

When you issue the `show clients` command on the PgBouncer administrative console, PgBouncer provides us with a list of clients that have been either using or waiting for a Postgresql connection. Some of the important columns that are displayed in the output of the `show clients` command are discussed in the following list:

- `User`: The value in this column displays the user that is connected to the database.
- `Database`: The value in this column displays the database name to which the client may be connected.
- `State`: The value in this column displays the session state of the currently connected user. The client connection can either be in an active, used, waiting, or idle state.
- `Connect_Time`: The value in this column indicates the time at which PgBouncer initiated the client connection to Postgresql.
- `Request Time`: The value in this column shows the timestamp of the latest client request.
- `Port`: The value in this column indicates the port to which the client is connected to.

We have the `show servers` command, which is used to display information about every connection that is being used to fulfill client requests. The `show servers` output contains similar columns that were discussed for `show clients`. The only difference is for the type column, if the value for the type column is `S`, it means it is a server entry. If the value for the type column is `C`, it means it is a client entry. Some of the other important columns for the `show servers` output are displayed in the following list:

- `User`: The value in this column displays the user that is connected to the database
- `Database`: The value in this column displays the name of the database to which the connection is attached to
- `State`: The value in this column displays the state of the PgBouncer server connection. The server state could be active, used, or idle
- `Connect_Time`: The value in this column indicates the time at which the connection was made
- `Request Time`: The value in this column shows the timestamp when the last request was issued
- `Port`: The value in this column indicates the port number of the Postgresql server

The `show pools` command displays a row for every database for which PgBouncer acts as a proxy. Some of the important columns in the `show pools` output are given in the following list:

- `cl_active`: The value in this column displays the number of clients that are currently active and that are assigned server connections.
- `cl_waiting`: The value in this column displays the number of clients waiting for a server connection.
- `sl_active`: The value in this column displays the number of server connections that are assigned to PgBouncer clients.
- `sl_idle`: The value in this column displays the number of idle server connections or the ones that are not in use.
- `sl_used`: The value in this column displays the number of used server connections. In effect these connections are actually idle, but they have not been yet marked by PgBouncer for reuse.

The `show stats` command displays the relevant connection pool statistics related to PgBouncer and for the databases for which PgBouncer was acting as a proxy. Some of the important columns in the `show stats` output are discussed here:

- `total_requests`: The value in this column displays the total number of SQL requests pooled by PgBouncer
- `total_received`: The value in this column displays the total volume of network traffic measured in bytes that has been received by PgBouncer
- `total_sent`: The value in this column displays the total volume of network traffic measured in bytes that has been sent by PgBouncer
- `total_query_time`: The value in this column displays the amount of time in microseconds that PgBouncer spent communicating with a client in this pool

Implementing partitioning

In this recipe we are going to cover table partitioning and show the steps that are needed to partition a table.

Getting ready

Exposure to database design and normalization is needed.

How to do it...

There are a series of steps that need to be carried out to set up table partitioning. Here are the steps:

1. The first step is to create a master table with all fields. A master table is the table that will be used as a base to partition data into other tables, that is, partitions. An index is optional here for a master table; however, since there are performance benefits of using an index, we are creating an index from a performance perspective:

   ```
   CREATE TABLE country_log (
       created_at TIMESTAMP WITH TIME ZONE DEFAULT NOW(),
       country_code char(2),
       content text
   );

   CREATE INDEX country_code_idx ON country_log USING btree
       (country_code);
   ```

2. The next step is to create child tables that are going to inherit from the master table:

   ```
   CREATE TABLE country_log_ru ( CHECK ( country_code = 'ru') )
   INHERITS (country_log);
   CREATE TABLE country_log_sa ( CHECK ( country_code = 'sa' ) )
   INHERITS (country_log);
   ```

3. The next step is to create an index for each child table:

   ```
   CREATE INDEX country_code_ru_idx ON country_log_ru
   USING btree (country_code);
   CREATE INDEX country_code_sa_idx ON country_log_sa
   USING btree (country_code);
   ```

4. The next step is to create a trigger function with the help of which data will be redirected to the appropriate partition table:

   ```
   CREATE OR REPLACE FUNCTION country_insert_trig() RETURNS TRIGGER AS
   $$
   BEGIN
       IF ( NEW.country_code = 'ru' ) THEN
           INSERT INTO country_log_ru VALUES (NEW.*);
       ELSIF ( NEW.country_code = 'sa' ) THEN
           INSERT INTO country_log_sa VALUES (NEW.*);
       ELSE
   ```

```
        RAISE EXCEPTION 'Country unknown';
    END IF;

    RETURN NULL;
END;
$$ LANGUAGE plpgsql;
```

5. The next step is to create a trigger and attach the trigger function to the master table:

```
CREATE TRIGGER country_insert
BEFORE INSERT ON country_log
FOR EACH ROW EXECUTE PROCEDURE country_insert_trig();
```

6. The next step is to insert data into the master table:

```
postgres=# INSERT INTO country_log (country_code, content)
VALUES ('ru', 'content-ru');

postgres=# INSERT INTO country_log (country_code, content)
VALUES ('sa', 'content-sa');
```

7. The final step is to select the data from both the master table and the child table to confirm partitioning of data in child tables:

```
postgres=# SELECT * from country_log;
          created_at          | country_code |   content
------------------------------+--------------+------------
 2014-11-30 12:10:06.123189-08 | ru           | content-ru
 2014-11-30 12:10:14.22666-08  | sa           | content-sa
(2 rows)

postgres=# select * from country_log_ru;
          created_at          | country_code |   content
------------------------------+--------------+------------
 2014-11-30 12:10:06.123189-08 | ru           | content-ru
(1 row)

postgres=# select * from country_log_sa;
          created_at          | country_code |   content
------------------------------+--------------+------------
 2014-11-30 12:10:14.22666-08  | sa           | content-sa
(1 row)
```

How it works...

The following is the detailed explanation for the steps carried out in the previous section:

1. PostgreSQL basically supports partitioning via table inheritance. Hence partitioning is set up in such a way that every child table inherits from the parent table. It is for this purpose that we created two child tables, that is, country_log_ru and country_log_sa in step 2 of the previous section. These child tables inherit from the parent or the master table country_log by using the keyword INHERITS against the master table country_log for the CREATE TABLE DDL statement for both the child tables. This was the initial setup.

2. The next step in our scenario was to build partitioning in such a way that logs by country are stored in a country-specific table. The case scenario that we used in the previous section was to ensure that all logs for Russia go in the country_log_ru table and all logs for South Africa go in the country_log_sa table. To achieve this objective we defined a trigger function country_insert_trig, which helps partition the data into a country-specific table whenever an INSERT statement is triggered on the country_log master table. The moment the INSERT statement gets triggered on the country_log master table, the country_log trigger gets fired upon, which it calls the country_insert_trig() trigger function. The country_insert_trig() trigger function checks the inserted records: if it finds records for Russia (checked by the NEW.country_code = 'ru' condition) in the country_log table then it inserts the said record in the country_log_ru child table; and if the inserted record in the country_log master table is for South Africa (NEW.country_code = 'sa') then it logs the same record in the country_log_sa child table. This way the trigger function partitions the data. The following is the section of code in the country_insert_trig() trigger function that uses the logic defined in the IF condition to partition the data into the child tables:

```
IF ( NEW.country_code = 'ru' ) THEN
      INSERT INTO country_log_ru VALUES (NEW.*);
   ELSIF ( NEW.country_code = 'sa' ) THEN
      INSERT INTO country_log_sa VALUES (NEW.*);
   ELSE
      RAISE EXCEPTION 'Country unknown';
   END IF;
```

3. Once the data has been partitioned into the child tables, the final step was to verify the data by comparing the records from the child tables and the master table, as shown in step 7 of the previous section.

There were initially two records inserted in the `country_log` master table. This can be confirmed by running the `SELECT` query against the `country_log` table. In the following snippet, we can see two log records in the `country_log` table, one for Russia identified by the country code `ru`, and one for South Africa identified by the country code `sa`:

```
postgres=# SELECT * from country_log;
          created_at          | country_code |  content
------------------------------+--------------+------------
 2014-11-30 12:10:06.123189-08 | ru          | content-ru
 2014-11-30 12:10:14.22666-08  | sa          | content-sa
(2 rows)
```

The next step is to run the `SELECT` queries against the respective child tables, `country_log_ru` and `country_log_sa`:

```
postgres=# select * from country_log_ru;
          created_at          | country_code |  content
------------------------------+--------------+------------
 2014-11-30 12:10:06.123189-08 | ru          | content-ru
(1 row)

postgres=# select * from country_log_sa;
          created_at          | country_code |  content
------------------------------+--------------+------------
 2014-11-30 12:10:14.22666-08 | sa          | content-sa
(1 row)
```

From the preceding output, we can see that there is only a record in each `country_log_ru` and `country_log_sa` child table. In effect the `country_insert_trig()` trigger function has partitioned the log data in country-specific tables. Entries for the `country_code  ru`, that is, for Russia go into the `country_log_ru` table, and entries for the `country_code sa`, that is, South Africa go into the `country_log_sa` child table.

> You may refer to the following links for more detailed explanations on implementing partitioning:
> `https://blog.engineyard.com/2013/scaling-postgresql-performanc` `e-table-partitioning`and `http://www.postgresql.org/docs/9.6/sta` `tic/ddl-partitioning.html`.

Managing partitions

In this recipe, we are going to show how the partitioning scheme remains intact when an existing partition is dropped or a new partition is added.

Getting ready

Refer to the first recipe, *Implementing partitioning*, before reading the steps outlined in this recipe.

How to do it...

There are two scenarios here. One is what happens when an existing partition is deleted and the other is what happens when a new partition is added. Let's discuss both cases:

1. In the first scenario we will drop an existing partition table. Here it is the `country_code_sa` table that will be dropped:

    Before dropping the `country_log_sa` child table, first see the records in the `country_log` master table:

    ```
    postgres=# SELECT * from country_log;
            created_at          | country_code |  content
    ----------------------------+--------------+------------
     2014-11-30 12:10:06.123189-08 | ru         | content-ru
     2014-11-30 12:10:14.22666-08  | sa         | content-sa
    (2 rows)
    ```

    The next step would be to drop the `country_log_sa` child table:

    ```
    postgres=# drop table country_log_sa;
    DROP TABLE
    ```

    As a final step we would again check the data in the `country_log` master table once the `country_log_sa` child table is dropped:

    ```
    postgres=# select * from country_log;
            created_at          | country_code |  content
    ----------------------------+--------------+------------
     2014-11-30 14:41:40.742878-08 | ru         | content-ru
    ```

2. Here in the second scenario we are going to add a partition. Let's add a new partition, `country_log_default`. The idea of creating this partition is that if there are tables for which the trigger function does not define any country codes those records should go into a default table partition:

> Before we create the child table, let's see the existing records in the country_log master table:

```
postgres=# select * from country_log;
         created_at          | country_code |   content
-----------------------------+--------------+------------
 2014-11-30 14:41:40.742878-08 | ru          | content-ru
```

> The next step would be to create a `country_log_sa` child table and create an index on the child table:

```
postgres=# CREATE TABLE country_log_sa ( ) INHERITS
  (country_log);
CREATE TABLE
postgres=# CREATE INDEX country_code_sa_idx ON country_log_sa
   USING btree          (country_code);
CREATE INDEX;
```

> Also, let's create another partition table called `country_log_default` where the rest of the transaction goes to that table. Let's modify our existing trigger function to define a condition to insert log records for those countries whose country codes are not explicitly defined to go into a country code-specific log table:

```
CREATE OR REPLACE FUNCTION country_insert_trig() RETURNS
  TRIGGER AS $$
BEGIN
    IF ( NEW.country_code = 'ru' ) THEN
        INSERT INTO country_log_ru VALUES (NEW.*);
    ELSIF ( NEW.country_code = 'sa' ) THEN
        INSERT INTO country_log_sa VALUES (NEW.*);
    ELSE
        INSERT INTO country_log_default VALUES (NEW.*);
    END IF;

    RETURN NULL;
END;
$$ LANGUAGE plpgsql;
```

Now let's insert records into the master table:

```
postgres=# INSERT INTO country_log (country_code, content)
   VALUES ('dk',          'content-dk');
INSERT 0 0
postgres=# INSERT INTO country_log (country_code, content)
   VALUES ('us',          'content-us');
INSERT 0 0
```

Let's now check the newly created records in the `country_log` master table and see if these records have been partitioned into the `country_log_default` child table:

```
postgres=# select * from country_log;
          created_at            | country_code |   content
-------------------------------+--------------+------------
 2014-11-30 14:41:40.742878-08 | ru           | content-ru
 2014-11-30 15:10:28.921124-08 | dk           | content-dk
 2014-11-30 15:10:42.97714-08  | us           | content-us
postgres=# select * from country_log_default;
          created_at            | country_code |   content
-------------------------------+--------------+------------
 2014-11-30 15:10:28.921124-08 | dk           | content-dk
 2014-11-30 15:10:42.97714-08  | us           | content-us
(2 rows)
```

How it works...

Let's first discuss the first scenario, where we are dropping the child partition table, `country_log_sa`. Here is the code snippet that was shown in the previous section:

```
postgres=# SELECT * from country_log;
          created_at            | country_code |   content
-------------------------------+--------------+------------
 2014-11-30 12:10:06.123189-08 | ru           | content-ru
 2014-11-30 12:10:14.22666-08  | sa           | content-sa
(2 rows)

postgres=# drop table country_log_sa;
DROP TABLE
postgres=# select * from country_log;
          created_at            | country_code |   content
-------------------------------+--------------+------------
 2014-11-30 14:41:40.742878-08 | ru           | content-ru
```

If you refer to the sequence of events in the preceding output, we can clearly see that once the `country_log_sa` child table got dropped its corresponding entry from the `country_log` master table also got removed. This technique really helps if there are large numbers of records to be pruned from the master table once the corresponding child table is dropped. This procedure is automatic and does not require DBA intervention. This way the partition structure and data can be easily managed and handled if any existing partition is dropped.

Similarly, data can be easily managed when a new partition is added. If you refer to step 2 in the How to do it section we are creating a new child table, `country_log_default`, which inherits from the `country_log` master table. Once the existing trigger function, `country_insert_trig()`, is modified to include the conditional-based insert for partitioning the data into the newly created partition, `country_log_default`, and once an `INSERT` statement is triggered on the `country_log` master table, and if the prevalent condition for inserting records into the `country_log_default` child table is fulfilled, then the records are inserted into the `country_log_default` child table. This can be seen from in step 2 of the How to do it section.

To manage partitions automatically, PostgreSQL offers an extension called `pg_partman`, which will create the required partition tables on the parent table automatically. Refer to the following URL for more information about this extension `https://github.com/keithf4/pg_partman`.

Installing PL/Proxy

PL/Proxy is a database partitioning system that is implemented as a PL language. PL/Proxy makes it straightforward to split large independent tables among multiple nodes in a way that almost allows unbounded scalability. PL/Proxy scaling works on both read and write workloads. The main idea is that the proxy function will be set up with the same signature as the remote function to be called, so only the destination information needs be specified inside the proxy function body.

In this recipe, we are going to show the steps required to install PL/Proxy.

How to do it...

The following are the steps to install PL/Proxy:

1. Go to the following website and download the latest tarball of PL/Proxy:
   `http://pgfoundry.org/projects/plproxy/`.

2. Once the latest version of PL/Proxy is downloaded, then the next step is to unpack the TAR archive:

   ```
   tar xvfz plproxy-2.5.tar.gz
   ```

3. Once the TAR archive has been unpacked, the next step is to enter the newly created directory and start the compilation process:

   ```
   cd   plproxy-2.5
   make  &&  make install
   ```

How it works...

Installing PL/Proxy is an easy task. Here we are downloading the source code from the website link given in step 1 of the preceding section. The latest version of PL/Proxy at this stage is 2.5 and we need to download the tarball containing version 2.5 of PL/Proxy. Once downloaded we need to compile and build it. This completes the installation of PL/Proxy.

You may also install `plproxy` from binary packages if prebuilt packages are available for your operating system.

Partitioning with PL/Proxy

In this recipe, we are going to cover horizontal partitioning with PL/Proxy.

Getting ready

PL/Proxy needs to be installed on the host machine. Refer to the previous recipe for more details on installing PL/Proxy.

How to do it...

The following are the steps that need to be carried out for horizontal partitioning using PL/Proxy:

1. Create three new databases: one proxy database named nodes, and two partitioned databases, `nodes_0000` and `nodes_0001`, respectively:

   ```
   postgres=# create database nodes;

   postgres=# create database nodes_0000;

   postgres=# create database nodes_0001;
   ```

2. Once you have created these databases the next step is to create a PL/Proxy extension:

   ```
   psql  -d  nodes

   nodes=# create extension plproxy;
   ```

3. The next step is to create the `plproxy` schema in the proxy database nodes:

   ```
   nodes=# create schema plproxy;
   ```

4. The next step is to execute the following mentioned file, `plproxy--2.5.0.sql`, on the proxy database nodes:

   ```
   cd  /usr/pgsql-9.6/share/extension

    psql -f plproxy--2.5.0.sql  nodes

   CREATE FUNCTION
   CREATE LANGUAGE
   CREATE FUNCTION
   CREATE FOREIGN DATA WRAPPER
   ```

5. The next step is to configure PL/Proxy using the configuration functions on the proxy database nodes:

   ```
   psql -d    nodes

   CREATE OR REPLACE FUNCTION
     plproxy.get_cluster_version(cluster_name text)
   RETURNS int AS $$
   ```

```
BEGIN
    IF cluster_name = 'nodes' THEN
        RETURN 1;
    END IF;
END;
$$ LANGUAGE plpgsql;


CREATE OR REPLACE FUNCTION
  plproxy.get_cluster_partitions(cluster_name
text) RETURNS SETOF text AS $$
BEGIN
    IF cluster_name = 'nodes' THEN
        RETURN NEXT 'host=127.0.0.1 dbname=nodes_0000';
        RETURN NEXT 'host=127.0.0.1 dbname=nodes_0001';
        RETURN;
    END IF;
    RAISE EXCEPTION 'no such cluster: %', cluster_name;
END;
$$ LANGUAGE plpgsql SECURITY DEFINER;


CREATE OR REPLACE FUNCTION plproxy.get_cluster_config
  (cluster_name text,
out key text, out val text)
RETURNS SETOF record AS $$
BEGIN
    RETURN;
END;
$$ LANGUAGE plpgsql;
```

6. The next step is to log in to the partitioned databases and create the users table in both of them:

```
psql -d nodes_0000

nodes_0000=# CREATE TABLE users (username text PRIMARY KEY);

psql -d  nodes_0001

nodes_0001=# CREATE TABLE users (username text PRIMARY KEY);
```

7. The next step is to create the following mentioned function, `insert_user()`, which will be used to insert usernames in the users table:

```
psql -d   nodes_0000

CREATE OR REPLACE FUNCTION insert_user(i_username text) RETURNS
text AS $$
BEGIN
    PERFORM 1 FROM users WHERE username = i_username;
    IF NOT FOUND THEN
        INSERT INTO users (username) VALUES (i_username);
        RETURN 'user created';
    ELSE
        RETURN 'user already exists';
    END IF;
END;
$$ LANGUAGE plpgsql SECURITY DEFINER;

psql  -d   nodes_0001

CREATE OR REPLACE FUNCTION insert_user(i_username text) RETURNS
text AS $$
BEGIN
    PERFORM 1 FROM users WHERE username = i_username;
    IF NOT FOUND THEN
        INSERT INTO users (username) VALUES (i_username);
        RETURN 'user created';
    ELSE
        RETURN 'user already exists';
    END IF;
END;
$$ LANGUAGE plpgsql SECURITY DEFINER;
```

8. The next step is to create a proxy function called `insert_user()` on the proxy database nodes:

```
psql -d nodes

CREATE OR REPLACE FUNCTION insert_user(i_username text) RETURNS
TEXT AS $$
    CLUSTER 'nodes'; RUN ON hashtext(i_username);
$$ LANGUAGE plproxy;
```

9. Check the `pg_hba.conf` file and you will need to set the authentication to trust and then restart the `postgresql` service.

10. The next step is to fill the partitions by executing the following query on the proxy database nodes:

```
nodes=#SELECT insert_user('user_number_'||generate_series::text)
FROM generate_series(1,10000);
```

11. Once the data has been inserted we are going to verify the corresponding records in the partitioned databases, `nodes_0000` and `nodes_0001`:

```
nodes_0000=# select count(*) from users;
 count
-------
  5106
(1 row)

nodes_0001=# select count(*) from users;
 count
-------
  4894
(1 row)
```

How it works...

Explanation for the preceding code output is given here:

1. Initially we created three databases, one as a proxy database named nodes and two other databases named `nodes_0000` and `nodes_0001` across which the data will be partitioned.

2. The next step was to create the `plproxy` extension.

3. As can be seen in step 5 in the preceding section, we are configuring PL/Proxy using the configuration functions on the proxy database nodes. The function `plproxy.get_cluster_partitions()` is invoked when a query needs to be forwarded to a remote database and is used by PL/Proxy to get the connection string to use for each partition. We also use the `plproxy.get_cluster_version()` function, which is called upon each request and is used to determine if the output from a cached result from `plproxy.get_cluster_partitions` can be reused. We also use the `plproxy.get_cluster_config()` function, which enables us to configure the behavior of PL/Proxy.

4. Once we are done with defining the configuration functions on the proxy database nodes, the next step was to create the table users in both the partitioned databases across which the data will be partitioned.

5. In the next step, we created an `insert_user()` function that will be used to insert usernames into the users table. The `insert_user()` function will be defined on both the partitioned databases `nodes_0000` and `nodes_0001`. This is shown in step 7 of the preceding section.

6. In the next step, we created an `insert_user()` proxy function inside the proxy database nodes. The proxy function will be used to send the `INSERT` to the appropriate partition. This is shown in step 8 of the preceding section.

7. Finally, we filled the partitions with random data by executing the `insert_user()` proxy function in the proxy database named nodes. This is seen in step 10 in the preceding section.

> For more detailed information on PL/Proxy, refer to the following web link:
> `http://plproxy.projects.pgfoundry.org/doc/tutorial.html`.

6

High Availability and Replication

In this chapter, we will cover the following:

- Setting up hot streaming replication
- Replication using Slony
- Replication using Londiste
- Replication using Bucardo
- Replication using DRBD
- Setting up a Postgres-XL Cluster

Introduction

Some of the most important components for any production database are there to achieve fault tolerance, availability 24 x 7, and redundancy. It is for this purpose we have different high availability and replication solutions available for PostgreSQL.

From a business perspective, it is important to ensure data availability 24 x 7 in the event of a disaster situation or in the event of a database crash due to disk or hardware failure. In such situations, it becomes critical to ensure that a duplicate copy of data is available on a different server or a different database so that the seamless failover could be achieved even when the primary server/database is unavailable.

In this chapter, we will talk about various high availability and replication solutions including some popular third-party replication tools such as Slony, Londiste, and Bucardo. We will also discuss block level replication using DRBD, and finally we will set up a PostgreSQL Highly Extensible Cluster, that is, Postgres-XC.

Setting up hot streaming replication

In this recipe, we are going to set up a master/slave streaming replication.

Getting ready

For this exercise, you need two Linux machines each with the latest version of PostgreSQL 9.6 installed. We will be using the following IP addresses for master and slave servers:

- Master IP address: `192.168.0.4`
- Slave IP address: `192.168.0.5`

How to do it...

The following steps show you how to set up master/slave streaming replication:

1. Set up password-less authentication between master and slave for the Postgres user.
2. First, we are going to create a user ID on the master, which will be used by the slave server to connect to the PostgreSQL database on the master server:

   ```
   psql -c "CREATE USER repuser REPLICATION LOGIN ENCRYPTED
   PASSWORD 'charlie';"
   ```

3. The next step is to allow the replication user that was created in the previous step to allow access to the master Postgresql server.

   This is done by making the necessary changes as in the `pg_hba.conf` file:

   ```
   Vi pg_hba.conf
   host     replication     repuser     192.168.0.5/32     md5
   ```

4. In the next step, we are going to configure parameters in the `postgresql.conf` file. These parameters are required to be set in order to get the streaming replication working:

   ```
   Vi /var/lib/pgsql/9.6/data/postgresql.conf
   listen_addresses = '*'
   wal_level = hot_standbymax_wal_senders = 3wal_keep_segments = 8
   archive_mode = on
   archive_command = 'cp %p /var/lib/pgsql/archive/%f && scp %p
     postgres@192.168.0.5:/var/lib/pgsql/archive/%f'
   ```

5. Once the parameter changes have been made in the `postgresql.conf` file in the previous step, the next step is to restart the PostgreSQL server on the master server in order to get the changes made in the previous step to come into effect:

```
pg_ctl -D /var/lib/pgsql/9.6/data restart
```

6. Before the slave can replicate the master, we need to give it the initial database to build off. For this purpose, we will make a base backup by copying the primary server's data directory to the standby:

```
psql -U postgres -h 192.168.0.4 -c "SELECT
  pg_start_backup('label', true)"

rsync -a /var/lib/pgsql/9.6/data/
  192.168.0.5:/var/lib/pgsql/9.6/data/
--exclude postmaster.pid

psql -U postgres -h 192.168.0.4 -c "SELECT pg_stop_backup()"
```

7. Once the data directory in the previous step is populated, the next step is to configure the following parameters in the `postgresql.conf` file on the slave server:

```
hot_standby = on
```

8. The next step is to copy the `recovery.conf.sample` in the `$PGDATA` location on the slave server and then configure the following parameters:

```
cp /usr/pgsql-9.6/share/recovery.conf.sample
/var/lib/pgsql/9.6/data/recovery.conf
standby_mode = on
primary_conninfo = 'host=192.168.0.4 port=5432 user=repuser
password=charlie'
trigger_file = '/tmp/trigger.replication'
restore_command = 'cp /var/lib/pgsql/archive/%f "%p"'
```

9. The next step is to start the slave server:

```
service postgresql-9.6 start
```

10. Now that the previously replication steps are set up, we will test for replication. On the master server, log in and issue the following SQL commands:

```
psql -h 192.168.0.4  -d postgres -U postgres -W

postgres=# create database test;

postgres=# \c test;

test=# create table testtable ( testint int, testchar
   varchar(40) );
CREATE TABLE
test=# insert into testtable values ( 1, 'What A Sight.' );
INSERT 0 1
```

11. On the slave server, we will now check if the newly created database and the corresponding table in the previous step are replicated:

```
psql -h 192.168.0.5  -d test -U postgres -W
test=# select * from testtable;
testint | testchar
---------+--------------------------
1 | What  A Sight.
(1 row)
```

12. The `wal_keep_segments` parameter ensures how many WAL files should be retained in the master `pg_xlog` in case of network delays. However, if you do not want to assume a value for this, you can create a replication slot, which makes sure the master does not remove the WAL files in `pg_xlog` until they have been received by standbys.

> For more information, visit the following link: `https://www.postgresql.org/docs/9.6/static/warm-standby.html#STREAMING-REPLICATION-SLOTS`.

How it works...

The following is the explanation given for the steps done in the preceding section:

- In the initial step of the preceding section, we created a user called repuser, which will be used by the slave server to make a connection to the primary server. In the second step of the preceding section, we made the necessary changes in the `pg_hba.conf` file to allow the master server to be accessed by the slave server using the userid repuser that was created in step 2.

- We then made the necessary parameter changes on the master in step 4 of the preceding section for configuring streaming replication. The following is a description for these parameters:
    - `Listen_Addresses`: This parameter is used to provide the IP address that you want to have PostgreSQL listen to. A value of * indicates all available IP addresses.
    - `wal_level`: This parameter determines the level of `wal` logging done. Specify `hot_standby` for streaming replication.
    - `wal_keep_segments`: This parameter specifies the number of 16 MB WAL files to retain in the `pg_xlog` directory. The rule of thumb is that more such files may be required to handle a large checkpoint.
    - `archive_mode`: Setting this parameter enables completed `wal` segments to be sent to archive storage.
    - `archive_command`: This parameter is basically a shell command that is executed whenever a WAL segment is completed. In our case, we are basically copying the file to the local machine and then we are using the secure copy command to send it across to the slave.
    - `max_wal_senders`: This parameter specifies the total number of concurrent connections allowed from the slave servers.

- Once the necessary configuration changes have been made on the master server, we then restart the PostgreSQL server on the master in order to get the new configuration changes to come into effect. This is done in step 5 of the preceding section.

- In step 6 of the preceding section, we were basically building the slave by copying the primary's data directory to the slave.

- Now with the data directory available on the slave, the next step is to configure it. We will now make the necessary parameter replication related parameter changes on the slave in the `postgresql.conf` directory on the slave server. We set the following parameter on the slave:
  - `hot_standby`: This parameter determines if we can connect and run queries during times when the server is in the archive recovery or standby mode.

- In the next step, we are configuring the `recovery.conf` file. This is required to be set up so that the slave can start receiving logs from the master. The following parameters are configured in the recovery.conf file on the slave:
  - `standby_mode`: This parameter when enabled causes Postgresql to work as a standby in a replication configuration.
  - `primary_conninfo`: This parameter specifies the connection information used by the slave to connect to the master. For our scenario, our master server is set as `192.168.0.4` on port `5432` and we are using the `userid` repuser with password charlie to make a connection to the master. Remember that the repuser was the `userid` that was created in the initial step of the preceding section for this purpose, that is, connecting to the master from the slave.
  - `trigger_file`: When the slave is configured as a standby it will continue to restore the XLOG records from the master. The `trigger_file` parameter specifies what is used to trigger a slave to switch over its duties from standby and take over as master or to be the primary server.

- At this stage, the slave has now been fully configured and we then start the slave server and then the replication process begins.

- In step 10 and 11 of the preceding section, we are simply testing our replication. We first begin by creating a database test and log into the test database and create a table by the name test table and then begin inserting some records into the test table. Now our purpose is to see whether these changes are replicated across the slave. To test this, we then log in into the slave on the test database and then query the records from the test table as seen in step 10 of the preceding section. The final result that we see is that all the records that are changed/inserted on the primary are visible on the slave. This completes our streaming replication set up and configuration.

Replication using Slony

In this recipe, we are going to set up a replication using Slony, which is a widely used replication engine. It replicates a desired set of table data from one database to another. This replication approach is based on a few event triggers that will be created on the source set of tables, which will log the DML and DDL statements into Slony catalog tables. By using Slony, we can also set up the cascading replication among multiple nodes.

Getting ready

The steps followed in this recipe are carried out on a CentOS version 6 machine.

We first need to install Slony.

The following are the steps needed to install Slony:

1. First, go to the following web link and download the given software: http://slo ny.info/downloads/2.2/source/

2. Once you have downloaded the software, the next step is to unzip the tarball and then go to the newly created directory:

   ```
   tar xvfj slony1-2.2.3.tar.bz2
   cd slony1-2.2.3
   ```

3. In the next step, we are going to configure, compile, and build the software:

   ```
   ./configure --with-pgconfigdir=/usr/pgsql-9.6/bin/
   ```

   ```
   make
   ```

   ```
   make install
   ```

How to do it...

The following are the sequence of steps required to replicate data between two tables using Slony replication:

1. First, start the PostgreSQL server if it is not already started:

   ```
   pg_ctl -D $PGDATA start
   ```

2. In the next step, we will be creating two databases, `test1`, and `test2`, which will be used as source and target databases:

```
createdb test1

createdb  test2
```

3. In the next step, we will create the table `t_test` on the source database, `test1`, and will insert some records into it:

```
psql -d test1

test1=# create table t_test (id numeric primary key, name
    varchar);

test1=# insert into t_test values(1,'A'),(2,'B'), (3,'C');
```

4. We will now set up the target database by copying the table definitions from the source database, `test1`:

```
pg_dump -s -p 5432 -h localhost test1 | psql -h localhost -p
    5432 test2
```

5. We will now connect to the target database, `test2`, and verify that there is no data in the tables of the `test2` database:

```
psql -d  test2

test2=# select * from t_test;
```

6. We will now set up a slonik script for master/slave, that is, the source/target setup:

```
vi init_master.slonik

  #! /bin/slonik
  cluster name = mycluster;
  node 1 admin conninfo = 'dbname=test1 host=localhost
port=5432 user=postgres password=postgres';
  node 2 admin conninfo = 'dbname=test2 host=localhost
port=5432 user=postgres password=postgres';
  init cluster ( id=1);
  create set (id=1, origin=1);
  set add table(set id=1, origin=1, id=1, fully qualified
name = 'public.t_test');
  store node (id=2, event node = 1);
```

```
    store path (server=1, client=2, conninfo='dbname=test1
host=localhost port=5432 user=postgres password=postgres');
    store path (server=2, client=1, conninfo='dbname=test2
host=localhost port=5432 user=postgres password=postgres');
    store listen (origin=1, provider = 1, receiver = 2);
    store listen (origin=2, provider = 2, receiver = 1);
```

7. We will now create a slonik script for subscription on the slave, that is, the target:

```
vi init_slave.slonik
#! /bin/slonik
 cluster name = mycluster;
 node 1 admin conninfo = 'dbname=test1 host=localhost
port=5432 user=postgres password=postgres';
 node 2 admin conninfo = 'dbname=test2 host=localhost
port=5432 user=postgres password=postgres';
 subscribe set ( id = 1, provider = 1, receiver = 2, forward
= no);
```

8. We will now run the `init_master.slonik` script created in step 6 and will run this on the master:

```
cd /usr/pgsql-9.6/bin
slonik init_master.slonik
```

9. We will now run the `init_slave.slonik` script created in step 7 and will run this on the slave, that is, the target:

```
cd /usr/pgsql-9.6/bin
slonik init_slave.slonik
```

10. In the next step, we will start the master `slon` daemon:

```
nohup slon mycluster "dbname=test1 host=localhost port=5432
user=postgres          password=postgres" &
```

11. In the next step, we will start the slave `slon` daemon:

```
nohup slon mycluster "dbname=test2 host=localhost port=5432
user=postgres          password=postgres" &
```

12. In the next step, we will connect to the master, that is, the source database, `test1`, and insert some records in the `t_test` table:

```
psql -d test1
test1=# insert into t_test values (5, 'E');
```

13. We will now test for replication by logging to the slave, that is, the target database, test2, and see if the inserted records in the t_test table in the previous step are visible:

```
psql -d test2
test2=# select * from t_test;
 id | name
----+------
  1 | A
  2 | B
  3 | C
  5 | E
(4 rows)
```

How it works...

We will now discuss the steps followed in the preceding section:

- In step 1, we started the Postgresql server if it was not already started.
- In step 2, we created two databases, namely test1 and test2, which will serve as our source (master) and target (slave) databases.
- In step 3, of the preceding section, we logged into the source database, test1, and created a table t_test and inserted some records into the table.
- In step 4, of the preceding section, we set up the target database, test2, by copying the table definitions present in the source database and loading them into the target database, test2, by using the pg_dump utility.
- In step 5, of the preceding section, we logged into the target database, test2, and verified that there were no records present in the table t_test because in step 5 we only extracted the table definitions into the test2 database from the test1 database.
- In step 6, we set up a slonik script for the master/slave replication setup. In the init_master.slonik file, we first defined the cluster name as mycluster. We then defined the nodes in the cluster. Each node will have a number associated to a connection string, which contains database connection information. The node entry is defined both for the source and target databases. The store_path commands are necessary so that each node knows how to communicate with the other.

- In step 7, we set up a slonik script for subscription of the slave, that is, the target database, test2. Once again the script contains information such as cluster name and node entries, which are designated a unique number related to the connect string information. It also contains a subscriber set.
- In step 8, of the preceding section, we ran the init_master.slonik on the master. Similarly in step 9, we ran the init_slave.slonik on the slave.
- In step 10, of the preceding section, we started the master slon daemon. In step 11 of the preceding section we started the slave slon daemon.
- The subsequent sections from step the 12-13 of the preceding section are used to test for replication. For this purpose in step 12 of the preceding section we first login into the source database test 1 and insert some records into the t_test table. To check if the newly inserted records have been replicated to the target database, test2, we log into the test2 database in step 13 and then the result set obtained by the output of the query confirms that the changed/inserted records on the t_test table in the test1 database are successfully replicated across the target database, test2.

> You may refer to the following link for more information regarding Slony replication:
> http://slony.info/documentation/tutorial.html.

Replication using Londiste

In this recipe, we are going to show how to replicate data using Londiste, which is based on a queue that is populated by a set of producers, and consumed by a set of consumers. It is also similar to Slony replication, which is needed to create a set of event triggers on source tables.

Getting ready

For this setup, we are using the same host CentOS Linux machine to replicate data between two databases. This can also be set up using two separate Linux machines running on Vmware or VirtualBox or any other virtualization software. It is assumed that Postgresql version 9.6 is installed. We have used CentOs version 6 as the Linux operating system for this exercise.

To set up Londiste replication on the Linux machine, follow these steps:

1. Go to the following link and download the latest version of skytools 3.2, that is, tarball `skytools-3.2.tar.gz`: `http://pgfoundry.org/projects/skytools/`

2. Extract the tar ball as follows:

   ```
   tar -xvf skytools-3.2.tar.gz
   ```

3. Go to the new location and build and compile the software:

   ```
   cd skytools-3.2

   ./configure  --prefix=/var/lib/pgsql/9.6/Sky -with
     pgconfig=/usr/pgsql-
   9.6/bin/pg_config

   make

   make install
   ```

4. Also set the environment variable, PYTHONPATH, as follows. Alternatively, you can also set it in the `.bash_profile` script as well:

   ```
   export PYTHONPATH=/opt/PostgreSQL/9.6/Sky/lib64/python2.6/site-
     packages/
   ```

How to do it...

We are going to follow these steps for setting up replication between two different databases using Londiste:

1. First create the two databases between which replication is to occur:

   ```
   createdb node1
   createdb node2
   ```

2. Populate the node1 database with data using the pgbench utility:

   ```
   pgbench -i -s 2 -F 80 node1
   ```

3. Add any primary key and foreign keys on the tables in the node1 database that are needed for replication. Create the following SQL file and add the following lines to it:

```
Vi /tmp/prepare_pgbenchdb_for_londiste.sql
- add primary key to history table
ALTER TABLE pgbench_history ADD COLUMN hid SERIAL PRIMARY KEY;
-- add foreign keys
ALTER TABLE pgbench_tellers ADD CONSTRAINT
  pgbench_tellers_branches_fk          FOREIGN KEY(bid)
    REFERENCES pgbench_branches;
ALTER TABLE pgbench_accounts ADD CONSTRAINT
  pgbench_accounts_branches_fk
FOREIGN KEY(bid) REFERENCES pgbench_branches;
ALTER TABLE pgbench_history ADD CONSTRAINT
  pgbench_history_branches_fk
FOREIGN KEY(bid) REFERENCES pgbench_branches;
ALTER TABLE pgbench_history ADD CONSTRAINT
  pgbench_history_tellers_fk
FOREIGN KEY(tid) REFERENCES pgbench_tellers;
ALTER TABLE pgbench_history ADD CONSTRAINT
  pgbench_history_accounts_fk
FOREIGN KEY(aid) REFERENCES pgbench_accounts;
```

4. We will now load the SQL file created in the previous step and then load it into the database:

```
psql node1 -f /tmp/prepare_pgbenchdb_for_londiste.sql
```

5. We will now populate the node2 database with table definitions from the tables in the node1 database:

```
pg_dump -s -t 'pgbench*' node1 > /tmp/tables.sql
psql  -f /tmp/tables.sql node2
```

6. Now start the process of replication. We will first create the configuration file, londiste.ini, with the following parameters for setting up the root node for source database, node1:

```
Vi londiste.ini
[londiste3]
job_name = first_table
db = dbname=node1
queue_name = replication_queue
logfile = /home/postgres/log/londiste.log
pidfile = /home/postgres/pid/londiste.pid
```

7. In the next step, we are going to use the configuration file, londiste.ini, created in the previous step to set up the root node for, database, node1, as follows:

```
[postgres@localhost bin]$ ./londiste3 londiste3.ini create-root
  node1
dbname=node1

2016-12-09 18:54:34,723 2335 WARNING No host= in public connect
  string,
bad idea
2016-12-09 18:54:35,210 2335 INFO plpgsql is installed
2016-12-09 18:54:35,217 2335 INFO pgq is installed
2016-12-09 18:54:35,225 2335 INFO pgq.get_batch_cursor is
  installed
2016-12-09 18:54:35,227 2335 INFO pgq_ext is installed
2016-12-09 18:54:35,228 2335 INFO pgq_node is installed
2016-12-09 18:54:35,230 2335 INFO londiste is installed
2016-12-09 18:54:35,232 2335 INFO londiste.global_add_table is
  installed
2016-12-09 18:54:35,281 2335 INFO Initializing node
2016-12-09 18:54:35,285 2335 INFO Location registered
2016-12-09 18:54:35,447 2335 INFO Node "node1" initialized for
  queue
"replication_queue" with type "root"
2016-12-09 18:54:35,465 2335 INFO Don
```

8. We will now run the worker daemon for the root node:

```
[postgres@localhost bin]$ ./londiste3 londiste3.ini worker
2016-12-09 18:55:17,008 2342 INFO Consumer uptodate = 1
```

9. In the next step, we will now create a configuration file, slave.ini, to create a leaf node for the target database, node2:

```
vi slave.ini
[londiste3]
job_name = first_table_slave
db = dbname=node2
queue_name = replication_queue
logfile = /home/postgres/log/londiste_slave.log
pidfile = /home/postgres/pid/londiste_slave.pid
```

10. We will now initialize the node in the target database:

```
./londiste3 slave.ini create-leaf node2 dbname=node2
-provider=dbname=node1
2016-12-09 18:57:22,769 2408 WARNING No host= in public connect
string, bad idea
2016-12-09 18:57:22,778 2408 INFO plpgsql is installed
2016-12-09 18:57:22,778 2408 INFO Installing pgq
2016-12-09 18:57:22,778 2408 INFO    Reading from
/var/lib/pgsql/9.6/Sky/share/skytools3/pgq.sql
2016-12-09 18:57:23,211 2408 INFO pgq.get_batch_cursor is
   installed
2016-12-09 18:57:23,212 2408 INFO Installing pgq_ext
2016-12-09 18:57:23,213 2408 INFO    Reading from
/var/lib/pgsql/9.3/Sky/share/skytools3/pgq_ext.sql
2016-12-09 18:57:23,454 2408 INFO Installing pgq_node
2016-12-09 18:57:23,455 2408 INFO    Reading from
/var/lib/pgsql/9.3/Sky/share/skytools3/pgq_node.sql
2016-12-09 18:57:23,729 2408 INFO Installing londiste
2016-12-09 18:57:23,730 2408 INFO    Reading from
/var/lib/pgsql/9.3/Sky/share/skytools3/londiste.sql
2016-12-09 18:57:24,391 2408 INFO londiste.global_add_table is
   installed
2016-12-09 18:57:24,575 2408 INFO Initializing node
2016-12-09 18:57:24,705 2408 INFO Location registered
2016-12-09 18:57:24,715 2408 INFO Location registered
2016-12-09 18:57:24,744 2408 INFO Subscriber registered: node2
2016-12-09 18:57:24,748 2408 INFO Location registered
2016-12-09 18:57:24,750 2408 INFO Location registered
2016-12-09 18:57:24,757 2408 INFO Node "node2" initialized for
   queue
"replication_queue" with type "leaf"
2016-12-09 18:57:24,761 2408 INFO Done
```

11. We will now launch the worker daemon for the target database, that is, `node2`:

```
[postgres@localhost bin]$ ./londiste3 slave.ini worker
2016-12-09 18:58:53,411 2423 INFO Consumer uptodate = 1
```

12. We will now create the configuration file, that is, `pgqd.ini`, for the ticker daemon:

```
vi pgqd.ini
[pgqd]
logfile = /home/postgres/log/pgqd.log
pidfile = /home/postgres/pid/pgqd.pid
```

13. Using the configuration file created in the previous step, we will now launch the ticker daemon:

```
[postgres@localhost bin]$ ./pgqd pgqd.ini
2016-12-09 19:05:56.843 2542 LOG Starting pgqd 3.2
2016-12-09 19:05:56.844 2542 LOG auto-detecting dbs ...
2016-12-09 19:05:57.257 2542 LOG node1: pgq version ok: 3.2
2016-12-09 19:05:58.130 2542 LOG node2: pgq version ok: 3.2
```

14. We will now add all the tables to replication on the root node:

```
[postgres@localhost bin]$ ./londiste3 londiste3.ini add-table
  -all
2016-12-09 19:07:26,064 2614 INFO Table added:
  public.pgbench_accounts
2016-12-09 19:07:26,161 2614 INFO Table added:
  public.pgbench_branches
2016-12-09 19:07:26,238 2614 INFO Table added:
  public.pgbench_history
2016-12-09 19:07:26,287 2614 INFO Table added:
  public.pgbench_tellers
```

15. Similarly, we will add all the tables to replication on the leaf node:

```
[postgres@localhost bin]$ ./londiste3 slave.ini add-table -all
```

16. We will now generate some traffic on the source database, node1:

```
pgbench -T 10 -c 5 node1
```

17. We will now use the compare utility available with the londiste3 command to check that the tables in both the nodes, that is, both the source database, node1, and destination database, node2, have the same amount of data:

```
[postgres@localhost bin]$ ./londiste3 slave.ini compare

2016-12-09 19:26:16,421 2982 INFO Checking if node1 can be used
  for copy
2016-12-09 19:26:16,424 2982 INFO Node node1 seems good source,
  using it
2016-12-09 19:26:16,425 2982 INFO public.pgbench_accounts:
  Using node
node1 as provider
2016-12-09 19:26:16,441 2982 INFO Provider: node1 (root)
2016-12-09 19:26:16,446 2982 INFO Locking
  public.pgbench_accounts
2016-12-09 19:26:16,447 2982 INFO Syncing
```

```
    public.pgbench_accounts
2016-12-09 19:26:18,975 2982 INFO Counting
    public.pgbench_accounts
2016-12-09 19:26:19,401 2982 INFO srcdb: 200000 rows,
checksum=167607238449
2016-12-09 19:26:19,706 2982 INFO dstdb: 200000 rows,
checksum=167607238449
2016-12-09 19:26:19,715 2982 INFO Checking if node1 can be used
    for copy
2016-12-09 19:26:19,716 2982 INFO Node node1 seems good source,
    using it
2016-12-09 19:26:19,716 2982 INFO public.pgbench_branches:
    Using node
node1 as provider
2016-12-09 19:26:19,730 2982 INFO Provider: node1 (root)
2016-12-09 19:26:19,734 2982 INFO Locking
    public.pgbench_branches
2016-12-09 19:26:19,734 2982 INFO Syncing
    public.pgbench_branches
2016-12-09 19:26:22,772 2982 INFO Counting
    public.pgbench_branches
2016-12-09 19:26:22,804 2982 INFO srcdb: 2 rows,
    checksum=-3078609798
2016-12-09 19:26:22,812 2982 INFO dstdb: 2 rows,
    checksum=-3078609798
2016-12-09 19:26:22,866 2982 INFO Checking if node1 can be used
    for copy
2016-12-09 19:26:22,877 2982 INFO Node node1 seems good source,
    using it
2016-12-09 19:26:22,878 2982 INFO public.pgbench_history: Using
    node
node1 as provider
2016-12-09 19:26:22,919 2982 INFO Provider: node1 (root)
2016-12-09 19:26:22,931 2982 INFO Locking
    public.pgbench_history
2016-12-09 19:26:22,932 2982 INFO Syncing
    public.pgbench_history
2016-12-09 19:26:25,963 2982 INFO Counting
    public.pgbench_history
2016-12-09 19:26:26,008 2982 INFO srcdb: 715 rows,
    checksum=9467587272
2016-12-09 19:26:26,020 2982 INFO dstdb: 715 rows,
    checksum=9467587272
2016-12-09 19:26:26,056 2982 INFO Checking if node1 can be used
    for copy
2016-12-09 19:26:26,063 2982 INFO Node node1 seems good source,
    using it
2016-12-09 19:26:26,064 2982 INFO public.pgbench_tellers: Using
```

```
       node
node1 as provider
2016-12-09 19:26:26,100 2982 INFO Provider: node1 (root)
2016-12-09 19:26:26,108 2982 INFO Locking
  public.pgbench_tellers
2016-12-09 19:26:26,109 2982 INFO Syncing
  public.pgbench_tellers
2016-12-09 19:26:29,144 2982 INFO Counting
  public.pgbench_tellers
2016-12-09 19:26:29,176 2982 INFO srcdb: 20 rows,
  checksum=4814381032
2016-12-09 19:26:29,182 2982 INFO dstdb: 20 rows,
  checksum=4814381032
```

How it works...

The following is an explanation regarding the steps done in the preceding section:

- Initially in step 1 of the preceding section we created two databases, that is, node1 and node2, which are to be used as source and target databases respectively from a replication perspective.

- In step 2 of the preceding section, we populated the node1 database using the pgbench utility. In step 3 of the preceding section, we added and defined the respective primary key and foreign key relationships on different tables and put these DDL commands in an SQL file. In step 4 of the preceding section, we executed these DDL commands stated in step 3 on the node1 database and thus this way we force, the primary key and foreign key definitions on the tables in the pgbench schema in the node1 database.

- In step 5 of the preceding section, we extracted the table definitions from the tables in the pgbench schema in the node1 database and loaded these definitions in the node2 database.

- We will now discuss steps 6-8 of the preceding section. In step 6, we created the configuration file, which is then used in step 7 to create the root node for the source database, node1. In step 8, we launched the worker daemon for the root node. With regards to the entries in the configuration file in step 6, we first defined a job that must have a name so that distinguished processes can be easily identified. Then we defined a connect string with information to connect to the source database, that is, node1, and then we defined the name of the replication queue involved. Finally, we defined the location of the log and PID file.

- We will now discuss steps 9-11 of the preceding section. In step 9, we defined the configuration file, which is then used in step 10 to create the leaf node for the target database, that is, node2. In step 11, we then launched the worker daemon for the leaf node. The entries in the configuration file in step 9 contain the jobname, connect string to connect to the target database, that is, node2, the name of the replication queue involved, and the location of the log and PID involved. The key part here in step 11 relates to the slave, that is, the target database, and where to find the master or provider, that is, the source database, node1.
- We will now talk about steps 12-13 of the preceding section. In step 12, we defined the ticker configuration with the help of which we launched the ticker process in step 13. Once the ticker has started successfully, we have all the components and processes set up and needed for the replication; however, we have not yet defined what the system needs to replicate.
- In steps 14 and 15 of the preceding section, we defined the tables to replication set on both the source and target database, that is, node1, and node2, respectively.
- Finally, we will talk about steps 16 -17 of the preceding section. Here, at this stage, we are testing for the replicate that was set up the between source database, node1, and the target database, node2. In step 16, we generated some traffic on the source database, node1, by running pgbench with five parallel database connections and generating traffic for 10 seconds. In step 17, we checked that the tables on both the source and target databases have the same data. For this purpose, we use the compare command on the provider and subscriber nodes and then count and checksum the rows on both sides. A partial output from the preceding section tells us that the data has been successfully replicated between all the tables that are part of the replication set up between the source database, node1, and the destination database, node2, as the count and checksum of rows for all the tables on source and target destination databases are matching:

```
2016-12-09 19:26:18,975 2982 INFO Counting
  public.pgbench_accounts
2016-12-09 19:26:19,401 2982 INFO srcdb: 200000 rows,
checksum=167607238449
2016-12-09 19:26:19,706 2982 INFO dstdb: 200000 rows,
checksum=167607238449

2016-12-09 19:26:22,772 2982 INFO Counting
  public.pgbench_branches
2016-12-09 19:26:22,804 2982 INFO srcdb: 2 rows,
  checksum=-3078609798
2016-12-09 19:26:22,812 2982 INFO dstdb: 2 rows,
  checksum=-3078609798
```

```
2016-12-09 19:26:25,963 2982 INFO Counting
  public.pgbench_history
2016-12-09 19:26:26,008 2982 INFO srcdb: 715 rows,
  checksum=9467587272
2016-12-09 19:26:26,020 2982 INFO dstdb: 715 rows,
  checksum=9467587272

2016-12-09 19:26:29,144 2982 INFO Counting
  public.pgbench_tellers
2016-12-09 19:26:29,176 2982 INFO srcdb: 20 rows,
  checksum=4814381032
2016-12-09 19:26:29,182 2982 INFO dstdb: 20 rows,
  checksum=4814381032
```

You may refer to the following links for more information regarding Londiste
replication: https://wiki.postgresql.org/wiki/Londiste_Tutorial_(Sk
ytools_2) and http://manojadinesh.blogspot.in/2012/11/skytools-
londiste-replication.html.

Replication using Bucardo

In this recipe, we are going to show the replication between two databases using Bucardo, which is another replication tool that replicates data among multiple master nodes. As with the other two tools, this tool is also dependent on triggers at the source tables.

Getting ready

This exercise is carried out in a Red Hat Linux machine.

Install the EPEL package for your Red Hat platform from the following URL: https://fed
oraproject.org/wiki/EPEL.

Then install these RPMs with the following yum command:

```
yum install perl-DBI perl-DBD-Pg perl-DBIx-Safe
```

If it is not already installed, download the Postgresql repository from the following web link: http://yum.pgrpms.org/repopackages.php

After this, install the following package. This is required because Bucardo is written in Perl:

```
yum install postgresql96-plperl
```

To install Bucardo, download it from the following web link: `http://bucardo.org/wiki/B ucardo`

Extract the tarball and go to the newly downloaded location and compile and build the software:

```
tar xvfz Bucardo-5.2.0.tar.gz

cd Bucardo-5.2.0

perl Makefile.PL

make
make install
```

How to do it...

The following are the steps to configure replication between two databases using Bucardo:

1. The first step is to install Bucardo, that is, create the main Bucardo database containing the information that the Bucardo daemon will need:

   ```
   [postgres@localhost ~]$ bucardo install --batch --quiet
   Creating superuser 'bucardo'
   ```

2. In the next step, we create source and target databases, that is, gamma1 and gamma2 respectively, between which the replication needs to be set up:

   ```
   [postgres@localhost ~]$ psql -qc 'create database gamma1'

   psql -d test1 -qc 'create table t1 (id serial primary key,
       email text)'

   [postgres@localhost ~]$ psql -qc 'create database gamma2
       template gamma1'
   ```

3. In the next step, we inform Bucardo about the databases that will be involved in the replication:

   ```
   postgres@localhost ~]$ bucardo add db db1 dbname=gamma1
   Added database "db1"

   [postgres@localhost ~]$ bucardo add db db2 dbname=gamma2
   Added database "db2"
   ```

4. In the next step, we create a herd and include those tables from the source database that will be part of the replication setup:

```
[postgres@localhost ~]$ bucardo add herd myherd t1

Created relgroup "myherd"
Added the following tables or sequences:
 public.t1 (DB: db1)
The following tables or sequences are now part of the relgroup
  "myherd":
 public.t1
```

5. In the next step, we create a source sync:

```
[postgres@localhost ~]$ bucardo add sync beta herd=myherd
  dbs=db1:source
Added sync "beta"
Created a new dbgroup named "beta"
```

6. In the next step, we create a target sync:

```
[postgres@localhost ~]$ bucardo add sync charlie herd=myherd
dbs=db1:source,db2:target
Added sync "charlie"
Created a new dbgroup named "charlie"
```

7. At this stage, we have the replication procedure set up, so the next step is to start the Bucardo service:

```
[postgres@localhost ~]$ bucardo start
Checking for existing processes
Removing file "pid/fullstopbucardo"
Starting Bucardo
```

8. The next step is to test our replication setup. For this purpose, we are going to insert some records in the t1 table on the source database, gamma1:

```
psql  -d  gamma1

gamma1=# insert into t1 values (1,'wallsingh@gmail.com');
INSERT 0 1
gamma1=# insert into t1 values (2,'neha.verma@gmail.com');
INSERT 0 1
```

9. Now that we have inserted some records in the source database in the previous step, we need to check if these changes have been replicated to the target database, gamma2:

```
psql  -d  gamma2


gamma2=# select * from t1;
 id |         email
----+---------------------
  1 | wallsingh@gmail.com
  2 | neha.verma@gmail.com
(2 rows)
```

How it works...

The following is the description of the steps from the preceding section:

- In step 1, of the preceding section, we first created the bucardo database that will contain information about the Bucardo daemon and will also create a superuser by the name of bucardo.

- In step 2, of the preceding section, we created our source and target databases for replication, that is, gamma1, and gamma2, respectively. We also created the table t1 on the gamma1 database, which will be used for replication.

- In step 3, of the preceding section, we tell Bucardo regarding the source and target databases, that is, gamma1, and gamma2 respectively, which will be involved in the replication.

- In step 4, of the preceding section, we created a herd by the name of myherd and included the table t1 from the source database, gamma1, which will be a part of the replication setup. Any changes made on this table should be replicated from the source to the target database.

- In steps 5 and 6, of the preceding section, we basically created a source and a target sync that will replicate the table t1 in the herd, myherd, and replicate it from the source database db1, that is, gamma1 to the target database, db2, that is, gamma2.

- With the replication set up configured, we started the Bucardo service in step 7 of the preceding section.

- We tested the replication setup in steps 8 and 9, of the preceding section.

- In step 8, we inserted some records in the t1 table on the gamma1 database and in step 9, we logged in to the gamma2 database and checked if the newly inserted records in the t1 table in the gamma database are replicated across the gamma2 database. The result set of the SELECT query from the t1 table in the gamma2 database confirms that the inserted records in the gamma1 database have been successfully replicated to the gamma2 database.

> You may refer to the following links for more information regarding Bucardo replication: http://blog.pscs.co.uk/postgresql-replication -and-bucardo/ and http://blog.endpoint.com/2014/06/bucardo-5-mu ltimaster-postgres-released.html.

Replication using DRBD

In this recipe, we are going to cover block level replication using DRBD for Postgresql.

Getting ready

A working Linux machine is required for this setup. This setup requires network interfaces and the cLusterIP. These steps are carried out in a CentOS version 6 machine. Having covered the PostgreSQL setup in previous chapters, it is assumed that the necessary packages and prerequisites are already installed.

We will be using the following setup in our hierarchy:

- Node1.author.org uses the LAN IP address 10.0.0.181 and uses 172.16.0.1 for crossover
- Node2.author.org uses the LAN IP address 10.0.0.182 and uses the IP address 172.16.0.2 for crossover
- dbip.author.org uses the cluster IP address 10.0.0.180

How to do it...

The following are the steps for block level replication using DRBD:

1. First, temporarily disable SELINUX and set SELINUX to disabled and then save the file:

   vi /etc/selinux/config
   SELINUX=disabled

2. In the next step, change the hostname and gateway for both the nodes, that is, the network interfaces:

   vi /etc/sysconfig/network

   For node 1:

   NETWORKING=yes
   NETWORKING_IPV6=no
   HOSTNAME=node1.author.org
   GATEWAY=10.0.0.2

   For node 2:

   NETWORKING=yes
   NETWORKING_IPV6=no
   HOSTNAME=node2.author.org
   GATEWAY=10.0.0.2

3. In the next step, we need to configure the network interfaces for the first node, that is, node1.

   We first configure the first node1:

   vi /etc/sysconfig/network-scripts/ifcfg-eth0

   DEVICE=eth0
   BOOTPROTO=static
   IPADDR=10.0.0.181
   NETMASK=255.255.255.0
   ONBOOT=yes
   HWADDR=a2:4e:7f:64:61:24

   We then configure the crossover/DRBD interface for node1:

   vi /etc/sysconfig/network-scripts/ifcfg-eth1
   DEVICE=eth1

```
BOOTPROTO=static
IPADDR=172.16.0.1
NETMASK=255.255.255.0
ONBOOT=yes
HWADDR=ee:df:ff:4a:5f:68
```

4. In step 4, we then configure the network interfaces for the second node, that is, node2:

```
vi /etc/sysconfig/network-scripts/ifcfg-eth0
DEVICE=eth0
BOOTPROTO=static
IPADDR=10.0.0.182
NETMASK=255.255.255.0
ONBOOT=yes
HWADDR=22:42:b1:5a:42:6f
```

We then configure the crossover/DRBD interface for node2:

```
vi /etc/sysconfig/network-scripts/ifcfg-eth1
DEVICE=eth1
BOOTPROTO=static
IPADDR=172.16.0.2
NETMASK=255.255.255.0
ONBOOT=yes
HWADDR=6a:48:d2:70:26:5e
```

5. The next step is to configure DNS:

```
vi /etc/resolv.conf
search author.org
nameserver 10.0.0.2
```

Also configure the basic hostname resolution:

```
vi /etc/hosts
127.0.0.1               localhost.localdomain localhost
10.0.0.181              node1.author.org        node1
10.0.0.182              node2.author.org        node2
10.0.0.180              dbip.author.org         node2
```

6. In the next step, we will check the network connectivity between the nodes. First we will ping node 2 from node 1 first through the LAN interface and then through the crossover IP:

```
root@node1 ~]# ping -c 2 node2
PING node2 (10.0.0.182) 56(84) bytes of data.
64 bytes from node2 (10.0.0.182): icmp_seq=1 ttl=64 time=0.089 ms
64 bytes from node2 (10.0.0.182): icmp_seq=2 ttl=64 time=0.082 ms
--- node2 ping statistics ---
2 packets transmitted, 2 received, 0% packet loss, time 999ms
rtt min/avg/max/mdev = 0.082/0.085/0.089/0.009 ms

[root@node1 ~]# ping -c 2 172.16.0.2
PING 172.16.0.2 (172.16.0.2) 56(84) bytes of data.
64 bytes from 172.16.0.2: icmp_seq=1 ttl=64 time=0.083 ms
64 bytes from 172.16.0.2: icmp_seq=2 ttl=64 time=0.083 ms
--- 172.16.0.2 ping statistics ---
2 packets transmitted, 2 received, 0% packet loss, time 999ms
rtt min/avg/max/mdev = 0.083/0.083/0.083/0.000 ms
```

Now we will ping node1 from node2 first via the LAN interface and then through the crossover IP:

```
[root@node2 ~]# ping -c 2 node1
PING node1 (10.0.0.181) 56(84) bytes of data.
64 bytes from node1 (10.0.0.181): icmp_seq=1 ttl=64 time=0.068 ms
64 bytes from node1 (10.0.0.181): icmp_seq=2 ttl=64 time=0.063 ms
--- node1 ping statistics ---
2 packets transmitted, 2 received, 0% packet loss, time 999ms
rtt min/avg/max/mdev = 0.063/0.065/0.068/0.008 ms
```

Now we will ping node1 through the crossover interface:

```
[root@node2 ~]# ping -c 2 172.16.0.1
PING 172.16.0.1 (172.16.0.1) 56(84) bytes of data.
64 bytes from 172.16.0.1: icmp_seq=1 ttl=64 time=1.36 ms
64 bytes from 172.16.0.1: icmp_seq=2 ttl=64 time=0.075 ms
--- 172.16.0.1 ping statistics ---
2 packets transmitted, 2 received, 0% packet loss, time 1001ms
rtt min/avg/max/mdev = 0.075/0.722/1.369/0.647 ms
```

7. After configuring network connectivity, we next set the initialization options and set the run level to 3:

```
vi /etc/inittab

id:3:initdefault:
```

8. Install the necessary packages:

```
yum install -y  drbd83 kmod-drbd83
```

9. In the next step, configure DRBD on both the nodes:

```
vi /etc/drbd.conf

global {
    usage-count no;
}
common {
    syncer { rate 100M; }
    protocol        C;
}
resource postgres {
    startup {
       wfc-timeout 0;
       degr-wfc-timeout
       120;
    }
    disk { on-io-error detach; }
    on node1.author.org {
       device      /dev/drbd0;
       disk        /dev/sdb;
       address     172.16.0.1:7791;
       meta-disk   internal;
    }
    on node2.author.org {
       device      /dev/drbd0;
       disk        /dev/sdb;
       address     172.16.0.2:7791;
       meta-disk   internal;
    }
}
```

10. Once the `drbd.conf` file is set up for both the nodes, we then metadata on the Postgres resource. Execute the following step on both the nodes:

```
[root@node1 ~]# drbdadm create-md postgres
Writing meta data...
initializing activity log
NOT initialized bitmap
New drbd meta data block successfully created.

root@node2 ~]# drbdadm create-md postgres
Writing meta data...
initializing activity log
NOT initialized bitmap
New drbd meta data block successfully created.
```

11. In the next step, we will bring up the resource. Execute the following step on both the nodes:

```
drbdadm up postgres
```

12. In the next step, we can make the initial sync between the nodes. This step can be done on the primary node and we set node 1 as the primary node:

```
drbdadm -- --overwrite-data-of-peer primary postgres
```

13. To monitor the progress of the sync and the status of the DRBD resource, look at the `/proc/drbd` file:

```
[root@node1 ~]# cat /proc/drbd
version: 8.3.8 (api:88/proto:86-94)
GIT-hash: d78846e52224fd00562f7c225bcc25b2d422321d build by
mockbuild@builder10.centos.org, 2016-10-04 14:04:09
0: cs:SyncSource ro:Primary/Secondary ds:UpToDate/Inconsistent C r-
---
ns:48128 nr:0 dw:0 dr:48128 al:0 bm:2 lo:0 pe:0 ua:0 ap:0 ep:1 wo:b
oos:8340188
[>....................] sync'ed:   0.6% (8144/8188)M delay_probe: 7
finish: 0:11:29 speed: 12,032 (12,032) K/sec
```

14. Once the sync process completes, we can take a look at both the status of the Postgres resource on both the nodes:

```
[root@node1 ~]# cat /proc/drbd
version: 8.3.8 (api:88/proto:86-94)
GIT-hash: d78846e52224fd00562f7c225bcc25b2d422321d build by
mockbuild@builder10.centos.org, 2016-10-04 14:04:09
```

```
0: cs:Connected ro:Primary/Secondary ds:UpToDate/UpToDate C r----
ns:8388316 nr:0 dw:0 dr:8388316 al:0 bm:512 lo:0 pe:0 ua:0 ap:0
ep:1 wo:b oos:0

[root@node2 ~]# cat /proc/drbd
version: 8.3.8 (api:88/proto:86-94)
GIT-hash: d78846e52224fd00562f7c225bcc25b2d422321d build by
mockbuild@builder10.centos.org, 2016-2016-10-04 14:04:09
0: cs:Connected ro:Secondary/Primary ds:UpToDate/UpToDate C r----
ns:0 nr:8388316 dw:8388316 dr:0 al:0 bm:512 lo:0 pe:0 ua:0 ap:0
ep:1 wo:b oos:0
```

15. In the next step, we are going to initiate DRBD services on both the nodes. Issue the following command:

```
/etc/init.d/drbd start
```

16. In order to initialize the data directory and to set up using DRBD, we would need to format and mount the DRBD device. And then we initialize the data directory.

    Issue the following commands on node1:

```
mkfs.ext3 /dev/drbd0
```

```
mount -t ext3 /dev/drbd0 /var/lib/pgsql/9.6
```

```
chown postgres.postgres /var/lib/pgsql/9.6
```

    Next we log in as the Postgres user on node1 and initialize the database:

```
su - postgres
initdb /var/lib/pgsql/9.6/data
exit
```

17. In the next step, we enable trusted authentication and we will configure the necessary parameters for setting up PostgreSQL in the postgresql.conf file. On node1, execute the following:

```
echo "host    all    all    10.0.0.181/32    trust" >>
/var/lib/pgsql/9.6/data/pg_hba.conf
echo "host    all    all    10.0.0.182/32    trust" >>
/var/lib/pgsql/9.6/data/pg_hba.conf
echo "host    all    all    10.0.0.180/32    trust" >>
/var/lib/pgsql/9.6/data/pg_hba.conf
```

Then we configure the necessary parameters in the `postgresql.conf` file:

```
vi /var/lib/pgsql/9.3/data/postgresql.conf
listen_addresses = '*'
```

18. Once the previously parameters have been changed in the `postgresql.conf` file, the next step would be to start PostgreSQL. Execute the following command on node1:

```
service postgresql-9.6 start
```

19. We will then create an admin user to manage PostgreSQL. On node 1, execute the following command:

```
su - postgres
createuser --superuser admin  --pwprompt
```

20. In the next step, we create a database and populate it with data. On node1 execute the following steps and then access the database:

```
su - postgres

createdb test

pgbench -i test

psql -U admin -d test

test=# select * from pgbench_tellers;

tid | bid | tbalance | filler
-----+-----+----------+--------
1 |   1 |        0 |
2 |   1 |        0 |
3 |   1 |        0 |
4 |   1 |        0 |
5 |   1 |        0 |
6 |   1 |        0 |
7 |   1 |        0 |
8 |   1 |        0 |
9 |   1 |        0 |
10 |   1 |        0 |
(10 registros)
```

21. In the next step, we will test the block-level replication and see if PostgreSQL will work on node2.

On node 1, execute the following commands:

1. We will first stop `postgresql` on `node1`:

    `service postgresql-9.6 stop`

2. Then we will unmount the DRBD device on `node1`:

    `umount /dev/drbd0`

3. Now we will set up `node1` as the secondary node:

    `drbdadm secondary postgres`

4. Now we will configure `node2` as the primary node:

    `drbdadm primary postgres`

5. In the next step, mount the DRBD device:

`mount -t ext3 /dev/drbd0 /var/lib/pgsql/9.6`

6. Then we start the postgresql service on `node2`:

    `service postgresql-9.6 start`

7. Now we will see if we are able to access the test database on `node2`:

    `psql -u admin -d test`

    `test=# select * from pgbench_tellers;`

    ```
    tid | bid | tbalance | filler
    ----+-----+----------+--------
     1 |  1 |        0 |
     2 |  1 |        0 |
     3 |  1 |        0 |
     4 |  1 |        0 |
     5 |  1 |        0 |
     6 |  1 |        0 |
     7 |  1 |        0 |
     8 |  1 |        0 |
     9 |  1 |        0 |
    10 |   1 |        0 |
    ```

How it works...

In the initial steps from steps 1 to 6, we configured the nodes, that is, `node1` and `node2`, we set up network connectivity, and also configured DNS. In step 6, we did the network connectivity test between `node1` and `node2` on the LAN interface as well as on the crossover interface. We received successful echo response messages after doing the ping request tests. This shows that the network connectivity is successfully configured.

In step 9, we set up the `drbd.conf` file on both the nodes. Here is an extract from the `drbd.conf` file:

```
global {
    usage-count no;
}
common {
    syncer { rate 100M; }
    protocol        C;
}
resource postgres {
    startup {
        wfc-timeout 0;
        degr-wfc-timeout
        120;
    }
    disk { on-io-error detach; }
    on node1.author.org {
        device      /dev/drbd0;
        disk        /dev/sdb;
        address     172.16.0.1:7791;
        meta-disk   internal;
    }
    on node2.author.org {
        device      /dev/drbd0;
        disk        /dev/sdb;
        address     172.16.0.2:7791;
        meta-disk   internal;
    }
}
```

Basically, resource from the previously configuration, we are setting up a Postgres and we are configuring a DRBD interface /dev/drbd0, which is set up on two nodes, node1 and node2. This is basically what causes the block level replication to be successful. We can see in step 12 of the preceding section that we have initially set up node1 as the primary node and node2 serves as the secondary node at that stage. Then we set up Postgresql on node1 from step 16 onwards. From step 21 onwards, we do failover testing. We first reset the node 1 as the secondary node, unmount the filesystem, and then set up node2 as the primary node, mount the filesystem, and bring up the Postgresql server. After that, we are testing for record visibility in node2. The database test that was created in step 20 of the preceding section is accessible in node2 and so are the tables in the pgbench schema in step 21. Thus DRBD provides for block level replication and in case one of the nodes is not available, we can then configure and continue to run Postgresql on the secondary node where it is going to take the role of the primary.

Setting up a Postgres-XL cluster

Here in this recipe, we are going to set up a Postgres XL cluster, which is a scalable PostgreSQL cluster, to solve the big data processing challenges.

Getting ready

Postgres-XL is a horizontally scalable open source cluster, which has a set of individual dedicated components to scale PostgreSQL to multiple nodes. Postgre-XL (extensible lattice) gives us more convenience in distributing the data across the nodes or replicating the data across the nodes.

How to do it...

Note that:

```
node1 -- ec2-54-164-174-117.compute-1.amazonaws.com -- 172-30-1-154
node2 -- ec2-54-152-235-194.compute-1.amazonaws.com -- 172-30-1-155
node3 -- ec2-54-165-7-151.compute-1.amazonaws.com -- 172-30-1-156
node4 -- ec2-54-152-210-130.compute-1.amazonaws.com -- 172-30-1-157
```

1. Create the PostgresXL user account and group:

```
sudo groupadd pgxl
sudo useradd -g pgxl pgxl
```

2. Install RPMS on all four servers. Copy the following RPMS to the server and make sure you are in the same location where the packages are before you run the following yum command:

```
yum install postgres-xl92-libs-9.2-34.1.x86_64.rpm \
postgres-xl92-9.2-34.1.x86_64.rpm \
postgres-xl92-server-9.2-34.1.x86_64.rpm \
postgres-xl92-contrib-9.2-34.1.x86_64.rpm \
postgres-xl92-gtm-9.2-34.1.x86_64.rpm
```

3. Verify installation. Check if it is installed properly on each server:

```
[centos@ip-172-30-1-157 ~]$ cd /usr/postgres-xl-9.2/
[centos@ip-172-30-1-157 postgres-xl-9.2]$ ls -ltrh
total 12K
drwxr-xr-x. 2 pgxl pgxl 4.0K Dec 3 05:32 lib
drwxr-xr-x. 7 pgxl pgxl 4.0K Dec 3 05:32 share
drwxr-xr-x. 2 root root 4.0K Dec 3 05:32 bin
```

4. Set up the environment variables in bash. Make sure you add the following lines in bash_profile of the pgxl user on each server:

```
export PATH=/usr/postgres-xl-9.2/bin:$PATH
export LD_LIBRARY_PATH=/usr/postgres-xl
   9.2/lib:$LD_LIBRARY_PATH
```

5. GTM and GTM-Proxy initialization (login as a pgxl user). Decide where to run the GTM server. Let's choose the ec2-54-164-174-117.compute-1.amazonaws.com server as the GTM.

Steps to start GTM:

```
mkdir data_gtm
initgtm -Z gtm -D /home/pgxl/data_gtm/
--- Modify the config:
[pgxl@ip-172-30-1-154 data_gtm]$ grep -v '^#' gtm.conf
nodename = 'gtm_node' # Specifies the node name.
# (changes requires restart)
listen_addresses = '*' # Listen addresses of this GTM.
# (changes requires restart)
port = 6666 # Port number of this GTM.
# (changes requires restart)
```

Start using:

```
[pgxl@ip-172-30-1-154 data_gtm]$ gtm -D /home/pgxl/data_gtm/ &
[1] 5938
```

```
[pgxl@ip-172-30-1-154 data_gtm]$
[pgxl@ip-172-30-1-154 data_gtm]$
[pgxl@ip-172-30-1-154 data_gtm]$ ps -ef|grep gtm
pgxl 5938 5909 0 06:23 pts/2 00:00:00 gtm -D
  /home/pgxl/data_gtm/
pgxl 5940 5909 0 06:23 pts/2 00:00:00 grep gtm
[pgxl@ip-172-30-1-154 data_gtm]$

[pgxl@ip-172-30-1-154 data_gtm]$ netstat -apn |grep 6666
(Not all processes could be identified, non-owned process info
will not be shown, you would have to be root to see it all.)
tcp 0 0 0.0.0.0:6666 0.0.0.0:* LISTEN 5938/gtm
tcp 0 0 :::6666 :::* LISTEN 5938/gtm
[pgxl@ip-172-30-1-154 data_gtm]$
[pgxl@ip-172-30-1-154 data_gtm]$
```

Steps to start `gtm-proxy`:

```
mkdir data_gtm_proxy
intigtm -Z gtm_proxy /home/pgxl/data_gtm_proxy
--- Modify config:
pgxl@ip-172-30-1-154 ~]$ grep -v "^#"
  data_gtm_proxy/gtm_proxy.conf
nodename = 'gtm_proxy_node' # Specifies the node name.
# (changes requires restart)
listen_addresses = '*' # Listen addresses of this GTM.
# (changes requires restart)
port = 6667 # Port number of this GTM.

gtm_host = 'localhost' # Listen address of the active GTM.
# (changes requires restart)
gtm_port = 6666 # Port number of the active GTM.
# (changes requires restart)
```

Start the `gtm_proxy`:

```
gtm_proxy -D /home/pgxl/data_gtm_proxy/ &
[pgxl@ip-172-30-1-154 ~]$ ps -ef|grep gtm
pgxl 7026 6952 0 16:58 pts/0 00:00:00 gtm -D
  /home/pgxl/data_gtm/
pgxl 7052 6952 0 17:05 pts/0 00:00:00 gtm_proxy -D
/home/pgxl/data_gtm_proxy/
pgxl 7059 6952 0 17:05 pts/0 00:00:00 grep gtm
```

6. Create and configure a data node on each of the servers.

On node1 (which is GTM):

```
mkdir data_node1
initdb -D /home/pgxl/data_node1/ --nodename datanode1
```

In the datanode1/postgresql.conf file:

```
listen_addresses='*'
port = 5432
gtm_host = '172.30.1.154'
gtm_port=6666
```

On node2:

```
mkdir data_node2
initdb -D /home/pgxl/data_node2/ --nodename datanode2
```

In the datanode2/postgresql.conf file:

```
listen_addresses='*'
port = 5432
gtm_host = '172.30.1.154'
gtm_port=6666
```

On node3:

```
mkdir data_node3
initdb -D /home/pgxl/data_node3/ --nodename datanode3
```

In the datanode3/postgresql.conf file:

```
listen_addresses='*'
port = 5432
gtm_host = '172.30.1.154'
gtm_port=6666
```

On node4:

```
mkdir data_node4
initdb -D /home/pgxl/data_node4/ --nodename datanode4
```

In the `datanode4/postgresql.conf` file:

```
listen_addresses='*'
port = 5432
gtm_host = '172.30.1.154'
gtm_port=6666
```

7. Create and configure coordinators on two nodes: in this case, `ec2-54-152-235-194.compute-1.amazonaws.com` (node2) and `ec2-54-165-7-151.compute-1.amazonaws.com` (node3).

    On node2:

```
mkdir coord1
initdb -D /home/pgxl/coord1/ --nodename coord1
```

    In `coord1/postgresql.conf` file:

```
listen_addresses='*'
port = 5433
gtm_host = '172.30.1.154'
gtm_port=6666
```

    On node3:

```
mkdir coord2
initdb -D /home/pgxl/coord2/ --nodename coord2
```

In the `coord2/postgresql.conf` file:

```
listen_addresses='*'
port = 5433
gtm_host = '172.30.1.154'
gtm_port=6666
```

8. Configure `hba.conf`. Add the following entries in `hba.conf` of all the data nodes and coordinators:

```
host all all 172.30.1.154/32 trust
host all all 172.30.1.155/32 trust
host all all 172.30.1.156/32 trust
host all all 172.30.1.157/32 trust
```

9. Start the data nodes and coordinators.

On node1:

```
postgres --datanode -D /home/pgxl/data_node1 &
```

On node2:

```
postgres --datanode -D /home/pgxl/data_node2 &
postgres --coordinator -D /home/pgxl/coord1 &
```

On node3:

```
postgres --datanode -D /home/pgxl/data_node3 &
postgres --coordinator -D /home/pgxl/coord2 &
```

On node4:

```
postgres --datanode -D /home/pgxl/data_node4 &
```

Example of processes, on the GTM and GTM proxy:

```
[pgxl@ip-172-30-1-154 ~]$ ps -ef|grep gtm
pgxl 7026 6952 0 16:58 pts/0 00:00:00 gtm -D /home/pgxl/data_gtm/
pgxl 7052 6952 0 17:05 pts/0 00:00:00 gtm_proxy -D
/home/pgxl/data_gtm_proxy/
pgxl 7152 6952 0 17:36 pts/0 00:00:00 grep gtm
```

On a data node ONLY node:

```
[pgxl@ip-172-30-1-154 ~]$ ps -ef|grep postgres
pgxl 7128 6952 0 17:26 pts/0 00:00:00 postgres --datanode -D
/home/pgxl/data_node1
pgxl 7129 7128 0 17:26 ? 00:00:00 postgres: logger process
pgxl 7131 7128 0 17:26 ? 00:00:00 postgres: pooler process
pgxl 7132 7128 0 17:26 ? 00:00:00 postgres: checkpointer process
pgxl 7133 7128 0 17:26 ? 00:00:00 postgres: writer process
pgxl 7134 7128 0 17:26 ? 00:00:00 postgres: wal writer process
pgxl 7135 7128 0 17:26 ? 00:00:00 postgres: autovacuum launcher
process
pgxl 7136 7128 0 17:26 ? 00:00:00 postgres: stats collector process
pgxl 7155 6952 0 17:37 pts/0 00:00:00 grep postgres
```

On a datanode and coordinator node:

```
[pgxl@ip-172-30-1-156 ~]$ ps -ef|grep postgres
pgxl 7151 6922 0 17:35 pts/0 00:00:00 postgres --datanode -D
/home/pgxl/data_node3
pgxl 7152 7151 0 17:35 ? 00:00:00 postgres: logger process
```

```
pgxl 7154 7151 0 17:35 ? 00:00:00 postgres: pooler process
pgxl 7155 7151 0 17:35 ? 00:00:00 postgres: checkpointer
  process
pgxl 7156 7151 0 17:35 ? 00:00:00 postgres: writer process
pgxl 7157 7151 0 17:35 ? 00:00:00 postgres: wal writer process
pgxl 7158 7151 0 17:35 ? 00:00:00 postgres: autovacuum launcher
  process
pgxl 7159 7151 0 17:35 ? 00:00:00 postgres: stats collector
  process
pgxl 7161 6922 0 17:35 pts/0 00:00:00 postgres --coordinator -D
/home/pgxl/coord2
pgxl 7162 7161 0 17:35 ? 00:00:00 postgres: logger process
pgxl 7164 7161 0 17:35 ? 00:00:00 postgres: pooler process
pgxl 7165 7161 0 17:35 ? 00:00:00 postgres: checkpointer
  process
pgxl 7166 7161 0 17:35 ? 00:00:00 postgres: writer process
pgxl 7167 7161 0 17:35 ? 00:00:00 postgres: wal writer process
pgxl 7168 7161 0 17:35 ? 00:00:00 postgres: autovacuum launcher
  process
pgxl 7169 7161 0 17:35 ? 00:00:00 postgres: stats collector
  process
pgxl 7171 6922 0 17:35 pts/0 00:00:00 grep postgres
```

10. Create the cluster node information on each `datanode` and `coordinator`:

```
CREATE NODE coord1
WITH (TYPE = 'coordinator', HOST = '172.30.1.155',
PORT = 5433);

CREATE NODE coord2
WITH (TYPE = 'coordinator', HOST = '172.30.1.156',
PORT = 5433);

CREATE NODE datanode1
WITH (TYPE = 'datanode', HOST = '172.30.1.154',
PORT = 5432);

CREATE NODE datanode2
WITH (TYPE = 'datanode', HOST = '172.30.1.155',
PORT = 5432, PRIMARY, PREFERRED);

CREATE NODE datanode3
WITH (TYPE = 'datanode', HOST = '172.30.1.156',
PORT = 5432);

CREATE NODE datanode4
WITH (TYPE = 'datanode', HOST = '172.30.1.157',
PORT = 5432);
```

11. Update the coordinators' information in `pgxc_node`.

    On `node2`:

```
psql -d postgres -p 5433
postgres=# begin;
BEGIN
postgres=# update pgxc_node set node_port=5433 where
  node_name='coord1';          -- check if it's updated or not
    before you commit.
UPDATE 1
postgres=# commit;
COMMIT
```

    On `node3`:

```
psql -d postgres -p 5433
postgres=# begin;
BEGIN
postgres=# update pgxc_node set node_host='172.30.1.156' where
node_name='coord2'; check if it's updated or not before you
  commit.
UPDATE 1
postgres=# commit;
```

12. Alter the data nodes information in `pgxc_node`:

    On `node1`:

```
psql -d postgres -p 5432
postgres=# begin;
BEGIN
postgres=# alter node datanode1 with (TYPE = 'datanode',
HOST = '172.30.1.154', PORT = 5432);
ALTER NODE
postgres=# select * from pg_catalog.pgxc_node ;
node_name | node_type | node_port | node_host | nodeis_primary|
nodeis_preferred | node_id
-----------+-----------+-----------+--------------+-----------
  ----
+-------------------+--------------
coord1 | C | 5433 | 172.30.1.155 | f | f | 1885696643
coord2 | C | 5433 | 172.30.1.156 | f | f | -1197102633
datanode2 | D | 5432 | 172.30.1.155 | t | t | -905831925
datanode3 | D | 5432 | 172.30.1.156 | f | f | -1894792127
datanode4 | D | 5432 | 172.30.1.157 | f | f | -1307323892
datanode1 | D | 5432 | 172.30.1.154 | f | f | 888802358
(6 rows)
```

```
postgres=# commit;
COMMIT
```

On node2:

```
psql -d postgres -p 5432
postgres=# begin;
BEGIN
postgres=# alter node datanode2 with (TYPE = 'datanode',
HOST = '172.30.1.155', PORT = 5432, PRIMARY, PREFERRED);
postgres=# select * from pgxc_node;
node_name | node_type | node_port | node_host | nodeis_primary|
nodeis_preferred | node_id
-----------+-----------+-----------+--------------+------------
    ----
+------------------+-------------
coord1 | C | 5433 | 172.30.1.155 | f | f | 1885696643
coord2 | C | 5433 | 172.30.1.156 | f | f | -1197102633
datanode1 | D | 5432 | 172.30.1.154 | f | f | 888802358
datanode3 | D | 5432 | 172.30.1.156 | f | f | -1894792127
datanode4 | D | 5432 | 172.30.1.157 | f | f | -1307323892
datanode2 | D | 5432 | 172.30.1.155 | t | t | -905831925
(6 rows)
postgres=# commit;
COMMIT
```

On node3:

```
psql -d postgres -p 5432
postgres=# begin;
BEGIN
postgres=# alter node datanode3 with (TYPE = 'datanode',
HOST = '172.30.1.156', PORT = 5432);
postgres=# select * from pgxc_node;
node_name | node_type | node_port | node_host | nodeis_primary|
nodeis_preferred | node_id
-----------+-----------+-----------+--------------+------------
    ----
+------------------+-------------
coord1 | C | 5433 | 172.30.1.155 | f | f | 1885696643
coord2 | C | 5433 | 172.30.1.156 | f | f | -1197102633
datanode1 | D | 5432 | 172.30.1.154 | f | f | 888802358
datanode2 | D | 5432 | 172.30.1.155 | t | t | -905831925
datanode4 | D | 5432 | 172.30.1.157 | f | f | -1307323892
datanode3 | D | 5432 | 172.30.1.156 | f | f | -1894792127
(6 rows)
postgres=# commit;
COMMIT
```

On `node4`:

```
psql -d postgres -p 5432
postgres=# begin;
BEGIN
postgres=#
postgres=# alter node datanode4 with (TYPE = 'datanode',
HOST = '172.30.1.157', PORT = 5432);
postgres=# select * from pgxc_node;
node_name | node_type | node_port | node_host | nodeis_primary|
nodeis_preferred | node_id
-----------+-----------+-----------+--------------+-----------]
  ----
+-------------------+--------------
coord1 | C | 5433 | 172.30.1.155 | f | f | 1885696643
coord2 | C | 5433 | 172.30.1.156 | f | f | -1197102633
datanode1 | D | 5432 | 172.30.1.154 | f | f | 888802358
datanode2 | D | 5432 | 172.30.1.155 | t | t | -905831925
datanode3 | D | 5432 | 172.30.1.156 | f | f | -1894792127
datanode4 | D | 5432 | 172.30.1.157 | f | f | -1307323892
(6 rows)
postgres=# commit;
COMMIT
```

13. For verification, log in to any of the coordinators on nodes 2 and 3. Distribute by replication on the coordinator:

```
create table dist_repl(id int) distribute by replication to
  node
(datanode1, datanode2, datanode3, datanode4);
insert into dist_repl values(generate_series(1,8));
```

On each datanode:

```
select * from dist_tab;
```

Distribute by hash on the coordinator:

```
create table dist_hash(id int) distribute by hash(id) to
node(datanode1, datanode2, datanode3, datanode4);
insert into dist_hash values(generate_series(1,8));
```

On the datanode:

```
select * from dist_hash;
```

7
Working with Third-Party Replication Management Utilities

In this chapter, we will cover the following:

- Setting up Barman
- Backup and recovery using Barman
- Setting up OmniPITR
- WAL management with OmniPITR
- Setting up Repmgr
- Using Repmgr to create Replica
- Setting up Walctl
- Using Walctl to create Replica

Introduction

Indexes are in essence a database structure that speeds up fetching the data access operations. Indexes are basically used to boost database performance by rapidly locating data without having to search every row in the database table every time it is accessed. Data access via indexes is known as an indexed scan and it is used to provide random lookups and organized access of ordered records.

In this chapter, we are going to talk about indexes, performing maintenance operations on indexes, and comparing indexed and sequential scans:

- One of the major responsibilities of a DB admin is to use some third-party tools to manage the database as not all can be done through scripting. Every tool is designed for a specific purpose and can be utilized as per our requirements.
- In this chapter, we are going to cover tools such as Barman and OmniPITR, which are related to backup/recovery and WAL management, repmgr for auto-failover and setting up replicas in an easy way, and Walctl to create replicas and manage WALs.

Setting up Barman

Barman, which stands for Backup And Recovery Manager, is a third-party tool developed by a company known as 2nd Quadrant and it serves as a complete backup management system for PostgreSQL.

Barman can be used to perform the following functions:

- It can be used to manage PostgreSQL server backups
- It can be used as a tool to perform and restore backup images for PostgreSQL databases
- It can be used to perform incremental and configure backup retention policies

Getting ready

The following are some of the prerequisites that are required before installing Barman:

- The system on which Barman needs to be installed must be either a Linux or a Unix system.
- The Python language version needs to either start with 2.6 or higher.
- The `rsync` command version needs to be higher than 3.0.4. On the latest operating systems this should be taken care of automatically.

For our requirement we will be using two servers. One will serve as a backup server and the other one will serve as a primary server. The backup server is named `pg-backup` and the primary server is named `pg-primary`.

How to do it...

The following are the series of steps that are required to be carried out to install and set up Barman:

1. If you are running a Red Hat-based distribution you should use the following command to install the Barman tool:

   `yum install barman`

   On Ubuntu-based systems you need to use the following command:

   `apt-get install barman`

   The next two steps talk about setting up SSH connectivity between the backup and the primary server.

2. In this step we log into the backup server as the barman user and we will execute the following commands to set up direct ssh access to the primary server:

   `ssh-keygen -t rsa -N ' '`

   `ssh-copy-id postgres@pg-primary`

3. Quite similar to the previous server, but in a vice versa manner we will now log into the primary server and set up ssh access to the backup server:

   `ssh-keygen -t rsa -N ' '`

   `ssh-copy-id barman@pg-backup`

4. We will now configure the primary server's firewall file to allow connectivity access to the backup server:

   `host all postgres pg-backup md5`

5. In the next step, we will enable the following PostgreSQL configuration parameters on the primary server:

   ```
   archive_mode = on
   archive_command = 'rsync -aq %p \ barman@pg-backup:primary/incoming/%f'
   ```

   Make sure you setup password less authentication between backup server and primary server.

6. In the next step on the backup server, we will enter the following line in the `.pgpass` file for the barman user:

```
*:*:*:postgres:postgres-password
```

7. In the next step, we will restart the PostgreSQL server on the primary for changes made to the server parameters in the previous step to come into effect:

```
pg_ctl -D /db/pgdata restart
```

8. In the next step, we are going to add the following steps at the end of the `barman.conf` configuration file, which resides in the `/etc/` or `/etc/barman` folder:

```
[primary]
description = "Primary PostgreSQL Server"
conninfo = "host=pg-primary user=postgres"
ssh_command = "ssh postgres@pg-primary"
```

9. In the next step, we are going to issue the following command from the backup server to see the primary server's barman configuration:

```
barman check primary
```

How it works...

The following is the explanation for steps carried out in the preceding section:

- In the first step of the preceding section, we installed the Barman toolkit and depending on whether the platform is a Red Hat distribution or an Ubuntu/Debian Linux distro the appropriate commands are given for the installation of the Barman tool for each platform.
- As mentioned in steps 2 and 3, we basically configured ssh access to and from the primary and the backup server. The barman user needs to fetch the PostgreSQL files from the primary server. In addition to this the Postgres user needs to be able to send files to the backup server using `rsync`. For this reason we set up passwordless SSH connectivity between the two servers for seamless interaction.
- In step 4, we basically modified the access control file `pg_hba.conf` of the primary server to allow the Postgres user to connect to primary from the backup server.

- In step 5, we enabled archiving by setting `archive_mode=on` and then we set `archive_command` in order to send the archived WAL files to the backup server so that Barman can find these WAL files in an appropriate directory.
- In step 6, we basically entering password credentials of the Postgres user in the `.pgpass` file.
- In step 7, we restart the PostgreSQL services on the primary server so that changes made in step 5 could come into effect straightaway.
- In step 8, we entered configuration information for Barman. The first parameter description is more like setting a named label so that Barman will know it is the primary server. The second line refers to the `conn_info` parameter, which specifies PostgreSQL server connection settings on the primary server that may be used internally by Barman 's Python libraries. The third line refers to the `ssh_command` parameter, which is more like stating to Barman the way to access files on the primary server as a Postgres user.
- Step 9 is more like checking Barman configuration that has been set up in all the previous steps of the preceding section. In essence, this step goes beyond just checking the Barman configuration and server status. It in fact creates different directories and tracking files that can be used to maintain PostgreSQL database server backups.

Backup and recovery using Barman

Now that we have installed and configured Barman it is now time to use Barman for its actual purpose, that is, taking backups with Barman and recovering PostgreSQL using the backups taken with Barman. This section is divided into two areas, first taking the backup and then testing its recovery.

Getting ready

All the steps in this recipe require Barman to be installed on the backup server. For restoring data we are going to use a new server named `pg-clone`.

How to do it...

The first part is to take backups, which will be done here. The following steps are all carried out on the backup server:

1. First, we create a Barman backup with the following command:

    ```
    barman backup primary
    ```

2. In the next step, we examine the list of backups with the following command:

    ```
    barman list-backup primary
    ```

3. In the third step, we check the metadata of the most recent backup:

    ```
    barman show-backup primary latest
    ```

4. In the next step, we see all files that were backed up with the most recent Barman backup:

    ```
    barman list-files primary latest
    ```

In the next series of steps we are restoring data with Barman. Here we are going to demonstrate how to restore data to the target server `pg-clone`:

1. The first step is to log into the backup server and enable SSH connectivity for the target `pg-clone` server:

    ```
    ssh-copy-id postgres@pg-clone
    ```

2. In the next step, we need to ensure that the data in the data directory of the target server is deleted/empty because using Barman we are going to restore the data to this directory:

    ```
    rm -Rf /db/pgdata
    ```

3. In the next step, we are going to send the data to the target server from the backup server and then we are going to recover the data:

    ```
    barman recover --remote-ssh-command "ssh postgres@pg-clone"
    primary latest /db/pgdata
    ```

4. In the final step, we start the PostgreSQL server on the target server having recovered the data:

    ```
    pg_ctl -D /db/pgdata start
    ```

How it works...

Here we are going to explain the steps carried out in the preceding section.

First we will talk about steps 1-4 of the preceding section:

- In step 1, we basically tell Barman to enter the backup mode with the backup command and the label primary is used to indicate to contact the primary server `pg-primary` and then contact with via ssh connectivity and take the backup of it and retrieve all the database files over SSH and save them in its repository.
- In step 2, we listed and examine the content of the backup made and that was stored in our barman repository.
- In step 3, we examine the metadata of the backup that was made. The metadata part includes the series of WAL log files produced during the backup and among other things the start and stop time of the backup.
- In step 4, we examine all the files that constituted as part of the barman backup command.
- In step 5, we configure SSH connectivity to the target server `pg-clone`. We basically do this by sending the SSH key to the target server using the `ssh-copy-id` command.
- In step 6, we remove any data existing on the data directory of the target server. This is done because we are going to restore the data directory from the backup made using Barman.
- In step 7, we basically use the barman-recover command to restore data. However, we are using the `-remote-ssh-command` option with this command. This is done because usually the recovery is done on the local server and with the usage o `-remote-ssh-` command we are basically initiating the recovery on the target server. We then specify primary as the label and we specify the latest ID of the backup to restore, that is, in short we are looking to restore the latest backup of the primary server onto the target. All these commands are fired from the terminal console of the backup server. Using the latest backup the restoration is eventually done to the data directory of the target server.
- In step 8, we now start the PostgreSQL server on the target having done full recovery of the primary on the target.

Setting up OmniPITR

OmniPITR is a third-party tool that consists of a set of scripts that are used to maintain and manage PostgreSQL database transaction log files, that is, WAL logs.

OmniPITR can also be used for initiating hot backups on master and slave PostgreSQL servers.

In this recipe, we are going to set up and install OmniPITR.

Getting ready

In this recipe, we are going to show how to install OmniPITR on a machine. However, this needs to be done on both the master and slave servers. For our exercise, the pg-primary serves as the master server and the pg-clone server serves as the slave server.

How to do it...

The following are the series of steps that are required to configure and install OmniPITR:

1. On both the master and slave machines we can install the OmniPITR as follows:

    ```
    $ git clone git://github.com/omniti-labs/omnipitr.git
    ```

2. In the next step, we run a sanity check to see if the omniPITR installation goes fine on both the machines:

    ```
    $ /opt/omnipitr/bin/sanity-check.sh
    Checking:
    - /opt/omnipitr/bin
    - /opt/omnipitr/lib
    5 programs, 9 libraries.
    All checked, and looks ok.
    ```

How it works...

In step 1 of the preceding section, we used the `git clone` command to copy an existing GIT repository on to the local machines, that is, the master and the slave server. Once that is done, in the next step we run a shell script named `sanity-check.sh`, which examines various sources and produces a report. If it is successful, the `sanity-check.sh` script gives an OK message, as seen in step 2 of the preceding section.

WAL management with OmniPITR

Transaction log files, that is WAL logs, play a significant role in different situations be it for backups, point in time recovery, replication, or even crash recovery.

Here we are going to utilize the OmniPITR tool to effectively manage WAL log files for archival and recovery purpose.

Getting ready

The prerequisites are that OmniPITR needs to be installed on all the participating servers. Here we are assuming three servers, one is the primary server, the next one is the slave server, and the other one is the backup server.

We also assume the following configuration on these servers.

On the master server, we should have or create the following directories that should be writeable by the postgres user:

- `/home/postgres/omnipitr`: Location of the data files stored by omnipitr
- `/home/postgres/omnipitr/log`: Location of the omnipitr log
- `/home/postgres/omnipitr/state`: Location of the omnipitr state files
- `/var/tmp/omnipitr`: Location of temporary files created by omniPITR

On the slave server we assume the following configuration:

- /home/postgres/wal_archive: Location where the master sends xlog segments for replication
- /home/postgres/omnipitr: Location of the data files stored by omnipitr
- /home/postgres/omnipitr/log: Location of the omnipitr log
- /home/postgres/omnipitr/state: Location of the omnipitr state files
- /var/tmp/omnipitr: Location of temporary files created by omniPITR

On the backup server we assume the following configuration:

- /var/backup/database: Directory for database backups
- /var/backup/database/hot_backup: Directory for hot backup files
- /var/backup/database/xlog: Directory for xlog segments

We are going to use direct rsync for transfers over servers for OmniPITR transfers.

We assume the following direct rsync paths:

- rsync://slave/wal_archive: This refers to /home/postgres/wal_archive on the slave server with write access to the master without a password
- rsync://backup/database: This refers to /var/backups/database on the backup server with write access to both the master and slave without a password

How to do it...

The following are the series of steps that need to be carried out on the master server for archival of xlogs from the master:

1. In the first step, we are going to configure archiving as follows by setting the following server parameter in the postgresql.conf file:

```
archive_mode = on
```

2. In the second step, we will set the archive_command parameter as follows:

```
archive_command = '/opt/omnipitr/bin/omnipitr-archive -l
 /home/postgres/omnipitr/log/omnipitr-^Y^m^d.log -s
 /home/postgres/omnipitr/state -dr
   gzip=rsync://slave/wal_archive/ -dr
 gzip=rsync://backup/database/xlog/ -db
```

```
/var/tmp/omnipitr/dstbackup -t
/var/tmp/omnipitr/ -v "%p"'
```

3. In the third step, we are going to set the `archive_timeout` parameter:

   archive_timeout = 60

4. In the final step, we are going to restart the master:

   pg_ctl -D /home/postgres/data restart

How it works...

Here we are going to discuss the steps mentioned in the preceding section:

- In step 1, we enabled WAL archiving by setting `archive_mode = on`.
- Once archiving is enabled in step 1, of the preceding section, we could then set the `archive_command` parameter, which invokes the `omnipitr-archive` command that is used to archive WAL logs and send them to the slave server from the master server. In step 3, we set the `archive_timeout` parameter to 60 seconds to force the PostgreSQL server to switch to a new WAL log after every 60 seconds. Finally, in step 4, we restarted the PostgreSQL server on the master so that the values set for the configuration parameters come into effect.

We will now discuss the options used in the `archive_command`:

- `-l /home/postgres/omnipitr/log/omnipitr-^Y^m^d.log`: This option refers to the log file path, which be rotated automatically on every date change
- `-s /home/postgres/omnipitr/state`: This option refers to the directory in which omnipitr keeps state information
- `-dr gzip=rsync://slave/wal_archive/`: This option sends the WAL segments in a compressed gzip format to the slave
- `-dr gzip=rsync://backup/database/xlog/`: This option send the compressed WAL segments to the backup server
- `-db /var/tmp/omnipitr/dstbackup`: Ideally this patch should not exist, but if it does it will be used as an additional location for the purpose of the `omnipitr-backup-master` program
- `-t /var/tmp/omnipitr/`: This option specifies where to keep large temporary files created by omniPITR

Setting up repmgr

repmgr is an open source tool developed by 2ndQuadrant for the purpose of managing replication and failover in a cluster of PostgreSQL servers. It builds on and enhances PostgreSQL server's existing capabilities to create new clones, that is, replicas, and add them to an existing cluster of PostgreSQL servers. In addition to this it is used to monitor replication setups and perform administrative tasks such as failover or manual switchover operations

In this recipe, we are going to set up the remgr tool.

How to do it...

There are two ways to install the repmgr tool:

1. Through operating system package manager tools such as `yum` or `apt-get install`.
2. Through the source installation by downloading the `tar.gz` from `https://gith ub.com/2ndQuadrant/repmgr/releases`. Or by downloading the GitHub repository via the `git clone` command from the repmgr GitHub page.

In this recipe, we will be using the standard package manager tools to install repmgr.

For this recipe we will need at least two servers. The primary PostgreSQL server will be named `pg-primary` and the replica server is named `pg-clone`. `/data` is our default data directory as defined by the `$PGDATA` environment variable:

1. On CentOS/Red Hat-based systems use the following command:

   ```
   sudo yum install repmgr
   ```

2. On Debian/Ubuntu based distributions you should use the following command:

   ```
   sudo apt-get install repmgr postgresql-9.4-repmgr
   ```

3. In the next step, we are going to copy the `repmgr` script from the `/init` directory to `/etc/init.d` on each server.

4. If the supplied init script was copied, execute these commands as a root-capable user:

```
sudo rm -f /etc/init.d/repmgrd
sudo chmod 755 /etc/init.d/repmgr
```

In the next series of steps we are going to configure the primary server.

5. Log in as the Postgres user and generate an RSA key pair and export the public key to the replica:

```
ssh-keygen -t rsa -N ' '
ssh-copy-id  postgres@pg-clone
```

6. In the next step, we need to modify `postgresql.conf` and set the following server parameters:

```
wal_level = hot_standy
archive_mode = on
archive_command = 'exit 0'
wal_keep_segments = 5000
hot_standby = on
```

7. In the next step, we will modify the `pg_hba.conf` file and add the following lines:

```
host      all            postgres    192.168.56.0/24    trust
host        replication    postgres    192.168.56.0/24    trust
```

8. In the next step, we will modify the `pg_hba.conf` file and add the following lines:

```
pg_ctl -D /data restart
```

9. Execute this command to find the binary path to PostgreSQL tools:

```
pg_config -bindir
```

10. We will now create the configuration file for repmgr, named `repmgr.conf`, with the following parameters:

```
cluster=pgnet
node=1
node_name=parent
conninfo='host=pg-primary dbname=postgres'
pg_bindir=[value from step 5]
```

11. We will now register the master node with the following command:

```
repmgr -f /etc/repmgr.conf master register
```

12. Finally, we will start the repmgr daemon:

```
sudo service repmgr start
```

How it works...

The following is a description for the preceding steps:

- In step 1 and step 2, we were installing repmgr using yum on CentOS. If you are using Ubuntu systems you may follow step 2 to install repmgr and you can skip step 1.
- In step 3 and 4 we were just daemonizing the service.
- The rest of the steps were meant only for the primary server.
- In step 5 we were setting some PostgreSQL server parameters such as `wal_level` to `hot_standby`, enabling `archive_mode` by setting it to on, and by setting `archiving_command` to exit 0 we are essentially stating that the system exits with a status of 0, which means that the system is working correctly. This will make PostgreSQL believe that the system is working correctly.
- We were also setting the value of `wal_keep_segments` to `5000`, which means that we are preserving a size of almost 80 GB of wal files on the primary server. This is essentially a requirement for repmgr because of the need to configure multiple replicas we need this much amount of WAL logs on the primary server.
- In the next step, we were setting our PostgreSQL authentication and accessing configuration file `pg_hba.conf` to allow the postgres user to connect to any database. We allow these connections to originate from anywhere within the `192.168.56.0` subnet.
- In the next step, we created a single file named `repmgr.conf` in the **/etc** directory. We named the repmgr cluster pgnet, noted that this is our first node, and named our node parent as it is easy to remember. The connection information needs to match our entry in `pg_hba.conf`; thus, we use the repmgr user that we added to the database earlier. Finally, we set `pg_bindir` so that repmgr always knows where to find certain PostgreSQL binaries. This setting is supposed to be optional, but we ran into several problems when we tried to omit this entry; just keep it for now.

- As a final step we registered the primary node and completed the installation process by creating various database objects. These steps are all performed by the repmgr command, provided we specify the configuration file with -f and use the master register parameter.

The repmgr system comes with a daemon that manages communication and controls behavior between other repmgr nodes. Whenever we start repmgr it will run in the background and await the arrival of new replicas/clones.

Using repmgr to create replica

As mentioned earlier in this chapter, repmgr is a management suite to manage replication setups and also to create replicas and add them to the existing PostgreSQL clusters. In this recipe, we are going to create a new clone of the primary server.

This recipe builds on from the previous recipe. Here we are going to create a replica of the primary server pg-primary and as we said we need two machines participating in this configuration. Our replica server will be titled pg-clone and the /data location will be our data directory.

How to do it...

All the following commands in this recipe are carried out in the replica server pg-clone. Here are the complete steps:

1. First log in as the Postgres user and generate a RSA key-pair and send the credentials to the primary server pg-primary:

```
ssh-keygen -t rsa -N ' '
ssh-copy-id postgres@pg-primary
```

2. In the next step, we are going to clone the data on the pg-primary server with the following command:

```
repmgr -D /data standby clone pg-primary
```

3. We are going to start the cloned server with the following command:

```
pg_ctl -D /data start
```

4. Execute this command to find the binary path to PostgreSQL tools:

    ```
    pg_config --bindir
    ```

5. We will now create the configuration file for repmgr named `repmgr.conf` with the following contents:

    ```
    cluster=pgnet
    node=2
    node_name=child1
    conninfo='host=pg-clone dbname=postgres'
    pg_bindir=[value from step 4]
    ```

6. In the next step, we are going to register the `pg-clone` with the primary server:

    ```
    repmgr -f /etc/repmgr.conf standby register
    ```

7. In the next step, we are going to start the `repgmr` service:

    ```
    sudo service repmgr start
    ```

8. In the final step, we connect to the Postgres database and view the standby node's replication lag with the following query:

    ```
    SELECT standby_node, standby_name, replication_lag FROM
    repmgr_pgnet.repl_status;
    ```

How it works...

Much of the preliminary work was done earlier in the previous recipe. Here in the preceding section all the steps are carried out on the replica server `pg-clone`.

In the first step, we were creating an SSH key and exporting it to the primary server.

Now that the SSH keys are established we are now cloning the primary server on the replica with the repmgr command.

Once the cloning is completed we are ready to launch the replica server. When you start the replica server it immediately connects to the primary server `pg-primary` and begins replication. It can do this because repmgr knows all of the connection information necessary to establish a streaming replication connection with pg-primary. During the cloning process, it automatically created a recovery.conf file suitable to start directly in replication mode.

In the next step, we configured repgmr to recognize the new replica. When we create /etc/repmgr.conf, we need to use the same cluster name as we used on pg-primary. We also tell repmgr that this is node 2, and it should be named child1. The conninfo value should always reflect the connection string necessary for repmgr to connect to PostgreSQL on the named node. As we did earlier, we set pg_bindir to avoid encountering possible repmgr bugs.

With the configuration file in place, we can register the new clone in a similar way to how we registered the primary. By calling the repmgr command with -f and the full path to the configuration file, there are several operations we can invoke. For now, we will settle with the standby register to tell repmgr that it should track pg-clone as a part of the pgnet cluster.

Once we start the repmgrd daemon, all nodes are aware of each other and the current status of each.

Setting up walctl

walctl is basically a WAL management system that either pushes or fetches WAL files from a remote central server. It is a substitute for archive_command or restore_command in handling WAL archival or recovery.

walctl also includes a utility to clone a primary server and create a replica.

How to do it...

For this recipe we are going to use three servers. The remote server that will handle archival is called pg-arc. The primary server will be named pg-primary and the standby server will be named pg-clone. Our assumption is that the data directory will be located at /data location and the same can be defined in the $PGDATA environment variable.

Here are the steps for this recipe:

1. On the primary server and standby run the following commands:

```
git clone https://github.com/OptionsHouse/walctl
cd walctl
sudo make install
```

2. On the archival server `pg-arc` create the wal storage directory:

```
sudo mkdir -m 0600 /db/wal_archive sudo chown postgres:postgres
/db/wal_archive
```

3. On the primary server, we are going to create an RSA key pair and export it to the archival and the standby server:

```
ssh-keygen -t rsa -N ' '
ssh-copy-id pg-arc
ssh-copy-id pg-clone
```

4. Similarly, on the standby server we are going to create an SSH key and export it to the primary and archival server:

```
ssh-keygen -t rsa -N ' ' ssh-copy-id pg-arc ssh-copy-id pg-
primary
```

5. On the primary server, we are then going to create a user for walctl usage:

```
CREATE USER walctl  WITH PASSWORD 'superb' SUPERUSER
REPLICATION;
```

6. In the next step, we are going to modify the `pg_hba.conf` file on primary to allow the connection from archival and standby servers:

```
host    replication    walctl    pg-clone      md5
host    replication    walctl     pg-arc       md5
```

7. On the `pg-clone` and `pg-primary` servers we are going to configure the password authentication file with the following entries:

```
*:*:*:walctl:superb
```

8. In this step, we are going to create the configuration file for walctl, titled `walctl.conf`, on the primary and standby server:

```
PGDATA=/data
ARC_HOST=pg-arc
ARC_PATH=/db/wal_archive
```

9. On the primary server, we need to execute the following command:

```
walctl_setup master
```

10. In the next step, we need to restart the database server on the primary server:

```
pg_ctl -D /data restart
```

How it works...

The following is the explanation of steps for the preceding section:

- In step 1, we were cloning the walctl from the GitHub repository and setting up the install process on the standby and the primary servers.
- In step 2, we were setting up the WAL storage directory that will be holding up the archived files on the archival server pg-arc.
- In step 3, we were creating the SSH keys on the primary server and exporting them to the archival and standby servers.
- Similar to step 3, we were creating the SSH keys on the standby and exporting them to the primary and archival servers.
- In step 5, we were creating a database user on the primary server by the name of walctl. The standby server will use this user to connect to the primary.
- In step 6, we modified the access regulation file pg_hba.conf on the primary to allow the standby server to connect to the primary with the help of the walctl user defined in the previous step.
- In step 7, we were creating a password file, pgpass, and storing the username and password credentials for the walctl user on both primary and standby servers.
- In step 8, we were creating the configuration file for walctl where we defined the data directory and the name of the archive host server and WAL archive path on the archive server pg-arc.
- In this step we were calling the watctl_setup command on the primary server. The purpose of this command is to prepare PostgreSQL for WAL integration. When it is called with the master parameter as we've done here, it modifies postgresql.conf so that WAL files are compatible with archival, and streaming replicas can connect. In addition, it enables archive mode and sets archive_command to invoke a walctl utility named walctl_push, which sends WAL files to the archive server.

Using walctl to create replica

In this recipe, we are going to use the `walctl_clone` utility to create a clone/replica

How to do it...

For this recipe only two servers are needed. One is the primary server and the other is the replica server. Our primary server will be named `pg-primary` and the replica will be named `pg-clone` server.

We need to execute the following command on the replica server:

```
walctl_clone pg-primary walctl
```

How it works...

`walctl_clone` has two parameters. The first parameter is supposed to be the hostname of the primary server and the second parameter should be the name of the database superuser with which we are going to create a backup.

Here are the series of actions that are performed on behalf of `walctl_clone`:

- It puts the primary server in the backup mode.
- It retrieves all files from the database. It will copy only the changed files if all the data files are residing in the data directory.
- Once it has copied the respective files it will end the backup mode on the primary server.
- It will automatically create a `recovery.conf` file that will retrieve files from the archive server `pg-arc` and connect as a streaming standby to the primary server `pg-primary`.
- Finally, it starts the PostgreSQL server on the replica.

8
Database Monitoring and Performance

In this chapter, we will cover the following recipes:

- Checking active sessions
- Finding out what the users are currently running
- Finding blocked sessions
- Dealing with deadlocks
- Studying table access statistics
- Routine reindexing
- Logging slow statements
- Determining disk usage
- Preventing page corruption
- Generating planner statistics
- Tuning with background writer statistics

Introduction

Monitoring plays a crucial role in defining the server capacity or defining the health of a database server. Monitoring a database server with a certain interval will give us some useful trend information about the server functionality as per the running business. As business grow continuously, the collected trend information will define the future database server capacity.

Server capacity may not be directly proportional to database performance. Since even if we have enough resources, a bug in a database engine's optimizer may drain out all the resources. Also, database performance may not be directly proportional to server capacity, since a kernel bug might cause all the resources to drain out in no time. To identify the underlying problems, monitoring trends information will be more useful. However, in this chapter, we are only covering what to monitor in PostgreSQL to check its behavior in a database server.

PostgreSQL provides a good number of catalog tables, views, and extensions to monitor the instance accurately. We are going to use these catalog views to monitor the server's live metrics.

Checking active sessions

Using this recipe, we will get all the active sessions from a PostgreSQL instance, which are utilizing the server resources.

Getting ready

Like other database management systems, PostgreSQL is also providing a set of catalog tables and views, which will help us to retrieve the current instance status. In this recipe, we will be discussing a catalog view, which every DBA/developer queries very frequently.

How to do it...

1. Connect to your database using the psql client as a superuser and check the track_activities parameter status:

   ```
   postgres=# SHOW track_activities;
   track_activities
   -------------------
   on
   (1 row)
   ```

2. Initiate the pgbench test as follows:

   ```
   $ pgbench -i; pgbench -c 4 -T 100
   creating tables...
   100000 of 100000 tuples (100%) done (elapsed 0.17
   ```

```
  s, remaining
  0.00 s)
vacuum...
set primary keys...
done.
starting vacuum...end.
```

3. Execute the following SQL query to get the list of active sessions along with the session's attributes using the psql connection:

```
postgres=# SELECT
   datname,
   usename,
   application_name,
   now()-backend_start AS "Session duration",
   pid
FROM
   pg_stat_activity
WHERE
   state='active';
 datname   |  usename  | application_name | Session duration | pid
-----------+-----------+------------------+------------------+----
 postgres  | postgres  | psql.bin         |  00:06:41.74497  |2751
 postgres  | postgres  | pgbench          |  00:00:46.884915 |2796
 postgres  | postgres  | pgbench          |  00:00:46.883277 |2797
 postgres  | postgres  | pgbench          |  00:00:46.881618 |2798
 (4 rows)
```

How it works...

In PostgreSQL, we have an independent statistics collection process called **statistics collector**, which will populate the dynamic information about the sessions. This process behavior is dependent on a set of track parameters, which guides the stats collector about which metrics it needs to collect from the running instance. By enabling the required tracking at instance level, it will reduce the overhead on query execution. To collect the preceding metrics from the processes, we need to enable a parameter called track_activities, which is on by default. If we turn off this parameter, the statistics collection process will not give us all the useful information such as session status, command and query duration, and so on.

It is not recommended to turn this parameter off, as it gives more useful monitoring information to the end users. In case you want to not allow any users to observe what queries are running on a database, then we have to use the following SQL statement to disable them:

```
ALTER DATABASE <database name> SET track_activities TO
false;
```

Once we have disabled this parameter, we need to depend on PostgreSQL log messages to track useful information about query duration. Besides, it will reduce the query execution overhead.

When an application makes a connection to PostgreSQL, the postmaster process will fork a new process for that connection, and keeps its properties information in memory. Using a dynamic view called `pg_stat_activity`, we can read the connection properties information directly from memory.

The `pg_stat_activity` is a dynamic statistics view, which was built based on a PostgreSQL internal function, `pg_stat_get_activity()`, which collects the information from memory.

Whenever we execute the preceding SQL query:

- It will execute the underlying `pg_stat_get_activity(NULL)` function, which will get all the sessions information
- On the result, the actual query filters the data based on the predicate in the `WHERE` clause, which will only give us the active sessions information

There's more...

The `pg_stat_activity` is a dynamic statistics view, which will show all kinds of session information such as active, idle, idle in transaction, and so on. Besides, it will also give all connection properties such as client IP address, the application name that is being occupied, the database connections, and so on.

PostgreSQL also provides a set of per backend connection statistics, which will also produce the similar information like `pg_stat_activity`.

You can find more information about this view at this URL, `https://www.postgresql.org/docs/9.6/static/monitoring-stats.html#PG-STAT-ACTIVITY-VIEW`.

Finding out what the users are currently running

Using this recipe, we will get all the current running SQL commands from the PostgreSQL instance.

Getting ready

In the previous recipe, we discussed how to get all the active sessions information, and now we are going to get all the SQL statements that the active sessions are executing.

How to do it...

1. Initiate `pgbench` as aforementioned.
2. Connect to the PostgreSQL database as either a superuser or database owner and execute the following SQL statement:

```
$ psql -h localhost -U postgres
postgres=# SELECT
  datname,
  usename,
  application_name,
  now()-backend_start AS "Session duration",
  pid,
  query
FROM
  pg_stat_activity
WHERE
  state='active';
-[ RECORD 1 ]----+--------------------------------
datname          | postgres
usename          | postgres
application_name | pgbench
Session duration | 00:00:08.470704
pid              | 29323
query            | UPDATE pgbench_tellers SET
  tbalance = tbalance + 2331 WHERE tid = 9;
-[ RECORD 2 ]----+--------------------------------
datname          | postgres
usename          | postgres
application_name | pgbench
```

```
Session duration | 00:00:08.466858
pid              | 29324
query            | UPDATE pgbench_tellers SET
   tbalance = tbalance + -1438 WHERE tid = 7;
-[ RECORD 3 ]----+-------------------------------
datname          | postgres
usename          | postgres
application_name | psql
Session duration | 00:00:05.234634
pid              | 29580
query            | SELECT
                 |    datname,
                 |    usename,
                 |    application_name,
                 |    now()-backend_start AS
                 |       "Session duration",
                 |  pid,
                 |  query
                 |  FROM
                 |  pg_stat_activity
                 |  WHERE
                 |  state='active';
```

How it works...

The aforementioned SQL command is similar to the SQL, which collects the `active` session information, except a new field called `query` from the `pg_stat_activity` dynamic view.

As the database postgres has the `track_activities` parameter enabled, the statistics collector also tracks the present running SQL commands.

> From the preceding results, we also got the executed SQL statement in the result, as it is running at that moment. If you want to exclude that SQL query, which is running to get all the current sessions information, then we have to add another predicate in the WHERE clause as AND `pid != pg_backend_pid()`.

Finding blocked sessions

In this recipe, we will be discussing how to verify the queries that are currently blocking the SQL queries.

Getting ready

In any database, sessions will be blocked due to multiple technical reasons, to avoid concurrent access on the same resource. In PostgreSQL, a session can be blocked due to an idle in transaction or due to concurrent access on the same resource or due to some prepared transactions. In this recipe, we will be discussing how to get all the blocked/waiting sessions from the currently running instance.

How to do it...

1. Initiate pgbench as follows:

```
$ pgbench -i; pgbench -c 4 -T 100
```

2. Connect to your database using the psql client as a superuser and execute the following SQL command:

```
$ psql -h localhost -U postgres
postgres=#
SELECT
  datname,
  usename,
  application_name,
  now()-backend_start AS "Session duration",
  pid,
  query
FROM
  pg_stat_activity
WHERE
  state='active'
AND wait_event IS NOT NULL;
-[ RECORD 1 ]----+--------------------------------
datname          | postgres
usename          | postgres
application_name | pgbench
Session duration | 00:01:37.019791
pid              | 17853
query            | UPDATE pgbench_tellers SET
  tbalance = tbalance + 3297 WHERE tid = 5;
-[ RECORD 2 ]----+--------------------------------
datname          | postgres
usename          | postgres
application_name | pgbench
Session duration | 00:01:37.016008
```

```
pid              | 17854
query            | UPDATE pgbench_branches SET
bbalance = bbalance + 2742 WHERE bid = 1;
```

How it works...

The previously mentioned SQL command is similar to the aforementioned SQL queries, except for an additional predicate in the WHERE clause as wait_event IS NOT NULL. The pg_stat_activity view has the wait_event column, which will differentiate the waiting and non-waiting sessions. If the wait_event field is set to NOT NULL, then that particular session is blocked due to some concurrent resource waiting. We can also get the lock type it held on a resource using the wait_event_type column from the pg_stat_activity view.

There's more...

Once we find that a session is blocked, then we need to identify why the session got blocked and on what resources it's been waiting for. Once we identify the underlying session or transaction that is blocking the particular session, then we can take further actions such as kill the blocking session, cancel the blocking transaction, or wait until the blocking session is complete.

Transactional locks

Transactional locks are the implicit locks that get acquired when any DML statement gets executed. To identify the blocking session information that holds the transactional locks, we have to use the following query:

```
postgres=#
 SELECT bl.pid              AS blocked_pid,
   a.usename              AS blocked_user,
   ka.query               AS
 current_or_recent_statement_in_blocking_process,
   ka.state               AS
     state_of_blocking_process,
   now() - ka.query_start AS blocking_duration,
   kl.pid                 AS blocking_pid,
   ka.usename             AS blocking_user,
   a.query                AS blocked_statement,
   now() - a.query_start  AS blocked_duration
 FROM  pg_catalog.pg_locks       bl
```

```
JOIN pg_catalog.pg_stat_activity a   ON a.pid =
  bl.pid
JOIN pg_catalog.pg_locks          kl ON
  kl.transactionid = bl.transactionid AND kl.pid
    != bl.pid
JOIN pg_catalog.pg_stat_activity ka ON ka.pid =
  kl.pid
WHERE NOT bl.GRANTED;
-[ RECORD 1 ]---------------------------+--------
blocked_pid                             | 8724
blocked_user                            |postgres
current_or_recent_statement_in_blocking_process
                                        |UPDATE
  pgbench_branches SET bbalance = bbalance +
    -1632 WHERE bid = 1;
state_of_blocking_process               | idle in
  transaction
blocking_duration                       |
  00:00:00.003981
blocking_pid                            | 8726
blocking_user                           |postgres
blocked_statement                       | UPDATE
  pgbench_tellers SET tbalance = tbalance + 4600
    WHERE tid = 3;
blocked_duration                        |
  00:00:00.00222
```

From the preceding query results, we can confirm that the session (`pid 8726`) is blocking the session (`pid 8724`) due to an idle in transaction. And the recent query that got executed in session `8726` was `UPDATE pgbench_branches SET bbalance = bbalance + -1632 WHERE bid = 1`.

> The previously mentioned SQL query is compatible with PostgreSQL version greater than 9.1. Refer to the following link if you need an SQL that is compatible with versions less than 9.2: `https://wiki.postgresql.org/wiki/Lock_Monitoring`.

Whenever we find the preceding kind of idle in transactions that are blocking the other transactions, then check the blocking duration of that statement using the preceding SQL statement. If you observe that the blocking duration is much higher, then it's recommended you kill that process using the `pg_terminate_backend()` function. However, it's expected to get these kinds of locks in databases with minimal `blocking_duration` time.

Table level locks

In other cases, a session can also be blocked due to table level locks, which are granted exclusively using the LOCK statement. To find this table level exclusive locks information, we have to use the following SQL query.

For example,

In session 1:

```
postgres=# BEGIN;
BEGIN
postgres=# LOCK TABLE test IN EXCLUSIVE MODE;
LOCK TABLE
```

In session 2:

```
postgres=# INSERT INTO test VALUES (10);
```

Session 2 will be in a waiting state until we close the transaction that we opened in session 1. In Session 3 execute the following SQL to identify which session is blocked and which one is blocking:

```
postgres=#
SELECT
  act1.query as blocking_query,
  act2.query as blocked_query,
  l1.pid AS blocked_pid,
  l2.pid AS blocking_pid,
  l1.relation::regclass
FROM
  pg_locks l1,
  pg_locks l2,
  pg_stat_activity act1,
  pg_stat_activity act2
WHERE
  l1.granted=true AND
  l2.granted=false AND
  l1.pid=act1.pid AND
  l2.pid=act2.pid AND
  l1.relation=l2.relation;

-[ RECORD 1 ]--+---------------------------------
blocking_query | LOCK TABLE test IN EXCLUSIVE
   MODE;
blocked_query  | INSERT INTO test VALUES(10);
blocked_pid    | 10417
blocking_pid   | 8913
```

```
relation        | test
```

In general, developers will not be using the preceding LOCK statements explicitly in their application code, until there is a specific requirement. Whenever you observe the preceding kinds of locks on a database, it would be good to consult the DBA before terminating the session. Since there might be chances that DBA is doing some kind of maintenance on the table, by holding an exclusive lock.

Prepared transaction locks

In some other cases, a session can also be blocked due to **2 PC's** (**two phase commit**) prepared transactions.

For example, let's create a prepared transaction on a table as follows.

In session 1:

```
postgres=# BEGIN;
BEGIN
postgres=# INSERT INTO test VALUES (10);
INSERT 0 1
postgres=# PREPARE TRANSACTION 'testing';
PREPARE TRANSACTION
postgres=# END;
WARNING:  there is no transaction in progress
COMMIT
postgres=# SELECT * FROM test;
t
---
(0 rows)
```

In session 2:

```
postgres=# ALTER TABLE test ADD col2 INT;
```

The preceding DDL operation in session 2 will be in waiting state, until we either commit or rollback the previous prepared transaction. If we run the previous SQL query, which shows the waiting sessions information, then the ALTER statement will be in waiting state, as shown here:

```
-[ RECORD 1 ]----+--------------------------------
datname          | postgres
usename          | postgres
application_name | psql
Session duration | 00:02:01.030429
pid              | 23223
```

```
query            | ALTER TABLE test ADD col2 INT;
wait_event       | relation
```

If we run the preceding SQL, which finds the blocking queries, we will get zero rows. This is because 2 PC won't store the process ID of a session that initiates the prepared transaction. To identify these blocking prepared transactions, we have to use a separate SQL query as follows:

```
postgres=# SELECT locktype, relation::regclass, virtualtransaction FROM
pg_locks WHERE locktype ='relation';
 locktype | relation | virtualtransaction
----------+----------+--------------------
 relation | pg_locks | 4/34
 relation | test     | -1/452455
(2 rows)
```

A prepared transaction holds a `relation` lock on all the tables, which we used in that particular prepared transaction. To identify the tables information, we have to query the `pg_locks`, as shown previously.

From the preceding results, we see that the table `test` has a `relation` lock, which associates to the transaction ID, `452455`. Now, let's query the `pg_prepared_xacts` view using the preceding transaction ID:

```
postgres=# SELECT * FROM pg_prepared_xacts WHERE
   transaction = '452455';
transaction |   gid   |       prepared          |  owner  |
database
------------+---------+-------------------------   +---------+---------
 -
452455      | testing | 2016-08-20 19:06:28.534232+05:30| postgres|
postgres
(1 row)
```

From the preceding results, we can confirm that the transaction `452455` is a prepared transaction, and its `gid` is `testing`. Once we find that the transaction is a prepared transaction, then we have to either commit or rollback the transaction, which unlocks the blocked sessions. To commit/rollback the previous prepared transaction we have to execute the `[COMMIT|ROLLBACK]PREPARED'testing'` statement.

Usage of SKIP LOCKED

As of now, we have been trying to collect all the blocked and blocking queries information, which will be useful to troubleshoot the database performance issues. Now, let's consider a real use case such as parallel workers could process a single dataset. In this situation, all the parallel workers should be smart enough to skip the data set that is already processing by the other worker process. To achieve this kind of requirement, PostgreSQL has a new feature called SKIP LOCKED, which skips the rows that are already locked by the other processes. That is, if we run a query such as SELECT jobid FROM dataset FOR UPDATE SKIP LOCKED LIMIT 1 in parallel from multiple workers, then each worker process gets a distinct jobid to process. Here SKIP LOCKED will skip the rows that have been locked by other sessions and will return the rows that are not locked. Let's see the demonstration of this feature, as shown here:

In session 1:

```
postgres=# BEGIN;
BEGIN
postgres=# SELECT jobid FROM dataset FOR UPDATE SKIP LOCKED LIMIT 1;
 jobid
-------
     1
(1 row)
```

In session 2:

```
postgres=# BEGIN;
BEGIN
postgres=# SELECT jobid FROM dataset FOR UPDATE SKIP LOCKED LIMIT 1;
 jobid
-------
     2
(1 row)
```

From the preceding examples, each session got a unique jobid without any waiting at session 2, by skipping the locked tuple jobid 1 in session 1.

> Read more information about this feature at this URL, http://blog.2ndqu adrant.com/what-is-select-skip-locked-for-in-postgresql-9-5.

Dealing with deadlocks

Using this recipe, we will be troubleshooting the deadlocks in PostgreSQL.

Getting ready

In any database management systems, deadlocks can occur due to concurrent resource locking. It is the database engines responsibility to detect the deadlocks, and its applications responsibility to prevent the deadlocks. The PostgreSQL engine has the ability to detect the deadlocks; it also provides a few features to the developers to prevent the deadlocks in their application code.

How to do it...

Let's produce a simple deadlock situation and we will see all the options that PostgreSQL provides to troubleshoot them:

Have two different database sessions and execute the SQL statements as follows:

Session 1	Session 2
`BEGIN;`	`BEGIN;`
`UPDATE test SET t=1 WHERE` `  t=1;`	`UPDATE test SET t=2 WHERE` `  t=2;`

`UPDATE test SET t=2 WHERE t=2; --Waiting`
`for the record 2 which is locked in`
`session 2`
	`UPDATE test SET t=1 WHERE t=1; --`
	`Waiting for the record 1   which is`
	`locked in session 1`

`ERROR:  deadlock detected`
`DETAIL:  Process 10417 waits for`
`ShareLock on transaction   452459;`
`blocked by process 8913.`
`Process 8913 waits for ShareLock on`
`transaction 452458;   blocked by process`
`10417.`
	`END;`

`ROLLBACK;`	

From the preceding example, in session 1 we got the deadlock error due to mutual locking between session 1 and 2. From the preceding DETAIL message, it clearly says that the process 8913 waits for the transaction that holds by the 10417 process, and the 10417 process is waiting for the transaction that holds by the 8913 process.

As you see from the preceding example, deadlocks will not cause any data loss and it will only cause a transaction failure. To avoid these deadlock situations, we have to use the pre-locking techniques, as mentioned in the following section.

Using FOR UPDATE

This is an approach that tries to avoid the deadlock issues, by pre-locking all the required records that it is going to update in that session. To pre-lock all the required tuples, we have to use the FOR UPDATE clause in the SELECT statement. Let's see how we are going to fix the preceding problem using this approach:

Session 1	Session 2

BEGIN;
 	
SELECT * FROM test WHERE t IN(1, 2) FOR UPDATE;
 	
UPDATE test SET t=1 WHERE t=1;
UPDATE test SET t=2 WHERE t=2;
END;
	BEGIN;
	
	SELECT * FROM test WHERE t IN(1, 2) FOR UPDATE; --Waiting for the session to release the lock on records 1, 2
	
	UPDATE test SET t=2 WHERE t=2; UPDATE test SET t=1 WHERE t=1;
	END;

From the preceding example, session 2 transaction will be in waiting until session 1 transaction is complete. Here, we just made the two transactions to run in serializable fashion. That means that the transactions will not conflict with each other. This approach cannot be implemented for the SQL queries, which deal with SET operations. That is, usage of FOR UPDATE is restricted in SQL queries that do UNION/INTERSECT/EXCEPT operations.

Advisory locks

PostgreSQL provides advisory locks, which is an external locking mechanism that we can enforce from the application level, to achieve the concurrent data access. Let's see how we will be avoiding deadlocks using advisory locks:

Session 1	Session 2

BEGIN
SELECT pg_advisory_lock(t) FROM test WHERE t IN (1,2);
 	
UPDATE test SET t=1 WHERE t=1;
UPDATE test SET t=2 WHERE t=2;
SELECT pg_advisory_unlock(t) FROM test WHERE t IN(1,2);
END;
	BEGIN
	SELECT pg_advisory_lock(t) FROM test WHERE t IN (1,2); --Waiting for the session1 to release lock
	
	UPDATE test SET t=2 WHERE t=2; UPDATE test SET t=1 WHERE t=1;
	SELECT pg_advisory_unlock(t) FROM test WHERE t IN(1,2);
	END;

In the preceding example, we are making the transactions as serialize, by using the advisory locks. The only disadvantage of using advisory locks is, we need an application to enforce the lock and unlock behavior. Also, the session level advisory locks will not release the lock, even if the transaction failed or rollbacked. However, when a session is closed, then all the associated advisory locks within that session will be released automatically.

> Refer to the following URL for more information about advisory locks: htt ps://www.postgresql.org/docs/9.6/static/explicit-locking.html.

Table access statistics

In this recipe, we will be discussing how to study the table access statistics by using PostgreSQL catalog views.

Getting ready

PostgreSQL's statistics collector process keeps track of all kinds of operations that are performing on any table or an index. These statistics will be helpful in determining the importance of an object in the business, and also defines whether the required maintenance operations are running on it when it is required.

How to do it...

Let's create a test table, which we will perform a few operations on:

```
postgres=# CREATE TABLE test (t INT);
CREATE TABLE
```

PostgreSQL provides a few catalog views, which we are going to query to analyze the statistics, which statistics collector process is collected in the background.

pg_stat_user_tables

This catalog view provides most of the transactional metrics as well as maintenance operations metrics. Now, let's go and perform a few transactions and see how they reflect in this view:

```
postgres=# INSERT INTO test VALUES(1);
INSERT 0 1
postgres=# UPDATE test SET t=10;
UPDATE 1
postgres=# DELETE FROM test;
DELETE 1
 postgres=#SELECT relname, n_tup_ins "Total Inserts", n_tup_upd "Total
Updates", n_tup_del "Total deletes" FROM pg_stat_user_tables WHERE
relname='test';
-[ RECORD 1 ]-+-----
relname       | test
Total Inserts | 1
Total Updates | 1
Total deletes | 1
```

From the preceding results, it seems like our sample transactions are reflected properly in `pg_stat_user_tables`. Now, let's query on this table and see the relation between `seq_scan` and `idx_scan`:

```
postgres=# SELECT relname, seq_scan, seq_tup_read, idx_scan, idx_tup_fetch
FROM pg_stat_user_tables WHERE relname='test';
-[ RECORD 1 ]-+--------
relname       | test
seq_scan      | 12
seq_tup_read  | 100004
idx_scan      | 4
idx_tup_fetch | 50003
```

From the preceding results, the table has gone through more sequential scans rather than index scans. Also, the sequential scans read more tuples from the disk rather than index scans. Now, let's perform a few updates on the test table and see the maintenance operation metrics:

```
postgres=# SELECT relname, last_autovacuum, last_autoanalyze,
autovacuum_count, autoanalyze_count FROM pg_stat_user_tables WHERE
relname='test';
-[ RECORD 1 ]-----+-----------------------------------
relname           | test
last_autovacuum   | 2016-09-08 13:31:45.313314+05:30
last_autoanalyze  | 2016-09-08 13:31:45.451255+05:30
autovacuum_count  | 2
autoanalyze_count | 2
```

From the preceding results, it seems that the autovacuum process is invoked two times after we perform few update operations on it. In PostgreSQL 9.4, we have a new monitoring metric called `n_mod_since_analyze`, which shows the number of modifications that happened from the last analyze operation on a table. Now, let's go and update the whole table, and see how many tuples were changed after the recent table analyze operation:

```
postgres=# UPDATE test SET t=1000;
UPDATE 100000
postgres=# SELECT relname, n_mod_since_analyze FROM pg_stat_user_tables
WHERE relname='test';
-[ RECORD 1 ]-------+-----------------------------------
relname             | test
n_mod_since_analyze | 100000
```

From the preceding results, the table had `100000` tuple modifications, which are not analyzed by either manual analyze or the auto vacuum process. This `n_mod_since_analyze` metric value also gives an idea about whether the table has healthy statistics for the optimizer or not. Once an autovacuum or a manualanalyze is complete on this table, the `n_mod_since_analyze` will be reset to 0. This view also provides manual vacuum/analyze metrics such as `last_vacuum`, `last_analyze`, and `vacuum_cost`, which are similar to autovacuum metrics. Using this view, we can also get the metrics of live tuples and dead tuples or unused storage, by using `n_live_tup` and `n_dead_tup fields`.

pg_statio_user_tables

This catalog view stores all the I/O related metrics, which were performed while scanning or updating the tables. That is, how many blocks a session read from the PostgreSQL's cache and how many blocks it read from the disk:

```
postgres=# SELECT relname, heap_blks_read "Disk blks", heap_blks_hit "Cache
blks" FROM pg_statio_user_tables WHERE relname = 'test';
-[ RECORD 1 ]--------
relname    | test
Disk blks  | 890
Cache blks | 1130524
```

From the preceding results, for all the queries that are executed on the table `test` took, `890` disk reads, and `1130524` cache block hits. These metrics will be helpful in defining the cache hit and miss ratios of any specific table. This view also provides the cache hit ratio of table's indexes and its toast tables too.

How it works...

By default, the PostgreSQL instance enables the `track_counts` setting, which is a hint to the statistics collector process. When this parameter is enabled, all the table and index access related statistics will be collected and will store into the `pg_stat_tmp` location in the form of `db_oid.stat` or `globals.stat`. Whenever we query the catalog views, it will fetch the information from these statistics files, which are frequently updated by the statistics collector process, with the latest statistical information. This statistics collector process also depends on a few other parameters such as `track_functions` (which collects the metrics about the function calls) and `track_io_timing` (which collects the information about I/O operations).

> Please refer to the following PostgreSQL official documentation URL, which gives much more information about the statistics collector process: `https://www.postgresql.org/docs/9.6/static/monitoring-stats.html`.

Logging slow statements

In this recipe, we will be discussing how to track the slow running SQL statements.

Getting ready

In any database management system, checking the database logs is a regular action by the developers/DBA to find the root cause, for any database related issues. PostgreSQL provides various log settings, which controls its logger process. By using proper logging settings, we can control the amount of log messages, and the format of the log content. In some cases, having proper logging settings will help in debugging the situations as mentioned here.

Sometimes, it is not an easy job to figure out why a query is running very slowly, as there could be many reasons behind the slowness of the execution. The reasons could be:

- Concurrent locks on the same table
- Volume of the data
- Bad execution plan for the query and so on

As we discussed previously, if you have proper logging settings, PostgreSQL will log some useful information such as query duration, process ID, client host details, number of temp files it generated, and so on, which will help us in debugging the preceding scenarios.

How to do it...

Login to the database as a superuser and then execute the following SQL statement:

```
postgres=# ALTER SYSTEM SET log_min_duration_statement to '5s';
ALTER SYSTEM
postgres=# SELECT pg_reload_conf();
 pg_reload_conf
----------------
 t
(1 row)
```

The preceding ALTER command changes the instance configuration to log all the SQL queries where the execution duration was greater than or equal to 5 seconds.

> It is always recommended to enable the following settings at instance level, which logs additional query behavior such as query waiting duration, and the amount of temporary files it generated during the query execution:
> `ALTER SYSTEM SET log_lock_waits to 'on'; ALTER SYSTEM SET log_temp_files to '0;.`

We can also track the slow running queries from the `pg_stat_activity` dynamic view by querying it as follows. This view will only give us the live information:

```
postgres=# SELECT now()-query_start Duration, query, pid FROM
pg_stat_activity WHERE pid!=pg_backend_pid();
     duration     |           query          | pid
------------------+--------------------------+------
 00:00:25.19148   | SELECT pg_sleep(1000);   | 2187
(1 row)
```

How it works...

As we discussed previously, `logger process` is an independent PostgreSQL child process, and its job is to receive the log content from each PostgreSQL backend and flush them into the log destinations such as `stderr`, `syslog`, `csvlog`, and `eventlog`.

When we execute the preceding ALTER statements, PostgreSQL writes all these settings into a new file called `postgresql.auto.conf`. When we do the instance reload or when we perform the instance restart, these parameters will override the `postgresql.conf` parameters. To remove the entries from `postgresql.auto.conf`, we have to specify RESET ALL in the ALTER SYSTEM command.

> Refer to the following URL for more information about various logging parameters: `https://www.postgresql.org/docs/9.6/static/runtime-config-logging.html`.

Determining disk usage

In this recipe, we will be discussing the PostgreSQL functionality that measures object size.

Getting ready

PostgreSQL follows a specific file storage layout, which stores data into multiple folders. The common directories that we see in the PostgreSQL data directory are:

- `base`: This folder contains the database subfolders and the subfolder will contain actual relational files
- `global`: This folder contains all the cluster level catalog information
- `pg_clog`: This folder contains the committed transactions information, which will be helpful during crash recovery
- `pg_xlog`: This folder contains the ongoing transactions information, which will be helpful during crash recovery
- `pg_tblsp`: This folder contains the symbolic link to tablespaces
- `pg_log`: This folder contains the database log files

PostgreSQL also has a few more additional directories, which also keep additional information about the running instance.

> Refer to this URL for more information about additional directories: `https://www.postgresql.org/docs/9.6/static/storage-file-layout.html`.

To determine the whole PostgreSQL cluster size, including all the directories and subdirectories, we have to use the native OS commands, such as `du` in Linux. And to determine any specific object size, we have to use PostgreSQL's predefined SQL functions, as mentioned in the following section.

How to do it...

Column size

PostgreSQL provides a utility function called `pg_column_size()`, which determines the compressed disk usage of a single column value. The usage of this function is demonstrated as follows:

```
postgres=# CREATE TABLE bigtable(c char(10240000));
CREATE TABLE
postgres=# INSERT INTO bigtable VALUES('a');
INSERT 0 1
```

```
postgres=# SELECT pg_column_size(c) FROM bigtable;
 pg_column_size
----------------
         117225
(1 row)
```

From the preceding result, the value a has acquired `117225` bytes to store its value.

Relation size

PostgreSQL provides a utility function called `pg_total_relation_size()`, which calculates the whole table size including its indexes, toast, and also along with its free space map files:

```
postgres=# SELECT pg_size_pretty(pg_total_relation_size('test'));
 pg_size_pretty
----------------
 15 MB
(1 row)
```

In the preceding query, we used the `pg_size_pretty()` function, which converts the number of bytes into a human readable format. PostgreSQL also provides another utility function called `pg_relation_size()`, which gives more flexibility in measuring the relation size. This function takes table/index/material view names as the first argument, and its fork attribute as another argument. The following are the relation fork files in PostgreSQL:

- `main`: It determines the size of actual table data
- `fsm`: It determines the size of free space map file of a relation
- `vm`: It determines the size of visibility map file of a relation
- `init`: It determines the size of the initialization file of an unlogged relation

If you are using the psql client to connect to PostgreSQL, then we can also determine the size of an object using the following meta commands:

- `\dt+ <Table name>`
- `\di+ <Index name>`
- `\dms+ <Materialized view name>`

Database size

To determine the size of a database, we have to use the catalog function
`pg_database_size()` as a superuser or as a database owner as follows:

```
postgres=# SELECT pg_size_pretty(pg_database_size('postgres'));
 pg_size_pretty
----------------
 2860 MB
(1 row)
```

The psql client provides a meta command `\l+ <Database name>`, which also determines
the database size.

Tablespace size

To determine the size of a tablespace, we have to use the catalog function
`pg_tablespace_size()` as a superuser as follows:

```
postgres=# SELECT pg_size_pretty(pg_tablespace_size('test'));
 pg_size_pretty
----------------
 3568 kB
(1 row)
```

The psql client provides a meta command `\db+ <Tablespace size>`, which also
determines the tablespace size.

How it works...

If we execute the preceding function, it reaches to the underlying disk and calculates the
disk usage of each object. For example, let's consider `pg_database_size('postgres')`,
which returns the disk size as 2860 MB. Let's calculate the same database disk usage using
native commands:

```
postgres=# SELECT oid FROM pg_database WHERE datname = 'postgres';
  oid
-------
 12641
(1 row)

$ cd ${PGDATA DIRECTORY}/base/12641/
$ du -h .
2.8G
```

From the preceding output, we got the same disk usage from the native and SQL commands.

Preventing page corruption

Database corruption is a major concern, since in a worst case scenario we may lose valuable customer related data. It is also a painful job, to recover the corrupted disk or restore the data from previous backups. Database corruption can happen due to the following reasons:

- Bad hardware
- Bug in database software
- Bug in a kernel
- Bad database configuration

As like other database management systems, PostgreSQL also provides few configuration settings, which will try to avoid the page corruption. If page corruption happens at disk level, then PostgreSQL has the ability to bypass the corrupted data, and return the uncorrupted data.

Getting ready

In this recipe, we will be discussing how to enable the checksums for each data block, and how to retain the uncorrupted data when any corruption happens.

To enable the checksums for each data block, we have to initialize the PostgreSQL cluster with the `--data-checksums` option using the `initdb` command. Adding this checksum option will take a few computational resources, while doing any operations on data blocks. Once we enable or disable (by default) the checksums options, then it is not possible to change it later on. So, we have to choose wisely about this feature by doing the proper benchmarking with and without enabling the checksum option. However, we always recommend enabling this checksum, which will identify the serious data corruption in the early stages.

How to do it...

To enable the checksums, we have to use the following syntax while initializing the cluster:

```
$ initdb -D pgdata --data-checksums
The files belonging to this database system will be owned by user
"postgres".
This user must also own the server process.
The database cluster will be initialized with locale "C".
The default database encoding has accordingly been set to "SQL_ASCII".
The default text search configuration will be set to "english".
    Data page checksums are enabled.
creating directory pgdata ... ok
creating subdirectories ... ok
...
...
```

From the preceding `initdb` command output, it is showing that checksums are enabled at cluster level. We can also get this confirmation from `pg_controldata`, from an existing cluster as follows:

```
$ pg_controldata pgdata|grep checksum
Data page checksum version:            1
```

From the preceding output, the checksum version is 1, which defines whether the cluster's checksum is enabled. If the value is 0, then the cluster was not initialized with the checksum option.

Now let's see how to handle the corrupted blocks. Once any table block is corrupted, then by default PostgreSQL will not allow us to query on the table by throwing the following error message:

```
postgres=# SELECT * FROM test;
ERROR:  invalid page in block 0 of relation base/215681/429942
```

The preceding error message is saying that the block 0 has an invalid page and that is the reason why the query has stopped to proceed with scanning the remaining blocks. PostgreSQL has a session level setting called `zero_damaged_pages`, which gives a hint to query process as, to continue its scanning operation on all uncorrupted blocks by skipping all corrupted blocks. For example, let's consider the following case:

```
postgres=# SET client_min_messages TO WARNING;
SET
postgres=# SET zero_damaged_pages to on;
SET
postgres=# SELECT COUNT(*) FROM test;
```

```
WARNING:   invalid page in block 0 of relation base/215681/429942; zeroing
out page
 count
--------
    776
(1 row)
```

From the preceding example, we configured `client_min_messages` as to receive warning messages from the database server. Also, we enabled the `zero_damaged_pages` setting, which skips all the damaged pages and will return the undamaged pages. A data block can also be corrupted, even checksums at cluster level enabled. Checksums will not prevent the corruption, and it will only prompt about the corruption during its first phase. Let's see how the checksums react when any corruption occurs:

```
postgres=# SELECT COUNT(*) FROM test;
WARNING:   page verification failed, calculated checksum 47298 but expected
18241
ERROR:   invalid page in block 0 of relation base/12411/16384
```

From the preceding warning message, it is saying that the checksum has failed because it expected the checksum value to be `18241` and got the bad checksum as `47298`. To ignore these checksum messages, we have to enable the `ignore_checksum_failure` parameter, as shown here at session level:

```
postgres=# SET ignore_checksum_failure TO true;
SET
postgres=# SET zero_damaged_pages TO on;
SET
postgres=# SELECT COUNT(*) FROM test;
WARNING:   page verification failed, calculated checksum 47298 but expected
18241
WARNING:   invalid page in block 24 of relation base/12411/16384; zeroing
out page
WARNING:   page verification failed, calculated checksum 44553 but expected
56495
WARNING:   page verification failed, calculated checksum 30647 but expected
42827
WARNING:   invalid page in block 24 of relation base/12411/16384; zeroing
out page
 count
--------
   9481
(1 row)
```

Once we initialize the instance with checksums, then the checksums will be calculated for the table's indexes and PostgreSQL catalog tables.

How it works...

Once we initialize the cluster with the checksums option, then PostgreSQL writes the checksum value in the page header, after calculating its page checksum value. As we discussed in the beginning, on each operation a page takes the checksum validation, and it returns the page if and only if the validation is successful. Now, let's evaluate the checksum value of a page using the pageinspect extension as follows:

```
postgres=# CREATE EXTENSION pageinspect;
CREATE EXTENSION
postgres=# SELECT * FROM page_header(get_raw_page('test', 0));
    lsn     | checksum | flags | lower | upper | special | pagesize |
version | prune_xid
------------+----------+-------+-------+-------+---------+----------+-------
--+-----------
 0/1ACE940 |    -9900 |     0 |    28 |  8160 |    8192 |     8192 |
4 |          0
(1 row)
```

From the preceding results, we can see that the checksum of a block 0 is -9900. This checksum value will always be 0 for the clusters that were not initialized with the checksums option.

If the cluster is not initialized with the checksum options, then it is recommended to run cluster level pg_dumpall with a certain interval, which identifies the page corruption in early stages.

There's more...

As of now, we have only discussed the user data corruption. However, corruption can also occur at PostgreSQL's catalog level as well. Dealing with catalog corruption is a different story, and it is not an easy to job to recover from catalog corruption. To deal with catalog corruption, we have a utility tool called pg_catcheck, which will identify the catalog corruption in the database.

Refer to the following URL for more information about the `pg_catcheck` extension: `https://github.com/EnterpriseDB/pg_catcheck/blob/mast er/README.md`.

As, like the `zero_damaged_pages` setting, PostgreSQL has the `ignore_system_indexes` setting, which ignores the corrupted catalog indexes while we are dealing with corrupted catalogs.

Routine reindexing

As like tables, an index also needs a special maintenance activity called reindex or rebuild. The job of reindex is to build a fresh index by replacing the existing index pages.

Getting ready

When we do the `DELETE`/`UPDATE` operation on a table, PostgreSQL will remove or update the corresponding entries from the table's indexes. Once it removes the entries from the index pages, there might be chances of increasing the leaf page fragmentation in `btree` indexes, which leads to more I/O while performing the index scan operations. This is because in the `btree` index all the index and row entries will be at the leaf node, where root and branch nodes will be helping the index scan to reach its index entries. In general, if a leaf page fragmentation of an index is more than 30% then it is recommended to do a `REINDEX` operation on it. For non `btree` indexes, it is not possible to identify the leaf page fragmentation as it maintains its own implementation.

Like a table, an index can also get bloated due to multiple `DELETE`/`UPDATE` operations. To reclaim these dead spaces at index level, we have to execute the `VACUUM` command on the corresponding table; otherwise an autovacuum process takes care of it. If the index is too bloated, then it is also recommended to do a `REINDEX` operation on it. To find the leaf fragmentation and bloat on an index, we have to use an extension called `pgstattuple`.

How to do it...

Let's create the `pgstattuple` extension and examine a sample index as follows:

```
postgres=# CREATE EXTENSION pgstattuple ;
CREATE EXTENSION
postgres=# SELECT * FROM pgstatindex('test_idx');
-[ RECORD 1 ]------+--------
version            | 2
tree_level         | 2
index_size         | 22478848
root_block_no      | 412
internal_pages     | 10
leaf_pages         | 2733
empty_pages        | 0
deleted_pages      | 0
avg_leaf_density   | 90.06
leaf_fragmentation | 0
```

From the preceding results, the `test_idx` index is healthy, as its leaf fragmentation is 0, and also it does not have any deleted pages in it. Now, let's see the performance of the index scan by executing a sample query:

```
postgres=# EXPLAIN ANALYZE SELECT * FROM test WHERE t BETWEEN 999 AND 9999;
                                           QUERY PLAN
------------------------------------------------------------------------------
---------------------------------------------------------
 Index Only Scan using test_idx on test  (cost=0.29..331.17 rows=9144
width=4) (actual time=0.063..3.765 rows=9001 loops=1)
   Index Cond: ((t >= 999) AND (t <= 9999))
   Heap Fetches: 9001
 Planning time: 0.585 ms
 Execution time: 4.124 ms
(5 rows)

Time: 5.804 ms
```

Now, let's perform some update operation on the `test` table, and observe the index fragmentation ration:

```
postgres=# UPDATE test SET t=1000 WHERE t%3=0;
UPDATE 33333
postgres=# EXPLAIN ANALYZE SELECT * FROM test WHERE t BETWEEN 999 AND 9999;
                                           QUERY PLAN
------------------------------------------------------------------------------
---------------------------------------------------------
 Index Only Scan using test_idx on test  (cost=0.29..448.85 rows=12178
```

```
   width=4) (actual time=0.095..21.316 rows=39333 loops=1)
      Index Cond: ((t >= 999) AND (t <= 9999))
      Heap Fetches: 42334
 Planning time: 0.084 ms
 Execution time: 22.682 ms
(5 rows)
Time: 30.249 ms

postgres=# SELECT * FROM pgstatindex('test_idx');
-[ RECORD 1 ]------+---------
version            | 2
tree_level         | 1
index_size         | 3219456
root_block_no      | 3
internal_pages     | 0
leaf_pages         | 392
empty_pages        | 0
deleted_pages      | 0
avg_leaf_density   | 62.88
leaf_fragmentation | 26.79
```

From the preceding stats, the same query took 30ms since we increased the number of rows in the table, and the value is between 999 and 9999. And also, the corresponding index is fragmented up to 26.79.

Now, let's go and REINDEX the index and observe its fragmentation ratio along with the query result time:

```
postgres=# REINDEX INDEX test_idx;
REINDEX

postgres=# SELECT * FROM pgstatindex('test_idx');
-[ RECORD 1 ]------+---------
version            | 2
tree_level         | 1
index_size         | 2252800
root_block_no      | 3
internal_pages     | 0
leaf_pages         | 274
empty_pages        | 0
deleted_pages      | 0
avg_leaf_density   | 89.33
leaf_fragmentation | 0

postgres=# EXPLAIN ANALYZE SELECT * FROM test WHERE t BETWEEN 999 AND 9999;
                               QUERY PLAN
-----------------------------------------------------------------------------
```

```
--------------------------------------------------------
  Index Only Scan using test_idx on test  (cost=0.29..1222.95 rows=39333
width=4) (actual time=0.035..8.646 rows=39333 loops=1)
    Index Cond: ((t >= 999) AND (t <= 9999))
    Heap Fetches: 0
 Planning time: 0.210 ms
 Execution time: 10.024 ms
(5 rows)

Time: 10.792 ms
```

From the preceding results, after performing the REINDEX operation on the index, the query response time decreased to 10ms from 30ms, which is a sign of good query performance.

> The pgstatindex() function only supports btree index types.

How it works...

When we initiate REINDEX, it acquires the access exclusive lock on the table, and will recreate a brand new index. Until this index operation is complete, all the incoming queries on the same table will be blocked. If the index size is huge in size, then the amount of time for the index creation will be increased. This will cause a serious application outage, as all the queries will be in a waiting state. As an alternative to this REINDEX operation, we have to create a new index concurrently on the same columns, then we have to drop the fragmented index concurrently and then use the ALTER command to rename the new index name as an old index name. However, we will be discussing more about this in further chapters.

There's more...

We can also perform the REINDEX operation on system/database/schema/table levels as well. If we do REINDEX on the system level, it will recreate the system catalog indexes. And REINDEX on the database regenerate all the indexes of all tables in it. And, REINDEX on a schema level regenerates all the indexes of all the tables in the given schema. And REINDEX on a table level regenerate all the indexes of the specified table.

Refer to the following URL for more information about the index
maintenance operations: `https://wiki.postgresql.org/wiki/Index_Ma`
`intenance`.

Generating planner statistics

In this recipe, we will be discussing how we can use PostgreSQL to generate statistics.

Getting ready

Database statistical information plays a crucial role in deciding the proper execution plan
for the given SQL statement. PostgreSQL provides a utility command called `ANALYZE`,
which collects statistics from tables and makes them available to the planner. PostgreSQL
also provides another utility background process called autovacuum, which does a similar
job to analyze. All these collected statistics will be stored into the PostgreSQL catalog tables.

How to do it...

Now, for demonstration let's create a test table and populate a few entries in it:

```
postgres=# CREATE TABLE test(t INT);
CREATE TABLE
postgres=# SELECT COUNT(*) FROM pg_stats WHERE tablename = 'test';
 count
-------
     0
(1 row)
postgres=# INSERT INTO test VALUES(generate_series(1, 1000));
INSERT 0 1000
postgres=# ANALYZE test;
ANALYZE
postgres=# SELECT COUNT(*) FROM pg_stats WHERE tablename = 'test';
 count
-------
     1
(1 row)
```

After inserting a few records and executing the ANALYZE command, we are able to see that pg_stats is reflected with test table information. If we do not execute the ANALYZE command on the test table, autoanalyze will update pg_stats with the test table information, when an autovacuum process runs on that table.

How it works...

The ANALYZE command scans the relation, and will populate each column's metrics into the pg_statistic catalog table using the following:

null_frac

The percentage of null values in that column. If the column does not have any null values, then this value will be set to 0.

avg_width

This is the average width of bytes of the whole column.

n_distinct

This value defines the number of distinct values that exist in the column. If this value is −1, then the column does not have any duplicate values in it. This value will be always set to −1 for the primary key constrained columns.

most_common_vals

This is an array that stores the most common or repeated values in the column.

most_common_freqs

This is an array that stores the most common or repeated values frequency.

histogram_bounds

This array stores special values, which can divide the table into equally sized datasets.

correlation

This defines whether the rows are stored in the table's column order or not.

most_common_elems

This defines the most repeated elements of non-scalar data types, such as arrays and vectors.

most_common_elem_freqs

This defines the repeated elements frequency of non-scalar data types.

When `ANALYZE` or `autoanalyze` run on a table, then it collects the preceding metrics and will keep them in the `pg_statistics` table. To limit the number of statistics to collect and store into these columns, we have to use the `default_statistics_target` parameter or we can also use the `ALTER TABLE ... ALTER COLUMN ... SET STATISTICS` syntax.

> Refer to the following URL for more information about statistical information: `https://www.postgresql.org/docs/9.5/static/view-pg-stats.html`.

Tuning with background writer statistics

In this recipe, we will be discussing how PostgreSQL's background writer (`bgwriter`) process plays an important role in fine tuning PostgreSQL memory and checkpoint related information.

Getting ready

The `bgwriter` process is a mandatory background process in a PostgreSQL instance. Its main responsibility is to flush the buffers from memory to disk. Besides, it will also keep the shared buffers ready by flushing the least used dirty buffers from memory to disk, based on `bgwriter_lru_maxpages`, `bgwriter_lru_multiplier` parameter settings. In PostgreSQL, checkpoint activity is a heavy process, as it is going to flush many dirty buffers into the physical disk, which will increase a great utilization in I/O.

When an explicit/implicit checkpoint is invoked, the bgwriter process will do most of the work. The pg_stat_bgwriter catalog view will show the cumulative statistics of the bgwriter and checkpoint statistics. If we can store this statistical information into a separate table using any scheduled process, then we can define that the configured memory and checkpoint parameters are fine tuned. Otherwise, we have to reset the stats before analyzing, and let the instance run with required load and then evaluate them as shown next.

How to do it...

Let's reset the pg_stat_bgwriter statistics and run a normal pgbench test as follows:

```
postgres=# SELECT pg_stat_reset_shared('bgwriter');
 pg_stat_reset_shared
-----------------------

(1 row)

$ cat /tmp/test.sql
INSERT INTO test VALUES(generate_series(1, 10000));
SELECT * FROM test ORDER BY t DESC LIMIT 1000;
DELETE FROM test WHERE t%7=0;
UPDATE test SET t=100;

$ bin/pgbench -c 90 -T 1000 -f /tmp/test.sql
```

While the precedingpgbench test is running, we may get many deadlocks due to concurrent row update/delete operations. So, ignore those errors and let the pgbench operation complete. Once the pgbench test completes, let's evaluate the pg_stat_bgwriter and view results as follows:

```
postgres=# SELECT * FROM pg_stat_bgwriter;
-[ RECORD 1 ]---------+-----------------------------------
checkpoints_timed     | 19
checkpoints_req       | 445
checkpoint_write_time | 551012
checkpoint_sync_time  | 48577
buffers_checkpoint    | 1974899
buffers_clean         | 150281
maxwritten_clean      | 1470
buffers_backend       | 1883063
buffers_backend_fsync | 0
buffers_alloc         | 1880980
stats_reset           | 2016-09-20 23:58:12.183039+05:30
```

How it works...

Now, let's evaluate each field from the preceding results.

checkpoints_timed

This defines the number of checkpoints occurs due to `checkpoint_timeout`. From the preceding statistics, an implicit checkpoint occurred 19 times. Now, let's check what the current `chekpoint_timeout` setting is:

```
postgres=# SHOW checkpoint_timeout;
 checkpoint_timeout
--------------------
 1min
(1 row)
```

It is not recommended to set this value as very low. This is because if a checkpoint invokes for every 1 minute, then it will use most of the I/O to sync the dirty buffers to disk, which significantly decreases the running queries response time. To tune this parameter, we have to consider the current `shared_buffers` setting and need to decide the proper interval value for the timed checkpoints. In case we have the current instance `shared_buffers` as 10 GB, and the amount of dirty buffers generated in 1 minute is 5 GB, then every 1 minute the checkpoint process will be flushing 5 GB to disk, which takes more I/O resources. If we configure this parameter properly, then we can expect the `checkpoint_req` value as 0 or as a minimal value.

checkpoints_req

This defines the number of checkpoints that occur due to the `max_wal_size` limit. That is, if the latest generated WAL files size is greater than the `max_wal_size`, then PostgreSQL executes an internal checkpoint. This is similar to the `checkpoint_segments` parameter, which we have in previous versions of PostgreSQL.

From the preceding statistics, implicit checkpoints occurred 445 times. Now, let's see the `max_wal_size` setting:

```
postgres=# SHOW max_wal_size;
 max_wal_size
--------------
 192MB
(1 row)
```

As per the configuration setting, an implicit checkpoint will be executed after the 192 MB WAL files got generated. In some cases, even if we configured this value with high data interval like 10 GB, and if we do a bulk `INSERT/UPDATE/DELETE` operations that generate several 10 GB in less time than the `checkpoint_timeout` interval, then it will execute implicit checkpoint operations multiple times, which automatically brings down the server performance. If we could avoid these kinds of checkpoints during the bulk operations, then the server will be in stable mode. If we can tune this `max_wal_size` parameter properly, then we can get the `checkpoints_req` value as either 0 or minimal value.

checkpoint_write_time

This defines the amount of milliseconds it took to write the dirty buffers into the disk, by using the `write()` system call. From the preceding statistics, this value is `551012`. That is, all the timed out and required checkpoints took 5,51,012 milliseconds to write `1974899` (`buffers_checkpoints`) number of blocks into the disk. Now, let's verify the `block_size` setting value:

```
postgres=# SHOW block_size;
 block_size
------------
 8192
(1 row)
```

So, to write `1974899*8192 = 16178372608` bytes into the disk, checkpoint operation is needed 551 seconds. That is, on an average the write speed is 28 MB per second from shared buffers into disk. The amount of time required to write the buffers into disk is directly proportional to the number of dirty blocks and the I/O wait.

checkpoint_sync_time

This defines the amount of milliseconds it took to sync OS cached data to disk, by using the `fsync()` system call. From the preceding statistics, this value is `48577`. That is, all checkpoints took 48 seconds to flush the cached data into the disk. Once the checkpoint completes its `write()` system call, then it initiates the `fsync()` call to flush the cache to disk.

buffers_checkpoint

This defines the number of buffers that the checkpoint processes flushes to disk. From the preceding statistics, this value is `1974899`. That is, *16178372608 ~ 15 GB*. Out of this 15 GB, let's calculate how much data is flushed due to `checkpoints_timed(19)` and how much with`checkpoints_req(445)`. That is, 5% of *15 GB ~ 0.75 GB* is flushed to disk due to `checkpoints_timed`, whereas 95% of *15 GB ~ 14.25 GB* is flushed to disk due to `checkpoints_req`.

As we discussed previously, we have to maintain the cluster to do its checkpoints based on its timeout rather the limit of `max_wal_size`. From the preceding calculations, we can confirm that most of the data it is flushing is due to `max_wal_size` rather than `checkpoint_timeout`. So we have to consider fine tuning these two parameters.

buffers_clean

This defines the number of buffers that got cleared by the `bgwriter` process by flushing the least recently used dirty buffers. To limit the number of blocks to flush to disk, it depends on the `bgwriter_lru_maxpages, bgwriter_lru_multiplier` settings. The `bgwriter_lru_maxpages` is the maximum page limit for the `bgwriter` process, whereas `bgwriter_lru_multiplier` will be helpful in calculating the number of pages to flush, based on the average recent needed buffers allocated to load data from disk to pages.

From the preceding statistics, this value is `150281`. That is, the `bgwriter` process flushed *150281*8192 ~ 1231101952* bytes into disk whenever it invoked. Now, let's see the `bgwriter_delay` setting and evaluate this value:

```
postgres=# SHOW bgwriter_delay ;
 bgwriter_delay
----------------
 10s
(1 row)
```

As we configured the delay as 10 seconds, the `bgwriter` process invokes in this interval and flushed *1231101952 ~ 1 GB* dirty buffers from memory to disk.

But the amount of standalone checkpoint process is flushed 15 GB of data, whereas in background as a parallel task, the `bgwriter` process also flushed 1 GB dirty buffers to disk. So, to distribute the amount of dirty buffers between the `checkpoint` and `bgwriter` processes, we have to make the `bgwriter` related settings aggressive. That is, we have to reduce the `bgwriter_delay` settings, besides we have to increase the limit for the maximum number of pages to flush using the `bgwriter_lru_maxpages` and `bgwriter_lru_multiplier` parameters. Now, let's check these current parameter settings:

```
postgres=# SHOW bgwriter_lru_maxpages ;
 bgwriter_lru_maxpages
-----------------------
 100
(1 row)

postgres=# SHOW bgwriter_lru_multiplier;
 bgwriter_lru_multiplier
-------------------------
 2
(1 row)
```

The reason to distribute the dirty buffers among the `checkpoint`, `bgwriter` process is to avoid the user's backend connection to flush the dirty buffers. When a backend connection tries to access multiple dirty buffers, then it is needed to flush those buffers into the disk in the first place, before doing any operation on it. In this case, we may get an inefficient query response time. To avoid this kind of situation, we need to use `bgwriter` to flush all the possible dirty buffers into disk, before any user's connection tries to access it.

max_written_clean

This defines the number of times the `bgwriter` processes reached the `bgwriter_lru_maxpages` limit, while flushing the dirty buffers into disk. From the preceding statistics, this value is `1470`. That is, the `bgwriter` process is stopped `1470` times, since it reached its max page limit. This value will be helpful in defining the work load of the `bgwriter` process. If we see that this count is increasing rapidly, then we have to consider fine tuning the background writer's `lru` related parameters. And if we see that this value is constant, then we have to check whether `bgwriter` is causing any I/O load spikes during its interval. If it is, then we have to reduce the values for the background writer's `lru` related parameters.

buffers_backend

This defines the number of buffers that got flushed into disk by the individual backend connection. That is, when any connection tries to hit a dirty buffer, then that process will sync the dirty buffer into disk, before doing any operations on it. This syncing operation may cause a delay while processing the given query. From the preceding statistics, this value is `1883063`. That is, *1883063*8192 ~ 15426052096* bytes, which is approximately 14 GB.

As per the `pgbench` test case against checkpoint settings, and the `bgwriter` delay and its `lru` parameter settings, the `pgbench` user connection processes flushed 14 GB of data into disk. Now, let's verify the `shared_buffers` setting what we have at instance:

```
postgres=# SHOW shared_buffers;
 shared_buffers
-----------------
 128MB
(1 row)
```

It is an inefficient test case that we ran with this `shared_buffers` setting. This is because all the connections that forked from `pgbench` were busy in acquiring the limited `shared_buffers`, besides flushing the dirty buffers to disk. If we ran another `pgbench` test case, which had a low number of connections and a low number of DML operations, then we might get this `buffers_backend` value as either zero or minimal.

In general, it is recommended to set the `shared_buffers` value as 25% of the RAM, to hold all the connection's transactions. As per the `shared_buffers` setting value, we also need to tune the `checkpoints` and `bgwriter` related parameters, to reduce the number of `buffers_backend`, which significantly improve the query response time.

buffers_backend_fsync

This defines the number of times the `fsync()` happened, when buffers flushed to disk by the backend connection process. In general, when a user connection flushes the buffers, then it will push an `fsync()` request into the `bgwriter` parameter's queue. When this queue is already filled, then it is the user connections responsibility to execute `fsync()` on updated files.

buffers_alloc

This defines the number of buffers allocated in shared buffers to load the data blocks from disk, when a cache miss happens. From the preceding statistics, this value is 1880980, which is approximately equal to buffers_backend. As we discussed previously, with the lack of enough shared_buffers, the backend connections were competing for the resources by flushing the dirty buffers into the disk.

stats_reset

This defines the beginning timestamp for all of these cumulative statistics.

There's more...

The preceding pgbench test case ran by resetting the bgwriter statistics. It would be more useful if we can store this statistics snapshot information into another table, based on an interval. Once we have this snapshot information, then we can identify the I/O usage and the behavior of bgwriter and checkpoint by comparing the delta between these snapshots, as discussed previously.

PostgreSQL provides a logging parameter called log_checkpoints, which will log detailed information about the checkpoint into the log files as follows:

```
LOG:   checkpoint starting: immediate force wait
 LOG:   checkpoint complete: wrote 14168 buffers (86.5%); 0 transaction log
file(s) added, 0 removed, 12 recycled; write=1.669 s, sync=0.221 s,
total=34.881 s; sync files=6, longest=0.116 s, average=0.036 s;
distance=200615 kB, estimate=200615 kB
```

From the preceding log message, immediate force wait defines that it is not a timed out checkpoint. Also, the log message contains some helpful information, such as total time it took to complete this checkpoint, how many buffers it flushed to disk, and so on, which will help us to understand the I/O utilization when a checkpoint occurs.

9
Vacuum Internals

In this chapter, we will cover the following recipes:

- Dealing with bloating tables and indexes
- Vacuuming and autovacuuming
- Freezing and transaction ID wraparound
- Monitoring vacuum progress
- Controlling bloat using transaction age

Introduction

PostgreSQL provides **MVCC (Multi Version Concurrency Control)** to achieve one of the ACID properties called isolation. Transactional isolation is nothing but achieving the maximum possible concurrency among concurrent transactions. PostgreSQL has implemented MVCC to achieve this concurrency by creating versions of each tuple when the tuple receives any modifications. For example, let's say that a tuple received n concurrent modifications. PostgreSQL will keep n versions of the same tuple and it will make the last committed modified tuple as visible to further transactions. Having both visible and non-visible tuples leads to more disk space utilization. However, PostgreSQL provides a few ways to reutilize the non-visible tuples for further write operations.

In this chapter, we will be discussing what PostgreSQL offers to clean the nonvisible tuples, and how they internally work.

Dealing with bloating tables and indexes

In this recipe, we will be discussing how to deal with bloats using PostgreSQL's garbage collector processes.

Getting ready

We all know that PostgreSQL's storage implementation is based on MVCC. As a result of MVCC, PostgreSQL needs to reclaim the dead space/bloats from the physical storage, using its garbage collector processes called vacuum or autovacuum. If we do not reclaim these dead rows, then the table or index will keep growing until the disk space gets full. In a worst case scenario, a single live row in a table can cause the disk space outage. We will discuss these garbage collector processes in more detail in the next recipe, but for now let's find out which tables or indexes have more dead space.

How to do it...

To identify the bloat of an object, we have to use the `pgstattuple` extension, otherwise we have to follow the approach that is mentioned at: `http://www.databasesoup.com/2014/10/new-table-bloat-query.html`:

```
postgres=# CREATE EXTENSION pgstattuple;
CREATE EXTENSION
postgres=# CREATE TABLE test(t INT);
CREATE TABLE
postgres=# INSERT INTO test VALUES(generate_series(1, 100000));
INSERT 0 100000
postgres=# SELECT * FROM pgstattuple('test');
-[ RECORD 1 ]------+--------
table_len          | 3629056
tuple_count        | 100000
tuple_len          | 2800000
tuple_percent      | 77.16
dead_tuple_count   | 0
dead_tuple_len     | 0
dead_tuple_percent | 0
free_space         | 16652
free_percent       | 0.46
```

From the preceding output from `pgstattuple()`, we do not have any dead tuples in the test table, and we also do not have a huge amount of free space in it. Now, let's delete a few rows from the table test, and see the result of `pgstattuple()`:

```
postgres=# DELETE FROM test WHERE t%7=0;
DELETE 14285
postgres=# SELECT * FROM pgstattuple('test');
-[ RECORD 1 ]------+---------
table_len          | 3629056
tuple_count        | 85715
tuple_len          | 2400020
tuple_percent      | 66.13
dead_tuple_count   | 14285
dead_tuple_len     | 399980
dead_tuple_percent | 11.02
free_space         | 16652
free_percent       | 0.46
```

From the preceding results, `pgstattuple()` returns the number of dead tuples and the percentage of dead tuples in the table test. To identify the bloats of an index, we have to use another function called `pgstatindex()`, as follows:

```
postgres=# SELECT * FROM pgstatindex('test_idx');
-[ RECORD 1 ]------+-----------
version            | 2
tree_level         | 2
index_size         | 105332736
root_block_no      | 412
internal_pages     | 40
leaf_pages         | 12804
empty_pages        | 0
deleted_pages      | 13
avg_leaf_density   | 9.84
leaf_fragmentation | 21.42
```

From the preceding results, the index has a deleted pages count of 13, which is a bloat of an index. Once we identify the set of tables or indexes that need to be vacuumed, we have to initiate a manual VACUUM operation on those tables. We could also take advantage of the autovacuum process, which automatically runs VACUUM on the required tables.

How it works...

The `pgstattuple`/`pgstatindex` function requires a complete table/index scan to calculate the accurate values. If the table or index is huge in size, then the execution of the function takes a long time and increases the significant I/O, so try to avoid executing this function on any tables during production hours. There is no harm in using the other approach, which calculates the bloat based on `pg_catalog` views.

In PostgreSQL 9.5, the pgstattuple extension introduced a new function called `pgstattuple_approx()`, which is an alternative to `pgstattuple()` and returns the approximated bloat, along with the estimated live tuples information. This function will not do the full table scan like `pgstattuple()`, so it returns the results faster than the `pgstattuple()` function.

> For more information about this function, refer to: `https://www.postgres ql.org/docs/9.6/static/pgstattuple.html`.

Vacuum and autovacuum

In this recipe, we will be discussing the importance of vacuum and autovacuum in achieving good PostgreSQL performance.

Getting ready

As aforementioned, PostgreSQL is based on MVCC. As a net result, we will have all the non-visible tuples beside visible tuples, which occupy the underlying disk storage. As of now, these non-visible tuples have no use, and if we could reclaim or reuse the non-visible tuple's disk storage, that would make the disk utilization more effective.

How to do it...

Let's experiment with the usage of VACUUM by creating a sample table and executing a few SQL statements that generate non-visible tuples or dead tuples.

Connect to your database using `psql` as a super user and then execute the following command:

```
$ psql -h localhost -U postgres
postgres=# CREATE EXTENTION  pg_freespacemap;
CREATE
```

Now create a test table as follows:

```
postgres=# CREATE TABLE test(t INT);
CREATE
```

For demonstration of the VACUUM process, let's turn off autovacuum on this table as follows:

```
postgres=# ALTER TABLE test SET(autovacuum_enabled=off);
ALTER TABLE
```

Now let's insert 1,000 rows into the table, and observe how many pages it occupies in the underlying disk storage:

```
postgres=# INSERT INTO test VALUES(generate_series(1, 1000));
INSERT 0 1000
postgres=# ANALYZE test;
ANALYZE
postgres=# SELECT relpages FROM pg_class WHERE relname='test';
 relpages
-----------
        5
(1 row)
```

From the preceding SQL query, PostgreSQL used five relpages to store `1000` integer records. Now, let's verify the free space available in the relation test using the `pg_freespace()` function:

```
postgres=# SELECT sum(avail) freespace FROM pg_freespace('test');
 freespace
------------
        0
(1 row)
```

Now, let's update all the 1,000 records and collect the relpages and freespace map information again:

```
postgres=# UPDATE test SET t=1000;
UPDATE 1000
postgres=# ANALYZE test;
ANALYZE
postgres=# SELECT relpages FROM pg_class WHERE relname='test';
```

```
       relpages
    -----------
              9
    (1 row)
    postgres=# SELECT sum(avail) freespace FROM pg_freespace('test');
       freespace
    -----------
              0
    (1 row)
```

From the preceding SQL statement result, we got four additional pages by executing the update on 1,000 tuples. That is, the table size is expanded by up to 80% in the disk storage as we updated the whole table. We can also collect the number of non-visible or dead tuples of the table from the `pg_stat_user_tables` view:

```
    postgres=# SELECT n_dead_tup FROM pg_stat_user_tables WHERE relname='test';
      n_dead_tup
    -------------
            1000
    (1 row)
```

Now let's execute VACUUM and then check the amount of free space available or the relation `'test'`:

```
    postgres=# VACUUM test;
    VACUUM
    postgres=# SELECT sum(avail) freespace FROM pg_freespace('test');
      freespace
    -----------
          33248
    (1 row)
```

From the preceding results, once we execute the VACUUM command, it gives us some free space that is available by logically cleaning the dead tuples. Now, let's insert an additional 1,000 records into the table, and then look at the relpages count and free space information:

```
    postgres=# INSERT INTO test VALUES(generate_series(1, 1000));
    INSERT 0 1000
    postgres=# ANALYZE test;
    ANALYZE
    postgres=# SELECT relpages FROM pg_class WHERE relname='test';
      relpages
    -----------
             9
    (1 row)
    postgres=# SELECT sum(avail) freespace FROM pg_freespace('test');
      freespace
```

```
-----------
       4320
(1 row)
```

From the preceding SQL statement result, the relpages count is not increased even after inserting an additional 1,000 records into the table, since we ran the VACUUM command before an insert operation. Also, we can clearly see that the free space that was logically removed by the previous VACUUM command has been utilized properly.

Now, let's repeat the same actions without using the VACUUM command before doing insert operations, and look at the disk usage:

```
postgres=# TRUNCATE test;
TRUNCATE TABLE
postgres=# ANALYZE test;
ANALYZE
postgres=# INSERT INTO test VALUES(generate_series(1, 1000));
INSERT 0 1000
postgres=# UPDATE test SET t=100;
UPDATE 1000
postgres=# INSERT INTO test VALUES(generate_series(1, 1000));
INSERT 0 1000
postgres=# ANALYZE test;
ANALYZE
postgres=# SELECT relpages FROM pg_class WHERE relname='test';
 relpages
-----------
         14
(1 row)
postgres=# SELECT sum(avail) freespace FROM pg_freespace('test');
 freespace
-----------
          0
(1 row)
```

From the preceding results, we can see that an additional insert operation after updating the table increased the table size by 50%. This is because the table has no free space map available, and it extended the table storage. In the previous example, after the insert operation is complete, the total table size takes nine pages, and in this case it takes 14 pages.

From all the preceding experiments, we can confirm that using the VACUUM operation on a table makes it reuse the table's dead tuple storage for any further incoming transactions. However, to run the VACUUM command explicitly on every insert/update/delete operation is not advisable. This is because VACUUM is a fairly heavy process that scans all the tuples in a table that gradually increases the I/O utilization. Also, it is not advisable to completely stop VACUUM on any table, since it will increase more dead tuples in your disk, which leads to ineffective disk utilization. Instead, we have to run the VACUUM process periodically, such as once in a day or once in a week, by scheduling the command in either crontab or using pgBucket.

> You can find more information about pgBucket at: `https://bitbucket.or g/dineshopenscg/pgbucket`.

From PostgreSQL 8.1 onwards, autovacuum background workers are turned on by default, which automatically run the VACUUM behavior in the background, and cleans the dead tuple storage from the database. We can consider that the autovacuum process is a lightweight vacuum process that keeps on running in the background with the interval of the `autovacuum_nap_time` setting.

How it works...

When we execute the VACUUM command on any table, it will request the postgres instance to send all the current running SQL queries at that moment. Once the vacuum process receives that list, it will go to identify the dead tuples that are not visible to the running SQL queries. Then it will use the configured `maintenance_work_mem` memory area, to load the relation into memory for identifying dead tuples. Once the vacuum process identifies all the dead tuples information, it will generate an **FSM (Free Space Map)** for that relation. This FSM file will be referred to reuse the dead tuple's disk storage for further transactions.

Another responsibility of the vacuum process is to update the table's each row transaction status by validating `pg_clog` and `pg_subtrans`. In PostgreSQL, every row header contains `xmin` and `xmax` values. The `xmin` and `xmax` values associate with the transaction statuses, such as `In progress`, `Committed`, or `Aborted` by referring to the status bits from `pg_clog`.

xmin

It keeps the transaction ID of an inserting transaction that is inserted due to insert/update operations.

xmax

It keeps the transaction ID of a deleting transaction, or a new transaction ID, which is inserted due to an update operation. By default, the value of xmax is 0.

VACUUM not only has the responsibility of cleaning the dead tuples and updating the status flags, it also has the responsibility of cleaning the tuples that are created due to an aborted transaction.

To initiate the vacuum operation at database level, we just have to execute a plain VACUUM command without any further arguments. By default, the VACUUM command will run on the entire database level by vacuuming tables one by one. PostgreSQL also provides a utility command called vacuumdb, which also executes the same VACUUM command by connecting to the given data source. In PostgreSQL 9.5, the vacuumdb utility command has parallel vacuum jobs, which execute vacuum operations concurrently on multiple relations, rather than doing them in a sequential manner.

For example, if we want to initiate four vacuum process concurrently, then we have to execute the vacuumdb command as follows:

```
$ vacuumdb -j 4
vacuumdb: vacuuming database "postgres"
```

Autovacuum

Autovacuum is a utility background worker that invokes vacuum automatically for every autovacuum_nap_time per database. We can also configure how many background worker processes we want by using the autovacuum_max_workers setting. Once an autovacuum worker process invokes, it will try to allocate the maintenance_work_mem memory area to do its vacuum operation. So it is advisable to revalidate the maintenanc_work_mem and autovacuum_max_workers parameters, while fine-tuning the PostgreSQL settings. We can also turn off this autovacuum job by making autovacuum=off in the postgresql.conf file, which needs an instance reload.

Even though, we turned off this autovacuum process at cluster level, autovacuum will invoke in a special case, namely when it tries to eliminate transaction ID wrap around an issue at database level. We will be discussing about the transaction ID wrap around in the further recipe, and for now will see how the autovacuum process works.

When an autovacuum invokes per a database, it will scan all the tables and will generate FSM for each table as like vacuum process. An additional responsibility of an autovacuum process is, it will also update the PostgreSQL catalog tables with the latest information. That is, internally autovacuum is running an ANALYZE operation on each table, and will update the statistics as well. By default, autovacuum process is not configured as aggressive in reclaiming the dead tuples. That means, autovacuum will only scan the all tables, when the n% of the table has dead tuples. PostgreSQL also provides table-level, database-level and cluster-level autovacuum settings, which helps us to drive autovacuum as needed.

In general, for every autovacuum job iteration it will collect the list of tables which needs to be vacuumed from the `pg_class` catalog table, by using the configured autovacuum settings. If any table's number of dead tuples crosses the threshold outlined in the following calculation, then autovacuum will trigger on that table, and will update its activity information in the `pg_stat_user_tables` catalog:

```
autovacuum_vacuum_scale_factor * total number of tuples +
autovacuum_vacuum_threshold
```

We can get the total number of tuples of any relation by using the `reltuples` field of `pg_class`, and we can get the dead tuples of any relation by using the `n_dead_tup` field of `pg_stat_user_table`.

Freezing and transaction ID wraparound

In this recipe, we will be discussing a few other aspects of the VACUUM process.

Getting ready

As we discussed in the previous recipe, each row in PostgreSQL contains `xmin` and `xmax` values in its header, which define the transaction status. For each implicit/explicit transaction, PostgreSQL allots a number to that transaction as a transaction ID. As transaction ID is a number, which should have its boundaries like the maximum and minimum values it should allow, since we cannot generate an infinite amount of numbers.

As any number should be a definite value, PostgreSQL chooses a 4-byte integer as a definite number for these transaction IDs. That is, the maximum transaction ID we can generate with 4 bytes is $2^{32} \sim 4294967296$, which is 4 billion transaction IDs. However, PostgreSQL is capable enough to handle the unlimited number of transactions with the 4-byte integer, by rotating the transaction IDs from 1 to $2^{31} \sim 2147483648$. That is, if PostgreSQL reaches to the transaction ID 2147483648, then it will allot transaction ID from 1 to 2^{31} for further incoming transactions. In PostgreSQL terminology, this kind of rotating the transaction ID is called as transaction ID wraparound.

In PostgreSQL, a tuple visibility is designed as follow.

A transaction can only see an old transaction's committed tuples as follows.

Session 1	Session 2
| ```
postgres=# BEGIN;
BEGIN
postgres=# SELECT txid_current();
 txid_current
---------------
       452516
(1 row)
postgres=# INSERT INTO test
VALUES(1);
INSERT 0 1
postgres=# END;
COMMIT
``` | ```
postgres=# BEGIN;
BEGIN
postgres=# SELECT txid_current();
 txid_current
---------------
       452517
(1 row)
postgres=# SELECT xmin, xmax, t FROM
test;
  xmin  | xmax | t
--------+------+---
 452516 |    0 | 1
(1 row)
postgres=# END;
COMMIT
``` |

From the preceding example, Session 2's transaction ID of 452517 is greater than the Session 1's transaction ID 452516, which is also committed. That is the reason we are able to see the tuple in Session 2 along with the xmin and xmax of the inserted record.

In some special cases, PostgreSQL will also allow the transaction to see its future transaction's committed tuples by referring the commit log files from `pg_clog`, as follows:

Session 1	Session 2

```postgres=# BEGIN;```
```BEGIN```
```postgres=# SELECT txid_current();```
``` txid_current```
```--------------```
```   452519```
```(1 row)```
 	
```postgres=# SELECT xmin, xmax, t FROM```
```test;```
`` xmin
	xmax	t```
		```--------+------+---```
		`` 452520
			0	1```
				```(1 row)```
				```postgres=# END;```
				```COMMIT```
					
					```postgres=# BEGIN;```
					```BEGIN```
					```postgres=# SELECT txid_current();```
					``` txid_current```
					```--------------```
					``` 452520```
					```(1 row)```
					```postgres=# INSERT INTO test```
					```VALUES(1);```
					```INSERT 0 1```
					```postgres=# END;```
					```COMMIT```

`pg_clog` stores the currently running transactions status, which will be helpful during PostgreSQL instance crash recovery. Also, `pg_clog` will only keep the minimum essential transactions information rather than storing all transactions from 1 to 2^31.

Now, let us consider a special case that will occur when a transaction ID is a wraparound. Let us assume the current transaction ID is 1, which we got it as a next transaction ID, after we reach the transaction limit *2^31*. As demonstrated earlier, the current transaction ID can only see its previous transaction ID's committed information. As we are at transaction ID 1, it is only able to see its previous transaction information and not the future transactions.

Since, all the transaction IDs from 2 to 2^31 are future ids for the current the transaction, and also `pg_clog` will not have any transaction status about those transactions, the current transaction ID 1 is not capable to see any rows in the database, which leads to a database unavailability. In PostgreSQL, we call this special case as transaction ID wraparound problem, and to prevent this issue, PostgreSQL provides an approach called freeze transaction ID.

How to do it...

Vacuum provides an another utility operation called freeze. When we execute vacuum along with the freeze option, it will remove dead tuples and freeze the transaction ID. This freeze will be helpful in preventing transaction ID wraparound.

The following command needs to be executed to freeze the transaction IDs:

```
postgres=# VACUUM FREEZE test;
VACUUM
```

The autovacuum process is also smart enough to do this freeze operation, even though we turned off this process at instance level.

How it works...

Freezing a transaction ID means converting the value of a transaction ID as less than the transaction ID 1. As we discussed previously, when we reached transaction ID 1 as a result of transaction wraparound, we cannot see all the further transactions that are committed from transaction ID 2 to 2^31. Since, all these transaction IDs are greater than the ID 1. So, if we could make all these IDs less than ID 1, then PostgreSQL will able to display all those committed transaction ID's information. This is exactly what a FREEZE operation perform against the table. It will convert all the previous transaction ID values as logically less than the transaction ID 1.

Once we execute the preceding VACUUM FREEZE command, PostgreSQL sets the vacuum_freeze_table_age to 0 and then it will proceed with the actual freezing operation. To do this freezing operation, VACUUM needs to visit each row in each page, and will freeze the transaction IDs. If a transaction ID has bulk operations like insert/update/delete, then vacuum freeze needs to convert all these row entries, which will increase the I/O load. If we do not run this VACUUM FREEZE, autovacuum will do the same freezing option to avoid the wraparound problem, when a database transaction ID age reaches to autovacuum_freeze_max_age. The age of a transaction ID is nothing but, how many transactions we performed in a table or database without any FREEZE being applied or after the FREEZE operation. Whenever the database transaction age reaches to autovacuum_freeze_max_age, then PostgreSQL will launch the autovacuum process instantly to perform the freeze operation on the whole database.

As the VACUUM FREEZE process is a bit expensive, we have to fine-tune this operation using the following parameters:

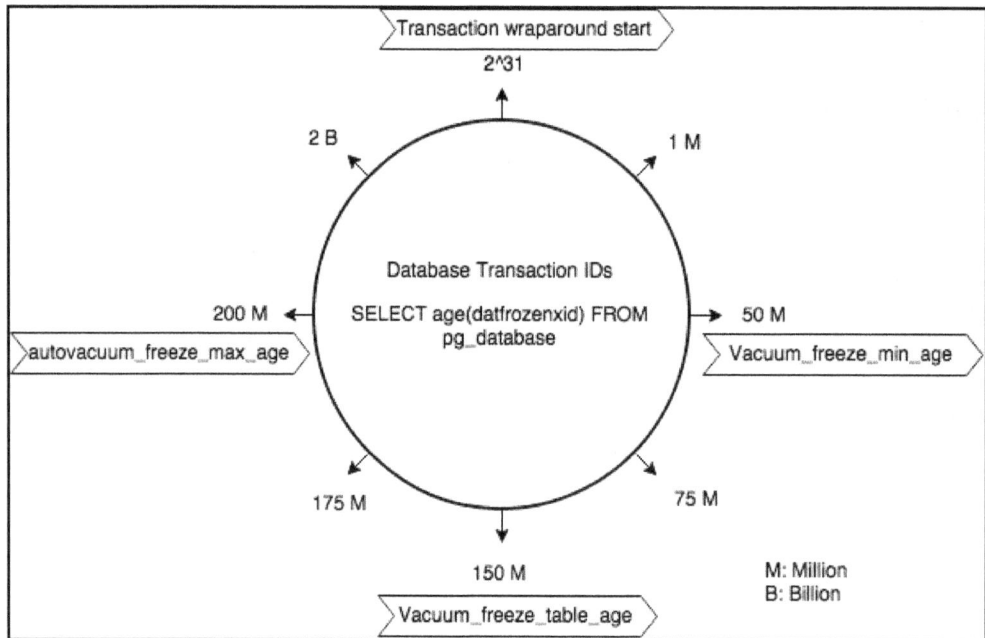

From the preceding pictorial representation contains the following parameters:

- **vacuum_freeze_min_age**: When an age of transaction reaches 50 million, then only perform the `FREEZE` operation on it. Once a `FREEZE` operation is done on a transaction ID, then, after 50 million transactions, it is eligible to freeze.

- **vacuum_freeze_table_age**: When the age of transaction IDs of a table reaches 150 million, then do a full table `FREEZE` operation, which will scan each and every row in a table. When we run `VACUUM FREEZE`, it will scan each and every row in a table to freeze the transaction IDs, and also with reclaim the dead tuples. In general, a plain `VACUUM` operation visits only the blocks, that have dead rows in them. so as to avoid the high I/O usage during the vacuum.

- **autovacuum_freeze_max_age**: When an age of database transaction ID reaches 200 million, then an autovacuum process will start forcefully and will perform `FREEZE` operation on all tables of a database. That is, autovacuum will be performing `FREEZE` operation approximately 10 times before we reach the transaction ID limit of *2^31*.

Fixing transaction ID wraparound

Transaction ID wraparound is a serious concern, since PostgreSQL needs to be shut down, which leads to a database outage. PostgreSQL will also throw the following kind of warning messages when transaction wraparound is about to happen:

```
WARNING: database "<database name>" must be vacuumed within XXX
transactions.
HINT: To avoid a database shutdown, execute a database wide VACUUM in that
database.
```

If we see the preceding kind of warning messages in a log file, as per the hint line we need to perform the `VACUUM` in the database. If we didn't notice the preceding warning messages from log file, we may hit the transaction wraparound limit and get the following error message in the log file:

```
ERROR: database is not accepting commands to avoid wraparound data loss in
database "<database name>"
HINT: Stop the postmaster and use a standalone backend to vacuum that
database.
```

The preceding hint line suggests that we have to use a standalone backend–such as the one shown here–to perform the vacuum.

```
$ bin/postgres --single -D <Data Directory Location> <database name>

PostgreSQL stand-alone backend 9.5.4
backend> VACUUM;
```

Once the vacuum operation is completed, use *Ctrl + D* to close this standalone connection, and then start the instance as usual.

Preventing transaction ID wraparound

To prevent a transaction id wraparound problem, it is always advisable to turn on the autovacuum process at cluster level. The autovacuum process plays a vital role in Postgres, which will update the statistics and perform VACUUM and do freezing operations online when it is required. Also, a periodic VACUUM ANALYZE operation in the required timings will also help the instance to be healthier.

Monitoring vacuum progress

In this recipe, we will be discussing the usage of the pg_stat_progress_vacuum catalog view, which gives some metrics about the ongoing vacuum process.

Getting ready

PostgreSQL 9.6 introduces a new catalog view, which provides some metrics about the ongoing vacuum processes. This view provides some metrics, along with different action phases, where vacuum/autovacuum performs internally on the table. This view currently does not track the metrics of VACUUM FULL operations, which might be available in future versions.

How to do it...

Let use VACUUM on any sample big table:

```
benchmarksql=# VACUUM bigtable;
```

In another terminal, let us query the view and put in the \watch mode, as shown here:

```
benchmarksql=# SELECT * FROM pg_stat_progress_vacuum;
(0 rows)
benchmarksql=# \watch 1 -[ RECORD 1 ]------+----------------- pid
 | 4785
datid               | 16405
datname             | benchmarksql
relid               | 16762
phase               | scanning heap
heap_blks_total     | 412830
heap_blks_scanned   | 393532
heap_blks_vacuumed  | 0
index_vacuum_count  | 0
max_dead_tuples     | 11184810
num_dead_tuples     | 1264
```

How it works...

The catalog view `pg_stat_progress_vacuum` is created based on an internal function, `pg_stat_get_progress_info`, which only takes VACUUM as an argument. This view provides statistical information about each vacuum/autovacuum backend process. At this moment, this function only tracks the information of VACUUM, and might be improved with more commands in future versions. From the preceding output, we can identify on what phase the current vacuum at this moment. There are a series phases a vacuum performs on a table in a sequential order, which helps us to identify which phase is taking more time during the vacuum.

> You can find more details about vacuum phases, and its counter values at: https://www.postgresql.org/docs/9.6/static/progress-reporting.html.

Control bloat using transaction age

In this recipe, we will be discussing how to control the generation of dead tuples using the snapshot threshold setting.

Getting ready

In earlier versions of PostgreSQL, the old version of a tuple could be visible to the snapshot until the transaction was completed. Once the tuple was not visible to any of the active transactions, then it would be removed logically by the autovacuum process. Also, we cannot limit the age of a transaction snapshot as we can in other database management systems. If we can restrict the age of a transaction, then we can prevent generating multiple versions of the tuples by throwing the `snapshot too old` error. This means that, if a transaction holds a set of tuples that were modified some time ago, then that transaction should not progress further. In PostgreSQL 9.6, we can achieve this by configuring the `old_snapshot_threshold` parameter.

How to do it...

To demonstration this feature, let us execute the following query and then restart the PostgreSQL instance:

```
postgres=# ALTER SYSTEM SET old_snapshot_threshold TO '1min';
ALTER SYSTEM
```

Let us execute transactions in two different sessions, as shown here:

Session 1	Session 2
| | ```
postgres=# BEGIN WORK;
BEGIN
postgres=# SET TRANSACTION ISOLATION LEVEL SERIALIZABLE;
SET
postgres=# SELECT * FROM test;
 t
----
 10
(1 row)
``` |
| ```
postgres=# UPDATE test SET t=10;
UPDATE 1
postgres=# SELECT pg_sleep(100);
 pg_sleep
----------
(1 row)
``` | |
| | ```
postgres=# UPDATE test SET t=10;
ERROR:  snapshot too old
``` |
```

How it works...

In PostgreSQL 9.6, whenever a transaction is started, it holds the transaction begin time as a snapshot time. For better understanding, let us call the snapshot time strx. Every statement that executes in the transaction, continues to update the recent transaction time. Let us call this transaction time ltrx. Whenever the statement in the transaction needs to visit the tuples, which were already modified by the other transactions, then it will compare the ltrx with the strx. If the delta of ltrx and strx is beyond the `old_snapshot_threshold`, then it will throw an error message as the snapshot is too old.

> At the moment, this new setting doesn't affect the tables that have hash indexes, and catalog tables.

10
Data Migration from Other Databases to PostgreSQL and Upgrading the PostgreSQL Cluster

In this chapter, we will cover the following recipes:

- Using the `pg_dump` to upgrade data
- Using the `pg_upgrade` utility for version upgrade
- Replicating data from other databases to PostgreSQL using Goldengate

Introduction

During the career of a database administrator, he/she will often be required to do major version upgrades of the PostgreSQL server. Over a period of time, new terminologies and features get added to PostgreSQL, and this results in a major version release. To implement the new features of the new version, the existing PostgreSQL setup needs to be upgraded to the new version. Database upgrades require proper planning, careful execution, and planned downtime. PostgreSQL offers two major ways to do a version upgrade:

- With the help of the `pg_dump` utility
- With the help of the `pg_upgrade` script

We will also cover the Oracle Goldengate tool in this chapter. **Goldengate** is a piece of heterogeneous replication software that can be used to replicate data between different databases. In this chapter, we are going to cover heterogeneous replication between Oracle and PostgreSQL.

Using pg_dump to upgrade data

In this recipe, we are going to upgrade the PostgreSQL cluster from version 9.5 to 9.6. We will utilize the pg_dump utility for this purpose.

Getting ready

The only prerequisites here are that an existing PostgreSQL cluster must be set up and running. The required version here is PostgreSQL Version 9.6. These steps are carried out on a 64 bit CentOS machine.

How to do it...

Here are the series of steps that need to be carried out for upgrading PostgreSQL from version 9.5 to 9.6 using pg_dump:

1. Back up your database using pg_dumpall:

   ```
   pg_dumpall >  db.backup
   ```

2. The next step would be to shut down the current PostgreSQL server:

   ```
   pg_ctl -D /var/lib/pgsql/9.5/data   stop
   ```

3. Rename the old PostgreSQL installation directory:

   ```
   mv /var/lib/pgsql   /var/lib/pgsql.old
   ```

4. Install the new version of PostgreSQL, which is PostgreSQL Version 9.6, by using either the yum command or the PostgreSQL binaries from: https://www.bigsql.org/postgresql/installers.jsp.

5. The next step would be to initialize the PostgreSQL Version 9.6 server:

   ```
   /usr/pgsql-9.6/bin/initdb -D  /var/lib/pgsql/9.6/data
   ```

6. Once the database cluster is initialized, the next step is to restore the configuration settings, such as `pg_hba.conf` and `postgresql.conf`, from 9.5 into 9.6.

7. Then start the PostgreSQL 9.6 database server:

```
pg_ctl -D /var/lib/pgsql/9.6/data   start
```

8. Finally, restore your data from the backup that was created in step 1:

```
/usr/pgsql-9.6/bin/psql   -d postgres   -f  db.backup
```

9. We can either remove the old version data directory or continue working alongside both the server versions.

10. If we choose to remove the old version as mentioned in step 9, we can then remove the respective old version packages by using the `yum remove` command, or the uninstaller file that BigSQL distribution creates in the local system.

How it works...

Here, initially we take a dump of all the databases in the existing PostgreSQL 9.6 version cluster. We then initiate a clean shutdown of the current PostgreSQL server and rename the existing PostgreSQL installation directory to avoid any conflicts with the new version of PostgreSQL, that is, the version 9.6 being installed. Once the respective packages of the new version are installed, we proceed with initializing a database directory for PostgreSQL 9.6 server. To ensure that the desired configuration settings come into effect, we will need to copy the configuration files from the old version's data directory to the new version's data directory, and then start the new version PostgreSQL server service using the configuration settings that were defined for the existing environment in the old server. Once the PostgreSQL server version 9.6 has been started, we can make connections to the databases on this server. Eventually, we restore all the tables and databases from the old PostgreSQL server 9.5 to the new PostgreSQL server version 9.6 using the backup that was made in step 1 of the previous section.

> You may refer to the link given here for a more detailed explanation on upgrading a PostgreSQL cluster using `pg_dump`: `http://www.postgresql.org/docs/9.6/static/upgrading.html`.

Using the pg_upgrade utility for version upgrade

Here in this recipe, we are going to talk about upgrading a PostgreSQL cluster using `pg_upgrade`. We will cover the upgrading of the PostgreSQL version from 9.5 to 9.6.

Getting ready

The only prerequisite here is that an existing PostgreSQL cluster must be up and running. The required version here is PostgreSQL Version 9.6. These steps are carried out on a 64 bit CentOS machine.

How to do it...

Here are the steps to upgrade a PostgreSQL machine from version 9.5 to version 9.6 using the `pg_upgrade` utility:

1. Take a full backup of the data directory using a filesystem dump, or use `pg_dumpall` to back up the data:

   ```
   cd  /opt/pgsql/9.5/

   tar -cvf data.tar data
   ```

2. The next step would to be install the new version of PostgreSQL 9.6, as mentioned previously.

3. Now that the new version of PostgreSQL is installed, we make the following configuration changes and then initialize the data directory for the new PostgreSQL Version 9.6 database:

   ```
   View /etc/init.d/postgresql-9.6

   PGDATA=/opt/pgsql/9.6/data
   PGLOG=/opt/pgsql/9.6/pgstartup.log
   PGPORT= 5433

   /etc/init.d/postgresql-9.6 initdb
   ```

4. Once the data directory has been initialized for the new PostgreSQL Version 9.6, the next step is to stop the existing PostgreSQL Version 9.5 server and then run the `pg_upgrade` utility to check whether the clusters are compatible or not:

```
Service postgresql-9.5  stop

cd  /usr/pgsql-9.6/bin

./pg_upgrade -v -b /usr/pgsql-9.5/bin/ -B /usr/pgsql-9.6/bin/ -
    d /opt/pgsql/9.5/data/ -D /opt/pgsql/9.6/data/ --check
```

5. Once the preceding command returns the compatible check as good, we need to run the same command without the `--check` option, which actually performs the upgrade operation.

6. Once the upgrade completes, it will generate two files, `analyze_new_cluster.sh` and `delete_old_cluster.sh`. These files are basically used to generate optimizer statistics and delete the old PostgreSQL cluster version's data files.

7. After this upgrade step, we would need to copy the configuration setup present in the configuration files in the old version to the new setup.

8. Next, we start the PostgreSQL server version 9.6 service:

```
service postgresql-9.6 start
```

9. Run the `analyze_new_cluster.sh` shell script that was generated at the end of step 5. This script is used to collect minimal optimizer statistics in order to get a working and usable PostgreSQL system:

```
./opt/pgsql/analyze_new_cluster.sh
```

10. Now remove the old PostgreSQL directory by running this script:

```
./delete_old_cluster.sh
```

How it works...

After installing the packages for PostgreSQL server version 9.6, what we are doing here is changing the location of the data directory in the startup script, as shown in step 4. After this is done, we initialize the data directory for the new PostgreSQL server. The difference between the steps here and the previous recipe is that here we are changing the location of the data directory, the log path, and port number of the new PostgreSQL server version; whereas in the earlier recipe, we renamed the existing PostgreSQL server version data directory. Once the data directory is initialized, we stop the current PostgreSQL server and then launch the `pg_upgrade` script to upgrade the existing setup to the new version. The `pg_upgrade` script requires specifying the path of old and new data directories and binaries. Once the upgrade completes, it generates two shell scripts, `analyze_new_cluster.sh` and `delete_old_cluster.sh` to generate statistics and delete the old version PostgreSQL directory. To preserve the existing configuration, we would need to move the `pg_hba.conf` and `postgresql.conf` files from the old version's data directory to the new version's data directory, as shown in step 6 in the preceding section. Then we can start the upgraded PostgreSQL server. Once the server is upgraded, we can then proceed to generate statistics via the `analyze_new_cluster.sh`, script and remove the old version directory, via the `delete_old_cluster.sh` script as shown in step 9 and 10, respectively.

> For more inputs, refer to `http://www.postgresql.org/docs/9.6/static/pgupgrade.html`.

Replicating data from other databases to PostgreSQL using Goldengate

In this recipe, we are going to cover heterogeneous replication using the Oracle Goldengate software. We are going to migrate table data from Oracle to PostgreSQL.

Getting ready

Since this recipe talks about replicating data from Oracle to PostgreSQL, it is important to cover the Oracle installation. Also, since Goldengate is the primarily tool that is used, we will cover the Goldengate installation for both Oracle and PostgreSQL.

To install the Oracle 11g software on the Linux platform, you may refer to either of the following web links: `http://oracle-base.com/articles/11g/oracle-db-11gr2-install ation-on-oracle-linux-5.php` and `http://dbaora.com/install-oracle-11g-release-2-11-2-on-centos-linux-7/`.

To install Goldengate for Oracle database, refer to: `http://docs.oracle.com/cd/E35209_01/doc.1121/e35957.pdf`.

Here are the high-level installation steps, given for the ease of the reader. Please refer to the aforementioned web link for more detailed information:

1. Log in to `edelivery.oracle.com`.
2. Select the product pack **Fusion Middleware** and the **Linux x86-64 platform**. Click on the **Go** button.
3. Choose the option with the description that says `Oracle GoldenGate on Oracle v11.2.1 Media Pack for Linux x86-64` and it will open a web link. Then download the file with the name `Oracle GoldenGate V11.2.1.0.3 for Oracle 11g on Linux x86-64`. Download the respective zip file.
4. As a next step, extract the downloaded file and change the directory to the new location. Then launch the Goldengate command-line interface using the `ggsci` command. Before launching the Goldengate command-line interface, set the Goldengate installation directory and library path in the `PATH` and `LD_LIBRARY_PATH` environment variables, respectively.

How to do it...

Given here is the complete sequence of steps required to migrate table data/changes from Oracle to PostgreSQL using Goldengate:

1. Connect as the superuser system by using the operating system authentication on the machine that hosts the Oracle database, using the `sqlplus` utility:

   sqlplus / as sysdba

2. Once logged in to the Oracle database, make the following parameter changes:

   ```
   SQL> alter system set
     log_archive_dest_1='LOCATION=/home/abcd/oracle/oradat
     /arch';
   ```

3. To make the aforementioned parameter changes come into effect, shut down and restart Oracle database:

```
SQL> shutdown immediate

SQL> startup mount
```

4. Configure archiving on the Oracle database to ensure that changes made by transactions are captured and logged in the archive log files:

```
SQL> alter database archivelog;
SQL> alter database open;
```

5. Enable minimum supplemental logging:

```
SQL> alter database add supplemental log data;

SQL> alter database force logging;

SQL> SELECT force_logging, supplemental_log_data_min FROM
  v$database;

FOR SUPPLEME
--- ---------
YES    YES
```

6. Add the Goldengate directory path to the PATH and LD_LIBRARY_PATH environment variables:

```
export
  PATH=$ORACLE_HOME/bin:$ORACLE_HOME/OPatch:$HOME/ggs:$PATH
export LD_LIBRARY_PATH=$ORACLE_HOME/lib:$HOME/ggs/lib
```

7. Launch the Goldengate command-line interface for Oracle:

```
./ggsci
```

8. The next step would to be create various subdirectories for Goldengate, such as directories for report files, database definition, and so on:

```
GGSCI> create subdirs

Creating subdirectories under current directory
  /home/abcd/oracle/ggs

Parameter files                    /home/abcd/oracle/ggs/dirprm:
                                   already exists
```

```
         Report files                  /home/abcd/oracle/ggs/dirrpt:
                                          created
         Checkpoint files              /home/abcd/oracle/ggs/dirchk:
                                          created
         Process status files          /home/abcd/oracle/ggs/dirpcs:
                                          created
         SQL script files              /home/abcd/oracle/ggs/dirsql:
                                          created
         Database definitions files    /home/abcd/oracle/ggs/dirdef:
                                          created
         Extract data files            /home/abcd/oracle/ggs/dirdat:
                                          created
         Temporary files               /home/abcd/oracle/ggs/dirtmp:
                                          created
         Stdout files                  /home/abcd/oracle/ggs/dirout:
                                          created
```

9. Create for the manager a parameter file that contains a port number for the manager. Here we enter port 7809 as the port number:

```
GGSCI > edit param mgr

GGSCI > view param mgr

PORT 7809
```

10. The next step would be to exit from the manager, start the manager, and then verify that it is running:

```
GGSCI > start mgr


GGSCI > info all

Program      Status       Group        Lag at Chkpt   Time Since
  Chkpt

MANAGER      RUNNING

GGSCI > info mgr

Manager is running (IP port 7809).
```

11. Log in to the server hosting the PostgreSQL server and write the Goldengate configuration steps there. First, add the Goldengate directory to the `LD_LIBRARY_PATH` and `PATH` environment variables:

```
export LD_LIBRARY_PATH=/usr/pgsql/lib:/usr/pgsql/ggs/lib
export PATH=/usr/pgsql/bin:/usr/pgsql/ggs:$PATH
```

12. Goldengate uses an ODBC connection to connect to the Postgres database. The next step is to create the ODBC file. The ODBC driver is shipped along with the installation on Linux/Unix; you only have to create just the configuration file. If the ODBC driver is not available, you may download the respective PostgreSQL driver from `http://www.uptimemadeeasy.com/linux/install-postgresql-odbc-driver-on-linux/`:

```
view odbc.ini

[ODBC Data Sources]
GG_Postgres=DataDirect 6.1 PostgreSQL Wire Protocol
[ODBC]
IANAAppCodePage=106
InstallDir=/usr/pgsql/ggs
[GG_Postgres]
Driver=/usr/pgsql/ggs/lib/GGpsql25.so
Description=DataDirect 6.1 PostgreSQL Wire Protocol
Database=test
HostName=dbtest
PortNumber=5432
LogonID=nkumar
Password=nkumar
```

13. Export the ODBC environment variable that is `ODBCINI` which should point to `odbc.ini` file that we created in the previous step:

```
export ODBCINI=/usr/pgsql/ggs/odbc.ini
```

14. Now that we have the ODBC setup completed, we start with the Goldengate setup for PostgreSQL. We will first launch the Goldengate command-line interpreter for PostgreSQL:

```
./ggsci
```

15. We will now create various subdirectories for Goldengate report, definition files, and so on:

```
GGSCI > create subdirs

Creating subdirectories under current directory /usr/pgsql/ggs

Parameter files                    /usr/pgsql/ggs/dirprm: already
                                     exists
Report files                       /usr/pgsql/ggs/dirrpt: created
Checkpoint files                   /usr/pgsql/ggs/dirchk: created
Process status files               /usr/pgsql/ggs/dirpcs: created
SQL script files                   /usr/pgsql/ggs/dirsql: created
Database definitions files         /usr/pgsql/ggs/dirdef: created
Extract data files                 /usr/pgsql/ggs/dirdat: created
Temporary files                    /usr/pgsql/ggs/dirtmp: created
Stdout files                       /usr/pgsql/ggs/dirout: created
```

16. The next step would be to create the manager parameter file with port number and then start the manager:

```
GGSCI > edit param mgr

GGSCI > view param mgr

PORT 7809
```

17. Once we've created the parameter file, we can start the manager and check its status:

```
GGSCI > start mgr

Manager started.

GGSCI > info all

Program       Status        Group         Lag at Chkpt   Time Since
  Chkpt

MANAGER       RUNNING


GGSCI > info mgr

Manager is running (IP port 7809).
```

18. We will now create a table both in Oracle and PostgreSQL and replicate the data between the two. Log in to the Oracle database and create the table:

```
sqlplus nkumar


SQL> create table abcd(col1 number,col2 varchar2(50));

Table created.

SQL> alter table abcd add primary key(col1);

Table altered.
```

19. Log in to the PostgreSQL database and create a similar table:

```
psql -U nkumar -d test -h dbtest

test=> create table "public"."abcd" ( "col1" integer NOT NULL,
    "col2" varchar(20),CONSTRAINT "PK_Col111" PRIMARY KEY
      ("col1"));
```

20. Log in to the Oracle database using the Goldengate command-line interface, list the tables, and capture and check their data types:

```
GGSCI > dblogin userid nkumar, password nkumar
Successfully logged into database.

GGSCI > list tables *
NKUMAR.ABCD
```

Found 1 tables matching list criteria:

```
GGSCI > capture tabledef nkumar.abcd
Table definitions for NKUMAR.ABCD:
COL1                         NUMBER NOT NULL PK
COL2                         VARCHAR (50)
```

21. In the next step, we will check our ODBC connection to the PostgreSQL database and use the Goldengate **command line interface (CLI)** to list the tables and capture the table definitions:

```
GGSCI > dblogin sourcedb gg_postgres userid nkumar

Password:

2014-11-04 17:56:35  INFO    OGG-03036  Database character set
```

```
    identified as UTF-8. Locale: en_US.

    2014-11-04 17:56:35 INFO    OGG-03037  Session character set
        identified as UTF-8.
    Successfully logged into database.


    GGSCI > list tables *
    public.abcd
    Found  1 table matching list criteria


    GGSCI > capture tabledef "public"."abcd"
    Table definitions for public.abcd:
    col1        NUMBER (10) NOT NULL PK
    col2        VARCHAR (20)
```

22. Now we will start the Goldengate extract process on the Oracle database. First we will create the extract process that captures the changes for the abcd table in the Oracle database and copy these changes directly to the PostgreSQL machine. Every process needs the configuration file, so we will create one for the extract process:

```
    GGSCI > edit param epos
```

The parameters created are shown here when viewing the parameter file:

```
    GGSCI > view param epos

    EXTRACT epos
    SETENV (NLS_LANG="AMERICAN_AMERICA.ZHS16GBK")
    SETENV
        (ORACLE_HOME="/home/abcd/oracle/product/11.2.0/dbhome_1")
    SETENV (ORACLE_SID="orapd")
    USERID nkumar, PASSWORD nkumar
    RMTHOST dbtest, MGRPORT 7809
    RMTTRAIL /usr/pgsql/ggs/dirdat/ep
    TABLE nkumar.abcd;
```

23. The extract process is called epos and it connects as user nkumar using the password nkumar to the Oracle database. Changes made on the Oracle table abcd will be extracted and this information will be put in a trail file in the PostgreSQL machine. Now that the parameter file has been created, we can add the extract process and start it:

```
    GGSCI > add extract epos, tranlog, begin now
    EXTRACT added.
```

```
GGSCI > add exttrail /usr/pgsql/ggs/dirdat/ep, extract epos,
    megabytes 5
EXTTRAIL added.


GGSCI > start epos

Sending START request to MANAGER ...
EXTRACT EPOS starting


GGSCI > info all

Program       Status       Group         Lag at Chkpt   Time Since
    Chkpt

MANAGER       RUNNING
EXTRACT       RUNNING      EPOS          00:00:00       00:00:00

GGSCI > info extract epos
```

24. Since we are replicating the data in the heterogeneous environment (that is, data replication is happening from Oracle to PostgreSQL), the process doing the loading in the PostgreSQL would need to provide more details about the data in the extract file. This is done by creating a definition file using the `defgen` utility:

```
GGSCI > view param defgen

DEFSFILE /home/abcd/oracle/ggs/dirdef/ABCD.def
USERID nkumar, password nkumar
TABLE NKUMAR.ABCD;
```

25. We can now exit from the Goldengate CLI, call the `defgen` utility on the command line to create the definition file, and add the reference to the `defgen` parameter file:

```
./defgen paramfile ./dirprm/defgen.prm

Definitions generated for 1 table in
    /home/abcd/oracle/ggs/dirdef/ABCD.def
```

26. The next step would be to copy the `defgen` file to the machine where the PostgreSQL database is hosted:

```
scp dirdef/ABCD.def postgres@dbtest:/usr/pgsql/ggs/dirdef
```

27. Start the PostgreSQL replicat process; and we are going to set up the parameter file for this and include the definition file that was copied from the server hosting the Oracle database to the server hosting PostgreSQL:

```
GGSCI > edit param rpos
```

The parameters created when viewing the parameter file are shown here.

```
GGSCI > view param rpos

REPLICAT rpos
SOURCEDEFS /usr/pgsql/ggs/dirdef/ABCD.def
SETENV ( PGCLIENTENCODING = "UTF8" )
SETENV (ODBCINI="/usr/pgsql/ggs/odbc.ini" )
SETENV (NLS_LANG="AMERICAN_AMERICA.AL32UTF8")
TARGETDB GG_Postgres, USERID nkumar, PASSWORD nkumar
DISCARDFILE /usr/pgsql/ggs/dirrpt/diskg.dsc, purge
MAP NKUMAR.ABCD, TARGET public.abcd, COLMAP
  (COL1=col1,COL2=col2);
```

28. In the next step, we create the replicat process, start it, and verify that it is running:

```
GGSCI > add replicat rpos, NODBCHECKPOINT, exttrail
  /usr/pgsql/ggs/dirdat/ep
REPLICAT added.


GGSCI > start rpos

Sending START request to MANAGER ...
REPLICAT RPOS starting

GGSCI > info all

Program       Status       Group        Lag at Chkpt   Time Since
  Chkpt

MANAGER       RUNNING
REPLICAT      RUNNING      RPOS         00:00:00       00:00:00


GGSCI > info all
Program       Status       Group        Lag at Chkpt   Time Since
  Chkpt

MANAGER       RUNNING
```

```
REPLICAT     RUNNING      RPOS          00:00:00       00:00:02
```

```
GGSCI > view report rpos
```

29. Now that the extract and replicat processes have been set up on Oracle and PostgreSQL Goldengate interfaces, the next step is to test the configuration. We first begin by logging in to the Oracle database and inserting records into the abcd table:

```
sqlplus nkumar

SQL> insert into abcd values(101,'Neeraj Kumar');

1 row created.

SQL> commit;

Commit complete.


SQL> select * from abcd;

COL1                 COL2
-----------          ---------------------------------------
101                  Neeraj Kumar
```

30. Now we will check if the corresponding changes/new records inserted into the abcd table in the Oracle database are visible in the corresponding abcd table in the PostgreSQL database:

```
psql -U nkumar -d test

test=> select * from abcd;
 col1 |       col2
------+-------------------
  101 |  Neeraj Kumar
(1 row)
```

This setup completes the heterogeneous testing scenario for migrating data/changes from Oracle to PostgreSQL.

How it works...

We are going to discuss steps of the preceding section in chunks:

1. We will first talk about steps 1 to 6. Initially, we make a superuser connection in Oracle with the `sysdba` privilege and make certain configuration changes. We first enable a destination for holding the archived logs; that is, logs that contain information about transactional changes are kept here in the location specified by the `log_archive_dest_1` initialization parameter as seen in step 2 of the previous section. We then shut down the database in order to ensure that the changes made in step 2 come into effect. Once the database is restarted, we configure archiving in the database and enable supplemental logging, as seen in step 4 and 5 of the preceding section. In step 6, we configure and include the Goldengate directory path and library path in the `PATH` and `LD_LIBRARY_PATH` environment variables.

2. We will now talk about steps 7 and 8 of the preceding section. After Goldengate is installed on the server hosting Oracle database, we launch the Goldengate CLI and then create various Goldengate subdirectories for holding parameter files, checkpoint files, database definition files, extract data files, and so on.

3. Now we will talk about steps 9 and 10. The Goldengate manager performs a number of functions like starting the Goldengate process, trail log file management, and reporting. The manager process needs to be configured on both source and target systems, and configuration is carried out with the help of the parameter file as shown in step 9 .We configure the parameter `PORT` to define the port on which the manager is running. Once the parameter file for the manager is set up on the source machine, we start the manager and verify if it is running. This is shown in step 10 of the preceding section.

4. We will now talk about steps 11 to 15 of the preceding section. Once Goldengate is installed on the machine where PostgreSQL server is hosted, we add the Goldengate directory and library path to the `PATH` and `LD_LIBRARY_PATH` environment variables. Goldengate basically uses an ODBC connection to connect to the PostgreSQL database. For this purpose, we set up an ODBC configuration file called `odbc.ini`, which contains connection information to connect to PostgreSQL server. This is shown in step 12. In the next step, we export the `ODBCINI` environment variable and include the path of the configuration file. Then from step 14 onwards, we launch the Goldengate command-line interface for PostgreSQL; and we create various subdirectories for holding parameter files, database definition files, and so on.

5. We will now talk about steps 16 and 17. Similar to what was performed in steps 9 and 10, on the source system for the manager process in Goldengate for Oracle, we configure the parameter file for the manager process in Goldengate the for target system, that is, PostgreSQL. Then we start the manager and verify it as shown in step 17. The only parameter that has been configured in step 16 is the PORT parameter, which identified the port on which the manager will listen.

6. We will now talk about steps 18 and 19 in the preceding section. Here we are create two tables of the same name and the same structure. One table will be created in the Oracle database and one will be created in PostgreSQL. The tables are created in this manner because the idea of this exercise is that any data/changes that happen on the table created in Oracle will be replicated/propagated in PostgreSQL. This is the heterogeneous replication concept.

7. Here we will talk about steps 20 and 21. Basically, in step 20, what we are doing is logging to the Oracle database using the Goldengate interface, and we capture the table definition for the table that was created in step 18 of the preceding section. Similarly, in step 21, we are checking the ODBC connectivity to PostgreSQL database from the Goldengate CLI, and once the connection is made, we capture the table definitions for the table created in step 19.

8. Here we are going to talk about steps 22 and 23 from the preceding section. In step 22, we create a parameter file for the extract process on the machine hosting Oracle database, since it is used as the source. The extract process happens on the source database. The extract process parameter file contains information regarding the Oracle environment, the target remote host, the manager port, the trail file, and the table for which the changes need to be captured. In step 23, we start the extraction process on the source Oracle database and we add the trail file. The extract process will extract any changes made to the Oracle table abcd and will put this information on the trail file that resides on the machine hosting PostgreSQL server.

9. Here we are going to talk about steps 24 and 25 from the preceding section; as the replication is happening in a heterogeneous environment (that is, from Oracle to PostgreSQL, in this scenario), it is important to get as many details as possible about the data in the extract file to make things clear for the process loading the data into the PostgreSQL database. For this to happen, we need to create a definition file that will be created on the Goldengate interface of the Oracle database and will then be shipped to the machine hosting PostgreSQL server. In step 24, we are basically creating a parameter file for the defgen utility. In step 25, we call the defgen utility to create the definition file, and we also add a reference to the parameter file created in step 24 of the preceding section.

10. In step 26 of the preceding section, we copy the definition file created in step 25 from the Oracle machine to the machine that hosts PostgreSQL server.

11. Here we are going to talk about steps 27 and 28. We start the replicat process. Replicat basically reads the changes from the trail file and distributes them to the PostgreSQL database. In step 27, we basically configure the parameter file for the replicat process. In step 28, we start the replicat process, add the trail file to the replicat process so that it can read changes from the trail file, and dump those changes to the PostgreSQL database.

12. Here we are going to talk about steps 29 and 30. Basically, we are going to test our configuration here. In step 29, we log in to the Oracle database, insert a record in the abcd table, and save the changes. Now, with the Goldengate extract and replicat processes running, the newly inserted record in the Oracle table should be replicated to the corresponding table in the PostgreSQL database. We confirm this by logging in to the PostgreSQL database and then selecting the records from the abcd table in step 30. We can see in step 30 that the records inserted in the Oracle table in step 29 are visible in the PostgreSQL database table abcd. This confirms the successful implementation of the heterogeneous replication from Oracle to PostgreSQL.

There's more...

Oracle also provides heterogeneous database connections to remote database instances. Configuring these kinds of database links from Oracle to PostgreSQL will also help us to migrate data instantly by using a trigger-based solution, as demonstrated at: http://manoj adinesh.blogspot.in/2014/12/heterogeneous-database-sync.html.

Also, there are few open source tools, such as SymmetricDS, which offers replication to multiple sources from different foreign databases. For more information about the tool: https://www.symmetricds.org/doc/3.8/html/user-guide.html.

11
Query Optimization

In this chapter, we will cover the following recipes:

- Using sample data sets
- Timing overhead
- Studying hot and cold cache behavior
- Clearing the cache
- Querying plan node structure
- Generating an explain plan
- Computing basic costs
- Running sequential scans
- Running bitmap heap and index scans
- Aggregate and hash aggregate
- Grouping
- Working with set operations
- Running a CTE scan
- Nesting loops
- Working with merge and hash join
- Working on semi and anti joins

Introduction

When an end user submits an SQL query to a database, in general any database engine does the parsing and then validates the syntax and semantics of the given query. Once the query passes through the parsing levels, it will enter into the optimizer section. This optimizer section is responsible for generating the execution plan of the submitted query, by reading the table statistics. An execution plan of the same query can be varied while executing the query multiple times. Since the plan that the optimizer is generating is based on the amount of data, the query is about to process. In this chapter, we will be discussing various aspects of the optimizer by discussing a few query processing algorithms.

Using sample data sets

There are enough sample data sets that are available for PostgreSQL, and most of the data sets are implemented by considering real-time business cases.

> Find the list of sample data sets that are available for postgres at this
> URL: https://wiki.postgresql.org/wiki/Sample_Databases.

Benchmarking tools such as pgBench and BenchmarkSQL will initiate a sample data set, on which they generate a real-time database load and do the benchmarking. In this chapter, to demonstrate a few aspects of the optimizer, let's choose the BenchmarkSQL's catalog tables, which will generate enough data load for this chapter's demonstrations.

Getting ready

BenchmarkSQL is an open source implementation of the popular TPC/C OLTP database benchmark, which supports Firebird, Oracle, and PostgreSQL and captures detailed benchmark results in CSV files, which can later be turned into an HTML report. BenchmarkSQL also captures the OS metrics, such as CPU and memory usages.

How to do it...

Let's download and build the BenchmarkSQL.

Download the source from the following URL: `https://bitbucket.org/o penscg/benchmarksql`.

Let's unzip the downloaded source file, and build the BenchmarkSQL as follows:

1. Create the `benchmarksql` database and user as follows:

```
$ psql postgres      postgres=# CREATE USER benchmarksql WITH
   ENCRYPTED PASSWORD 'benchmarksql';
postgres=# CREATE DATABASE benchmarksql OWNER benchmarksql;
```

2. Run the `ant` command to build the BenchmarkSQL:

```
$ ant
Buildfile: /Users/dineshkumar/Downloads/benchmarksql-
   5.0/build.xml
init:
compile:
   [javac] Compiling 11 source files to
      /Users/dineshkumar/Downloads/benchmarksql-5.0/build
dist:
   [jar] Building jar:
      /Users/dineshkumar/Downloads/benchmarksql
         5.0/dist/BenchmarkSQL-5.0.jar
BUILD SUCCESSFUL
Total time: 2 seconds
```

3. Let's create the benchmark configuration file using the `run/sample.postgresql.properties` file as follows:

```
$ cp run/sample.postgresql.properties
   run/postgres_benchmark.prop
```

4. Let's update `run/postgres_benchmark.prop` with the local BenchmarkSQL database JDBC URI as follows:

```
$ cat postgres_benchmark.prop
db=postgres
driver=org.postgresql.Driver
conn=jdbc:postgresql://localhost:5432/benchmarksql
user=benchmarksql
password=benchmarksql
. . .
. . .
```

5. Let's build the BenchmarkSQL database using the following command. The following database build command will take some time to generate and load sample data into the database:

```
$ ./runDatabaseBuild.sh  postgres_benchmark.prop
# ------------------------------------------------------------
# Loading SQL file ./sql.common/tableCreates.sql
# ------------------------------------------------------------
. . .
. . .
Worker 000: Loading ITEM
Worker 001: Loading Warehouse        1
Worker 002: Loading Warehouse        2
Worker 003: Loading Warehouse        3
Worker 000: Loading ITEM done
Worker 000: Loading Warehouse        4
. . .
. . .
# ------------------------------------------------------------
# Loading SQL file ./sql.postgres/buildFinish.sql
# ------------------------------------------------------------
-- ----
-- Extra commands to run after the tables are created, loaded,
-- indexes built and extra's created.
-- PostgreSQL version.
-- ----
vacuum analyze;
```

6. Let's check the BenchmarkSQL database after it builds with sample data:

```
postgres=# SELECT
  pg_size_pretty(pg_database_size('benchmarksql'));
pg_size_pretty
----------------
1150 MB
(1 row)
```

How it works...

BenchmarkSQL is a brand new benchmarking tool for databases such as PostgreSQL and Oracle. Using this tool, we can simulate the TPC-C environment. That is, this tool simulates an e-ordering environment by creating sample warehouses, customers, and order delivery status data.

Refer to the following URL for more information about TPC-C: `http://ww w.tpc.org/tpcc/`.

The `runDatabaseBuild.sh` command generates the sample dataset based on the given properties file. The given property file `postgres_benchmark.prop` has all the default options such as `warehouses=10`, `loadworkers=3`, and `terminals=10`. Based on these settings, BenchmarkSQL generates 1.1 GB data. Please refer to the `sample.postgresql.properties` file for the BenchmarkSQL supported parameters and their usage.

Timing overhead

In this recipe, we will be discussing overhead of system timing calls.

Getting ready

In general, operating systems maintain a set of clock sources that monotonically increase the time value. When we execute any time-related commands such as date, then the operation system reads the date time value from the underlying hardware clock and then returns the output in human readable format. The clock sources are designed as it should maintain its consistency throughout all of its system time calls. In any case, the clock source should not give us any time value that is in the past. That is, the clock time should be an atomically incremental value. If the clock source loses its consistency due to a bad hardware time keeper, then we also lose the system stability.

While running the `EXPLAIN ANALYZE` command, PostgreSQL needs to run multiple system time calls, which keep tracking each node type start and end execution time. When the system loses its consistency in keeping its time value, then `EXPLAIN ANALYZE` may take more time than the actual query execution.

How to do it...

PostgreSQL provides a contributed module called `pg_test_timing`, which makes multiple system time calls and will observe the system clock behavior. If the system clock is going backwards, then it will return the `Detected clock going backwards in time` error message.

1. Let's run the sample `pg_test_timing` command, as shown in the following snippet, to calculate the timing overhead in the system:

```
$ pg_test_timing -d 3
Testing timing overhead for 3 seconds.
Per loop time including overhead: 52.83 nsec
Histogram of timing durations:
 < usec    % of total         count
       1      94.78551      53828766
       2       5.21020       2958875
       4       0.00084           475
       8       0.00077           436
      16       0.00229          1300
      32       0.00028           157
      64       0.00007            41
     128       0.00001             7
     256       0.00002            13
     512       0.00000             1
    1024       0.00001             4
    2048       0.00000             1
    4096       0.00001             4
```

If the system clock source is consistent then, 90% of the system timing calls should fall in under 1 microsecond.

How it works...

The `pg_test_timing` module is especially designed to identify the timing overhead in the clock source. It makes several system clock calls and will identify the delta between its previous value and current value. That is, it just simulates the system calls that EXPLAIN ANALYZE generates during the plan generation.

On Unix systems, EXPLAIN ANALYZE is designed to calculate the timings based on the `gettimeofday()` function call, whereas on Windows systems it uses the `QueryPerformanceCounter()` function. These system calls will be performed for each node type during the plan generation.

Refer to the following URL for more information about the timing overhead calculations on the system:
`https://www.postgresql.org/docs/9.6/static/pgtesttiming.html`.

Studying hot and cold cache behavior

Database cache plays a vital role in the query performance. In this recipe, we will be discussing the hot and cold cache impact on the submitted SQL.

Getting ready

Cold cache is the behavior when the submitted SQL does not find its required data in memory, which leads to process to read the data from the disk into the memory. Hot cache is vice versa to the cold cache. If the SQL's required data is found in the memory, then it is a hot cache behavior, which will avoid the disk read operations, and also improves the query response time. The query performance is directly proportional to the amount of data we have in the memory. That is, if we can make less I/O operations then performance will improve automatically.

How to do it...

PostgreSQL provides a few extensions such as `pg_prewarm`, `pg_buffercache`, which will help us to deal with cache. So, let's create these two extensions as follows:

```
benchmarksql=# CREATE EXTENSION pg_buffercache ;
CREATE EXTENSION
benchmarksql=# CREATE EXTENSION pg_prewarm ;
CREATE EXTENSION
```

Cold cache

1. Let's check if any BenchmarkSQL tables are cached in memory or not by using the following SQL statement:

```
benchmarksql=# SELECT COUNT(*) FROM pg_buffercache WHERE
relfilenode::regclass::text ~ 'bmsql_';
count
--------
   0
(1 row)
```

2. It seems like no BenchmarkSQL tables are cached in memory. Let's also validate the heap_blks_read, heap_blks_hit from pg_statio_user_tables by taking bmsql_customer as a sample table:

```
benchmarksql=# SELECT heap_blks_read, heap_blks_hit FROM
pg_statio_user_tables WHERE relname = 'bmsql_customer';
heap_blks_read | heap_blks_hit
----------------+---------------
             0 |             0
(1 row)
```

3. Let's run an EXPLAIN ANALYZE along with the BUFFERS option on the bmsql_customer table and validate the results:

```
benchmarksql=# EXPLAIN (ANALYZE, BUFFERS) SELECT * FROM
  bmsql_customer ;
                                                   QUERY PLAN
-----------------------------------------------------------------
 Seq Scan on bmsql_customer   (cost=0.00..28211.00 rows=300000
   width=557) (actual time=39.086..3211.754 rows=300000 loops=1)
    Buffers: shared read=25211
 Planning time: 94.650 ms
 Execution time: 3232.508 ms
(4 rows)
```

4. From the preceding execution plan, we can see that all buffers are read from the disk and that no single buffer is read. This causes the query to take 3232.508 ms. Also, let's validate heap_blk_read, heap_blks_hit from the pg_statio_user_tables catalog view again:

```
benchmarksql=# SELECT heap_blks_read, heap_blks_hit FROM
  pg_statio_user_tables WHERE relname = 'bmsql_customer';
```

```
heap_blks_read | heap_blks_hit
----------------+----------------
         25211 |               0
(1 row)
```

The catalog view is also showing the number of heap blocks it read from the disk and the number of blocks it read from the buffers. In this case, there are no blocks read from the memory, this is the reason we have the `heap_blks_hit` value as 0.

This is a demonstration of cold cache behavior. During the cold cache, it is an expected behavior of getting slow response from a query.

Hot cache

Once PostgreSQL reads any table data from disk, then it keeps those buffers in the memory area called **shared buffers**. If we execute the same query again, then it tries to avoid the disk I/O by looking for the previous buffers in the memory. Let's check how many buffers there are in shared buffers for the `bmsql_customers` table using the following SQL statement:

```
benchmarksql=# SELECT COUNT(*) FROM pg_buffercache WHERE
relfilenode::regclass::text = 'bmsql_customer';
count
-------
32
(1 row)
```

It seems as if PostgreSQL keeps 32 blocks in shared buffers when the previous query was executed. Let's run the same explain analyze command to see how many buffers it is going to read from disk and how many buffers it is going to hit from the cache:

```
benchmarksql=# EXPLAIN (ANALYZE, BUFFERS) SELECT * FROM bmsql_customer;
QUERY PLAN
-----------------------------------------------------------------------
--------------------------------------------------------
Seq Scan on bmsql_customer   (cost=0.00..28211.00 rows=300000 width=557)
(actual time=0.034..92.899 rows=300000 loops=1)
Buffers: shared hit=32 read=25179
Planning time: 0.066 ms
Execution time: 111.866 ms
(4 rows)
```

From the preceding results, we read the 32 blocks from memory and the remaining blocks from disk or OS cache. As we read a few blocks from cache, the query performance has also increased significantly. These 32 allocated blocks in shared buffers will be refreshed with other table information by using the clock sweep algorithm.

By using the pg_prewarm extension we can also keep the whole table information in either shared buffers or at OS cache. Let's load the whole table into shared buffers, as shown in the following snippet, and let's see the query performance:

```
benchmarksql=# SELECT * FROM pg_prewarm('bmsql_customer', 'buffer');
pg_prewarm
------------
25211
(1 row)
benchmarksql=# SELECT COUNT(*) FROM pg_buffercache WHERE
relfilenode::regclass::text = 'bmsql_customer';
count
-------
16319
(1 row)
```

Using the pg_prewarm function, we loaded the whole table into shared buffers. That is, the total number of blocks 25211 are loaded into the shared buffers. But the pg_buffercache view is showing only 16319 blocks. The bmsql_customer table size is 25,211 * 8,192(block size) ~ 196MB and the amount of table that is loaded into the shared buffers is 16,319 *,8,192 ~ 127MB. That is approximately 65% of the table loaded into the shared buffers. Let's see the actual shared buffers setting the value as follows:

```
benchmarksql=# SHOW shared_buffers ;
shared_buffers
----------------
128MB
(1 row)
```

It seems as if we do not have enough shared buffers to hold the 196MB data and that is the reason why pg_prewarm has only loaded 127MB of the relation. Let's run the same explain query and see the query performance:

```
benchmarksql=# EXPLAIN (ANALYZE, BUFFERS) SELECT * FROM bmsql_customer ;
                                    QUERY PLAN
-----------------------------------------------------------------------------
-----------------------------------------------------------
 Seq Scan on bmsql_customer  (cost=0.00..28211.00 rows=300000 width=557)
(actual time=0.022..81.067 rows=300000 loops=1)
   Buffers: shared hit=16318 read=8893
 Planning time: 0.065 ms
```

```
Execution time: 100.300 ms
(4 rows)
```

From the preceding explain output, we hit 65% of table data, which is in memory and the rest of the data is read from disk or OS cache. As most of the data is in cache, we got a better query response time.

How it works...

As previously mentioned, whenever a query execution tries to fetch its required data then it looks for it in the buffers. If the required data is found, then it is a cache hit, otherwise it is a cache miss. Also, shared buffers will not keep all of its data permanently as it has a cache eviction policy based on clock sweep. Once cache is evicted from shared buffers then it goes to OS cache level from which queries try to fetch the data if data is not found in allocated shared buffers. PostgreSQL provides another extension called `pgfincore`, which provides information about OS cache.

> Refer to the following URL that has excellent information about pgfincore: `http://fibrevillage.com/database/128-postgresql-database-buffer-cache-and-os-cache`.

Clearing the cache

In this recipe, we will be discussing how to clean the cache from databases at operating system level.

Getting ready

In PostgreSQL, we do not have any predefined functionality to clear the cache from the memory. To clear the database level cache, we need to shut down the whole instance and to clear the operating system cache, we need to use the operating system utility commands.

> **TIP**
> Do not run any of the following operations in any production servers as it will cause production outage.

How to do it...

1. Let's load some sample data into the database cache by using the `pg_prewarm` function:

```
benchmarksql=# SELECT pg_prewarm('bmsql_customer', 'buffer');
pg_prewarm
------------
   25211
(1 row)
```

2. Let's validate whether we are able to hit the buffers, which are loaded using the `pg_prewarm` function:

```
benchmarksql=# EXPLAIN (ANALYZE, BUFFERS) SELECT * FROM
  bmsql_customer;
                                             QUERY PLAN
---------------------------------------------------------------------
-----------------------------------------------------
 Seq Scan on bmsql_customer  (cost=0.00..28211.00 rows=300000
 width=557) (actual time=0.013..65.337 rows=300000 loops=1)
  Buffers: shared hit=16101 read=9110
 Planning time: 204.910 ms
 Execution time: 83.123 ms
(4 rows)
```

3. As we have cached the `bmsql_customer` table data in buffers, we got the query response in `83 milliseconds`. If the data is not cached then the query could have taken more than `83 milliseconds`, which we are trying to reproduce by flushing all the shared buffers and OS cache. As previously mentioned, to clear the shared buffers, we do not have any predefined utility except instance shutdown. So let's shut down the PostgreSQL cluster to clear the database cache:

```
$ pg_ctl -D data stop -mf
waiting for server to shut down...... done
server stopped
```

4. To clear the operating system cache, we have to use OS utility commands as follows:

```
# sync
# echo 3 >/proc/sys/vm/drop_caches
```

5. As we cleared both the database and operating system cache, it is time to start the PostgreSQL instance to observe the cold cache behavior:

```
$ pg_ctl -D data start
server starting
```

6. Let's execute the preceding SQL command and see the query response time and cache hit ratio:

```
benchmarksql=# EXPLAIN (ANALYZE, BUFFERS) SELECT * FROM
bmsql_customer;
                                              QUERY PLAN
----------------------------------------------------------------------
--------------------------------------------------------------
    Seq Scan on bmsql_customer  (cost=0.00..28211.00 rows=300000
      width=557) (actual time=29.491..1451.221 rows=300000
        loops=1)
     Buffers: shared read=25211
    Planning time: 3.430 ms
    Execution time: 1488.079 ms
    (4 rows)
```

As expected with cold cache, the executed SQL statement read all its required blocks from disk rather from buffers. As it read from disk, the query response time is also increased when compared with the previous hot cache behavior.

How it works...

When we shut down the PostgreSQL instance, the postmaster process takes the responsibility of closing all the PostgreSQL background processes, besides cleaning the allocated shared buffers memory. The sync command does the flush, which writes all the modified memory blocks from the user space cache to respective data files and the echo 3 > /proc/sys/vm/drop_caches command drops most of the unused buffers without touching the modified buffers, which are in kernel cache. That is the reasons we used the sync command followed by drop_cache, which will clear both the modified and unmodified cached buffers.

There's more...

If any production maintenance activity is required for the system restart, and once the PostgreSQL is restarted and available for the application servers, then for a couple of hours we may hit performance problems due to cold cache behavior. To avoid these kinds of performance issues, it is recommended to load all the hot tables data into the shared buffers or operation system cache using the pg_prewarm function, during the maintenance window.

Query plan node structure

In this recipe, we will be discussing the explain plan tree structure.

Getting ready

PostgreSQL generates a set of plans before choosing an optimal plan that it is going to execute, based on the collected statistics about the relations. That is, the plan we are going to get when we use the EXPLAIN command along with the SQL statement is the optimal plan for that query. We also used EXPLAIN statements extensively on previous topics, and now we are going to understand the plan structure, and the significance of each value in it.

How to do it...

Let's run a basic EXPLAIN query and evaluate it as follows:

```
benchmarksql=# EXPLAIN SELECT * FROM bmsql_customer WHERE c_id=0;
                                   QUERY PLAN
    ----------------------------------------------------------------------
    ----------------------------
    Index Scan using bmsql_customer_pkey on bmsql_customer  (cost=0.42..7092.08
    rows=98 width=557)
    Index Cond: (c_id = 0)
    (2 rows)
```

In the preceding plan, we have only one node type called Index Scan on the given table and the scan is performed on is its primary key index.

The structure of the plan is a tree of node types and the leaf node always deals with accessing the data from the relations using different access methods. That is, by using sequential or index or bitmap index scans, PostgreSQL fetches the raw data from disk pages and feeds this raw data to its parent nodes such as nested loops, merge joins, hash joins, and so on. To demonstrate this, let's extend the preceding SQL query by adding a join condition as follows:

```
benchmarksql=# EXPLAIN SELECT * FROM bmsql_customer, bmsql_warehouse
WHERE c_id=0 AND c_w_id=w_id ORDER BY c_since;
                                        QUERY PLAN
------------------------------------------------------------------------
----------------------------------------
     Sort   (cost=6328.89..6329.14 rows=98 width=637)
       Sort Key: bmsql_customer.c_since
       ->  Nested Loop   (cost=0.42..6325.65 rows=98 width=637)
             ->  Seq Scan on bmsql_warehouse   (cost=0.00..1.10 rows=10
width=80)
             ->  Index Scan using bmsql_customer_pkey on bmsql_customer
(cost=0.42..632.36 rows=10 width=557)
                   Index Cond: ((c_w_id = bmsql_warehouse.w_id) AND (c_id =
0))
     (6 rows)
```

From the preceding example, the leaf node types are Index Scan, and Seq Scan and the parent node type is Nested Loop, which is a child node to the node type Sort. That is, the raw data that is fetched using different scans will feed to the parent node Sort, which returns the sorted output.

How it works...

As we discussed earlier, the PostgreSQL optimizer generates a set of plans for the submitted SQL and it will choose the optimal plan among them for the final execution. That is, from all the plans that are generated by the optimizer, it will only choose the plan that has the minimal cost value at the top most node type.

In the EXPLAIN text output format, each row defines a specific node type along with arbitrary cost values. In some cases, a node type can also be associated with labels such as Filter, Index Cond, and so on. From the preceding example, in the node type Index Scan we have cost values such as 0.42 ..632.36. Here, 0.42 defines the cost that is required to fetch the first raw record from the relation and 632.36 defines the cost that is needed to fetch the final record from the relation. From the preceding plan, rows=10 is an estimated number of values that we will be getting from the relation using the Index Condition c_w_id = bmsql_warehouse.w_id AND c_id =0. In the preceding plan, width=80 is an estimated average number of bytes that each row will be returning from the relation bmsql_customer. All these numbers are the arbitrary cost values, which PostgreSQL assumes. To track these actual timings, we have to use the ANALYZE option along with the EXPLAIN command as follows:

```
benchmarksql=# EXPLAIN ANALYZE SELECT * FROM bmsql_customer,
bmsql_warehouse WHERE c_id=0 AND c_w_id=w_id ORDER BY c_since;

QUERY PLAN
    ----------------------------------------------------------------------
    ----------------------------------------------------------------------
    ----
    Sort   (cost=6328.89..6329.14 rows=98 width=637) (actual
time=34.858..34.858 rows=0 loops=1)
        Sort Key: bmsql_customer.c_since
        Sort Method: quicksort  Memory: 25kB
        -> Nested Loop  (cost=0.42..6325.65 rows=98 width=637) (actual
time=34.853..34.853 rows=0 loops=1)
            -> Seq Scan on bmsql_warehouse  (cost=0.00..1.10 rows=10
width=80) (actual time=0.002..0.015 rows=10 loops=1)
            -> Index Scan using bmsql_customer_pkey on bmsql_customer
(cost=0.42..632.36 rows=10 width=557) (actual time=3.471..3.471 rows=0
loops=10)
                Index Cond: ((c_w_id = bmsql_warehouse.w_id) AND (c_id =
0))
    Planning time: 0.292 ms
    Execution time: 34.917 ms
(9 rows)
```

From the preceding results we can observe that each node type has additional information along with cost values. Here, actual time shows the time it took to process the records in milliseconds along with the actual number of rows it processed.

It is always recommended to run the `EXPLAIN ANALYZE` operation on any `DML` statements in a transaction. This is because `ANALYZE` actually runs the given SQL statement, which may affect the rows as per the `DELETE/INSERT/UPDATE` operations. If you do not want these changes to affect the database, then we can `ROLLBACK` the transaction after getting the execution plan for the statement.

Generating an explain plan

In this recipe, we will be discussing various supported formats of the `EXPLAIN` command.

Getting ready

The `EXPLAIN` command provides multiple formats of the plan output, which gives more flexibility in parsing the explain plan. In PostgreSQL 9.6, `EXPLAIN` supports the following formats:

- TEXT
- XML
- YAML
- JSON

How to do it...

1. Let's generate the XML formatted explain plan as follows:

```
benchmarksql=# EXPLAIN (FORMAT XML) SELECT * FROM bmsql_customer;
                    QUERY PLAN
-----------------------------------------------------------
<explain xmlns="http://www.postgresql.org/2009/explain">+
 <Query>                                                  +
  <Plan>                                                  +
    <Node-Type>Seq Scan</Node-Type>                       +
    <Relation-Name>bmsql_customer</Relation-Name>         +
    <Alias>bmsql_customer</Alias>                         +
    <Startup-Cost>0.00</Startup-Cost>                     +
    <Total-Cost>28218.00</Total-Cost>                     +
    <Plan-Rows>300000</Plan-Rows>                         +
    <Plan-Width>559</Plan-Width>                          +
```

```
      </Plan>                                    +
      </Query>                                   +
    </explain>
    (1 row)
```

2. Let's generate the YAML formatted explain plan as follows:

```
benchmarksql=# EXPLAIN(FORMAT YAML) SELECT * FROM bmsql_customer;
                QUERY PLAN
----------------------------------------
- Plan:                          +
    Node Type: "Seq Scan"        +
    Relation Name: "bmsql_customer"+
    Alias: "bmsql_customer"      +
    Startup Cost: 0.00           +
    Total Cost: 28218.00         +
    Plan Rows: 300000            +
    Plan Width: 559
  (1 row)
```

3. Let's generate the JSON formatted explain plan as follows:

```
benchmarksql=# EXPLAIN(FORMAT JSON) SELECT * FROM bmsql_customer;
                QUERY PLAN
----------------------------------------
    [                                        +
      {                                      +
        "Plan": {                            +
          "Node Type": "Seq Scan",           +
          "Relation Name": "bmsql_customer",+
          "Alias": "bmsql_customer",         +
          "Startup Cost": 0.00,              +
          "Total Cost": 28218.00,            +
          "Plan Rows": 300000,               +
          "Plan Width": 559                  +
        }                                    +
      }                                      +
    ]
    (1 row)
```

How it works...

All the previously mentioned approaches provide us with a way to parse the explain plan using the XML, YAML, or JSON libraries. By default, explain only provides a text tree node type structure where each node describes each specific node type.

There's more...

We can also generate and log the plan for each query automatically by using the `auto_explain` module. This extension logs the query along with its explain plan into the log files, which gives us information about what the plan was when the query took a long time to complete its execution. This extension also supports various formats, as we've discussed previously.

> Refer to the following URL for more information about the `auto_explain` extension: `https://www.postgresql.org/docs/9.6/static/auto-explain.html`.

Computing basic cost

In this recipe, we will be discussing how the optimizer chooses the optimal plan from the set of plans that it generates.

Getting ready

PostgreSQL generates a set of plans based on the optimizer attributes such as `enable_seqscan`, `enable_indexscan`, and so on. Among these generated sets of plans, PostgreSQL will only choose the plan that has the minimum cost value when compared with the other plans.

How to do it...

1. Let's generate a simple plan, as shown in the following snippet, and evaluate it:

```
benchmarksql=# SHOW seq_page_cost;
seq_page_cost
----------------
1
(1 row) benchmarksql=# EXPLAIN SELECT * FROM bmsql_customer;
                           QUERY PLAN
------------------------------------------------------------------
------

Seq Scan on bmsql_customer  (cost=0.00..28218.00 rows=300000
  width=559)
```

```
(1 row)
```

2. The numbers that we are seeing in the preceding plan are all arbitrary cost values. That is, assumed cost values to process the sequential scan on the whole table. Let's increase the optimizer cost setting seq_page_cost to 2.0 and see the same plan:

```
benchmarksql=# SET seq_page_cost TO 2;
SET
benchmarksql=# EXPLAIN SELECT * FROM bmsql_customer;
                         QUERY PLAN
------------------------------------------------------------------
------
 Seq Scan on bmsql_customer   (cost=0.00..53436.00 rows=300000
   width=559)
(1 row)
```

3. Let's extend the same example to the index scan and evaluate the cost values for it, as shown in the following snippet. To fetch required tuples from the table using an index, PostgreSQL needs to perform two different scans. One scan fetches the matching records from the index, and another scan fetches the required tuples from the table. The index scan cost calculation will include both cost calculations:

```
benchmarksql=# EXPLAIN SELECT * FROM bmsql_customer WHERE c_id = 1;
                              QUERY PLAN
------------------------------------------------------------------
------------------------------------------------
 Index Scan using bmsql_customer_pkey on bmsql_customer
 (cost=0.42..7096.24 rows=98 width=557)
   Index Cond: (c_id = 1)
(2 rows)
```

How it works...

From the preceding sequential, index scan examples, let us discuss how the optimizer chooses the cost values, and what are all the setting values it considers during the cost estimation are.

Sequential scan

1. From the previous sequential scan query, the optimizer returned the cost value as `53436`. Let us discuss how the optimizer calculates this value as follows:

```
benchmarksql=# SELECT reltuples, relpages FROM pg_class WHERE
relname='bmsql_customer';
reltuples | relpages
-----------+----------
300000 |    25218
(1 row)
```

2. The cost value `53436.00` was calculated based on the number of `relpages` along with the `cpu_tuple_cost`, `seq_page_cost` value. The default `cpu_tuple_cost` value is `0.01`, which is an estimated arbitrary cost value to fetch each tuple from the `relpages`. The sequential scan cost value will be calculated as `relpages*seq_page_cost + cpu_tuple_cost*reltuples` and the evaluation for it is as follows:

```
benchmarksql=# SELECT (25218*2 + 0.01*300000) seq_scan_cost;
seq_scan_cost
----------------
53436.00
(1 row)
```

3. Let's add a predicate and evaluate the cost value to the same SQL query:

```
benchmarksql=# EXPLAIN SELECT * FROM bmsql_customer WHERE
c_city = 'San Mateo';
                          QUERY PLAN
-----------------------------------------------------------------

Seq Scan on bmsql_customer  (cost=0.00..54186.00 rows=9 width=559)
Filter: ((c_city)::text = 'San Mateo'::text)
(2 rows)
```

4. From the preceding plan, the cost `54186.00` was calculated using
   `relpages*seq_page_cost + cpu_tuple_cost*reltuples + cpu_operator_cost*reltuples`. The default value of the
   `cpu_operator_cost` parameter is `0.0025`, which is an estimated abstract cost
   value to compare single tuple with the string `San Mateo`. The following is a
   pictorial representation of this sequential scan cost estimation:

```
bmsql_customer

Tuple 300000    Page 25218

Tuple 285547    Page 25217

                ...
                ...
                ...
                ...
                ...
                ...

                Page 2

Tuple 100       Page 1

Tuple 2
Tuple 1
```

Total page visting cost	2 * 25218	= 50436
Total tuple visiting cost	0.01 * 300000	= 3000
Total predicate checking cost	0.0025 * 300000 =	750
Total estimated cost for seq scan	SUM (50436, 3000, 750) =	54186

Index scan

The index scan calculation is not straightforward like a sequential scan cost calculation. As
we've discussed previously, an index scan cost calculation has two phases.

Phase I

In this phase, it will only calculate the cost that is required to process the index pages. In PostgreSQL, this will be calculated using the internal functions that are stored in the `pg_am` catalog. For each type of an index, there is an individual cost calculator. Let's find out what index cost calculators are available in PostgreSQL 9.6 using the following SQL query:

```
benchmarksql=# SELECT amname, amcostestimate FROM pg_am;
 amname  |  amcostestimate
---------+------------------
 btree   | btcostestimate
 hash    | hashcostestimate
 gist    | gistcostestimate
 gin     | gincostestimate
 spgist  | spgcostestimate
 brin    | brincostestimate
(6 rows)
```

For the preceding index scan example, the `btcostestimate` method will be used to find the cost to read the index pages. This method will consider `random_page_cost`, `cpu_index_tuple_cost`, the height of the index tree, and the arbitrary cost of each `WHERE` clause condition in estimating the index tuple scan cost.

Phase II

In this phase, it will verify few aspects before fetching the data from the actual table. That is, the optimizer verifies whether the table order is similar to an index order. If the order is not similar, then PostgreSQL prefers to fetch the pages randomly, which automatically increases the cost value. If the order is similar (`CLUSTER` table), then PostgreSQL prefers to fetch the pages sequentially, which costs less. If the table is partially ordered, then PostgreSQL chooses an average cost from the preceding two cost values. If the index scan is an Index Only Scan type, then it will add different cost levels for this node type. In Index Only Scans, PostgreSQL does not need to visit the actual table `relpages`. To calculate the cost for this phase, the optimizer needs table `relpages`, `index relpages`, and `effective_cache_size` values.

Running sequential scans

In this recipe, we will be discussing sequential scans.

Getting ready

Sequential scans are a mechanism, and PostgreSQL tries to read each tuple from the relation. The best example for the sequential scan is reading an entire table without any predicate. Sequential scans are always preferred over index scans, when a query is reading most of the data from the table, which will avoid the index lookup overhead.

Reading pages in sequential order takes less effort when compared with reading pages in random order. This is because, in sequential file reading, we do not need to set the file pointer to any specific location. However, during the index scan, PostgreSQL needs to read random pages from the file as per the index results. That is, during the index scan we move the file read pointer to multiple pages. This is the reason why the arbitrary cost parameter seq_page_cost value 1 is always less than the random_page_cost value 4.

How to do it...

1. Let's run a query that reads the complete table as follows:

```
benchmarksql=# EXPLAIN SELECT * FROM bmsql_customer;
                          QUERY PLAN
-------------------------------------------------------------------
 Seq Scan on bmsql_customer  (cost=0.00..28218.00 rows=300000
   width=559)
(1 row)
```

2. As expected, the preceding query went to perform the full table sequential scan. Let's add a predicate to the preceding query and see the execution plan:

```
benchmarksql=# EXPLAIN SELECT * FROM bmsql_customer WHERE
  c_city = 'San Mateo';
                          QUERY PLAN
-------------------------------------------------------------------
 Bitmap Heap Scan on bmsql_customer  (cost=4.49..40.09 rows=9
   width=559)
 Recheck Cond: ((c_city)::text = 'San Mateo'::text)
 ->  Bitmap Index Scan on city_idx  (cost=0.00..4.49 rows=9
   width=0)
      Index Cond: ((c_city)::text = 'San Mateo'::text)
(4 rows)
```

3. As we are only fetching the `San Mateo` city records from the `bmsql_customer` table, the optimizer decided to go with an index scan rather than a sequential scan. Let's force this query to take a sequential scan over an index scan, by increasing the `random_page_cost` value to some higher number:

```
benchmarksql=# SET random_page_cost TO 10000;
SET
benchmarksql=# EXPLAIN SELECT * FROM bmsql_customer WHERE
  c_city =    'San Mateo';
                          QUERY PLAN
---------------------------------------------------------------
-----
Seq Scan on bmsql_customer   (cost=0.00..28961.00 rows=9
  width=557)
 Filter:  ((c_city)::text = 'San Mateo'::text)
(2 rows)
```

From the preceding plan, the cost of a sequential scan is `28961` and the cost of a previous index scan is `40.09`. That is the reason why the optimizer chooses the index scan over the sequential scan. This is the plan we will be getting, if we do not have an index on the `c_city` column.

How it works...

Once the plan is generated for the submitted SQL query, then Postgres will start executing the plan node types. Sequential scans will try to fetch each heap tuple from the relation, by checking each given predicate in the SQL query, and it will update the number of tuples it reads from the relation. Once a sequential scan completes getting the whole matching records from the table, then postgres tries to keep the tuples in the shared buffers by storing the number of tuples it processed in catalog tables. A simple pictorial representation of a sequential scan is as follows:

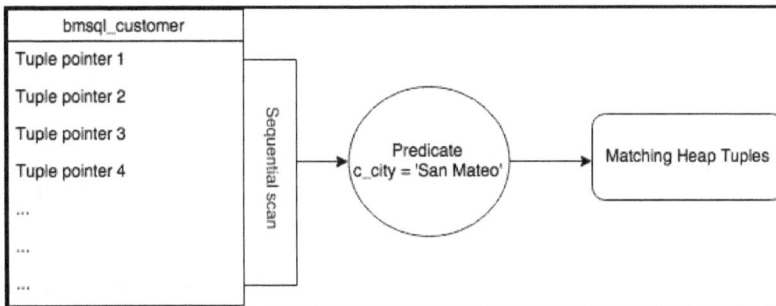

Running bitmap heap and index scan

In this recipe, we will be discussing bitmap heap scans and index scans.

Getting ready

PostgreSQL does not support creating bitmap indexes on tables. However, it will generate bitmap pages while scanning the index, which will be utilized during the table scan. PostgreSQL does not generate bitmap pages for every index scan, and it will only generate them if the number of fetching rows from the query is high enough. This bitmap page is unique to each query execution, and the scope of the bitmap page is the end of the query execution.

Bitmap heap scans will always be the parent node type to the bitmap index scan, which takes the bitmap pages as an input, and sorts the index pages as the physical table page order, and then fetches the tuples from the relation.

How to do it...

1. For demonstration purposes, let's consider the following example, which generates the bitmap heap scan:

```
benchmarksql=# EXPLAIN SELECT * FROM bmsql_customer WHERE
c_city = 'San Mateo';
                          QUERY PLAN
-----------------------------------------------------------------
------
 Bitmap Heap Scan on bmsql_customer  (cost=4.49..40.09 rows=9
   width=559)
   Recheck Cond: ((c_city)::text = 'San Mateo'::text)
   ->  Bitmap Index Scan on city_idx  (cost=0.00..4.49 rows=9
   width=0)
         Index Cond: ((c_city)::text = 'San Mateo'::text)
(4 rows)
```

2. From the preceding plan, the optimizer is expected to fetch 9 rows for the city San Mateo from the index. Let's add the ANALYZE option for the preceding plan, and see how many rows we will be getting in the final result:

```
benchmarksql=# EXPLAIN ANALYZE SELECT * FROM bmsql_customer
WHERE c_city = 'San Mateo';
```

```
                                                    QUERY PLAN
-------------------------------------------------------------------
---------------------------------------------------------
Bitmap Heap Scan on bmsql_customer   (cost=4.49..40.09 rows=9
  width=559)
(actual time=4.243..4.243 rows=0 loops=1)
Recheck Cond: ((c_city)::text = 'San Mateo'::text)
-> Bitmap Index Scan on city_idx   (cost=0.00..4.49 rows=9
  width=0)
(actual time=4.239..4.239 rows=0 loops=1)
      Index Cond: ((c_city)::text = 'San Mateo'::text)
Planning time: 0.092 ms
Execution time: 4.278 ms
(6 rows)
```

3. From the preceding results, the bmsql_customer table does not have any rows where the city belongs to San Mateo. But the estimated number of rows is calculated as 9 and the actual number of rows we have is 0. If PostgreSQL does not have enough statistical information, then we can expect these kinds of estimation mismatches. Let's increase the default_statistics_target to its maximum, and run the same query:

```
benchmarksql=# SET default_statistics_target TO 10000;
SET
benchmarksql=# ANALYZE bmsql_customer ;
ANALYZE
benchmarksql=# EXPLAIN SELECT * FROM bmsql_customer WHERE
c_city = 'San Mateo';
                                  QUERY PLAN
-------------------------------------------------------------------

Index Scan using city_idx on bmsql_customer   (cost=0.42..28.53
  rows=6
width=558)
Index Cond: ((c_city)::text = 'San Mateo'::text)
(2 rows)
```

4. From the preceding demonstration, after increasing the statistics limit value, the optimizer chooses the Index Scan over the Bitmap Index Scan node type. This is because there are not enough estimated tuples to build the bitmap pages.

> It is not recommended to set the default_statistics_target value to its maximum as the analyze operation will take more time to generate the statistics for each table. Also, it will increase the time to generate the execution plan of the query.

How it works...

For demonstration purposes, let's add another predicate to the preceding SQL query, and see the explain plan:

```
benchmarksql=# EXPLAIN SELECT * FROM bmsql_customer WHERE c_city = 'San
Mateo' or c_city='San Francisco';
                                              QUERY PLAN
-------------------------------------------------------------------------
-----------------------
Bitmap Heap Scan on bmsql_customer  (cost=8.94..56.34 rows=12 width=558)
Recheck Cond: (((c_city)::text = 'San Mateo'::text) OR ((c_city)::text =
'San Francisco'::text))
->  BitmapOr  (cost=8.94..8.94 rows=12 width=0)
->  Bitmap Index Scan on city_idx  (cost=0.00..4.47 rows=6 width=0)
Index Cond: ((c_city)::text = 'San Mateo'::text)
->  Bitmap Index Scan on city_idx  (cost=0.00..4.47 rows=6 width=0)
Index Cond: ((c_city)::text = 'San Francisco'::text)
(7 rows)
```

In the preceding example, we are fetching all the customer information whose city is either San Mateo or San Francisco. As per the preceding plan, the optimizer has generated two bitmap pages for each city from the `city_idx` index. And these two bitmap pages are merged using the `BitmapOr` operation, and the result is forwarded to the bitmap heap scan.

Once the bitmap index is created, the bitmap heap scan will perform sorting on the bitmap page, and then fetch the records from the relation in the sequential order. In the preceding example, the optimizer has created two bitmap pages for each city, and we can limit this number by using the IN operator. The bitmap heap scan cost is indirectly proportional to the number of bitmap pages. Let's observe the following query, which retrieves similar results to the previous example:

```
benchmarksql=# EXPLAIN SELECT * FROM bmsql_customer WHERE c_city IN
('San Mateo','San Francisco');
                                              QUERY PLAN
-------------------------------------------------------------------------
----------------
    Bitmap Heap Scan on bmsql_customer  (cost=8.94..56.30 rows=12
width=558)
        Recheck Cond: ((c_city)::text = ANY ('{"San Mateo","San
Francisco"}'::text[]))
        ->  Bitmap Index Scan on city_idx  (cost=0.00..8.94 rows=12 width=0)
            Index Cond: ((c_city)::text = ANY ('{"San Mateo","San
Francisco"}'::text[]))
    (4 rows)
```

The following is a sample pictorial representation of a bitmap heap scan:

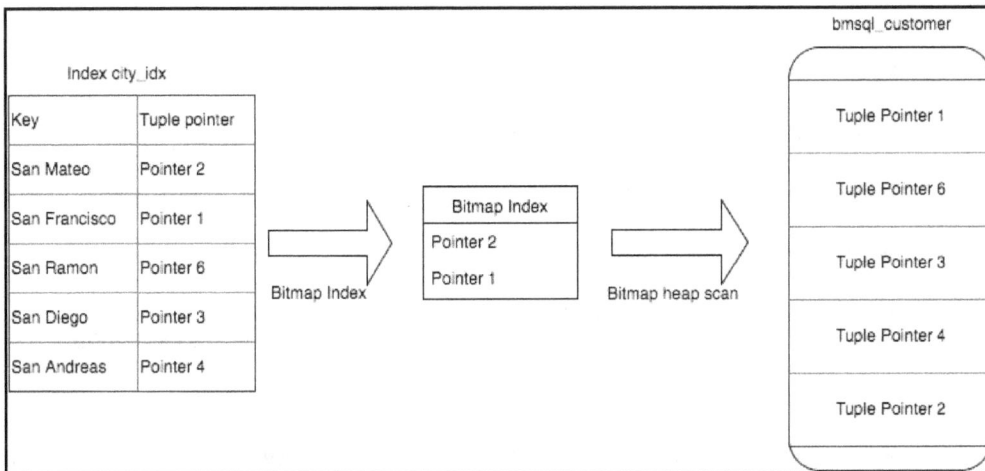

As illustrated in the preceding figure, the index will be scanned to generate a bitmap index in buffers. Later, the generated bitmap index will be used to fetch the required tuples from the table.

Aggregate and hash aggregate

In this recipe, we will be discussing aggregate and hash aggregate mechanisms in PostgreSQL.

Getting ready

Aggregate is a node type that only evaluates the aggregate operators. Some of the aggregate operators are SUM, MIN, MAX, and so on.

Hash aggregate is a node type that requires an aggregate operator, and a group key column. In general, we see this node type being utilized during the GROUP BY, DISTINCT, or set operations.

How to do it...

Aggregate

1. To demonstrate the aggregates behavior, let's query the `benchmarsql` as follows:

```
benchmarksql=# EXPLAIN SELECT max(i_price) FROM bmsql_item;
                         QUERY PLAN
-----------------------------------------------------------------
-----

 Aggregate  (cost=2549.00..2549.01 rows=1 width=6)
   ->  Seq Scan on bmsql_item  (cost=0.00..2299.00 rows=100000
      width=6)
 (2 rows)
```

2. From the preceding plan, as expected we got the aggregate node type, which is followed by a full table sequential scan. PostgreSQL will also choose different node types for the aggregate operators, when it can produce the result in less time. Let's create an ordered index on the `i_price` column, and see the execution plan for the same query:

```
benchmarksql=# CREATE INDEX pric_idx ON bmsql_item(i_price
  DESC);
CREATE INDEX
benchmarksql=# EXPLAIN SELECT max(i_price) FROM bmsql_item;
                                         QUERY PLAN
-----------------------------------------------------------------
------------------------------------
 Result  (cost=0.32..0.33 rows=1 width=0)
 InitPlan 1 (returns $0)
   ->  Limit  (cost=0.29..0.32 rows=1 width=6)
         ->  Index Only Scan using pric_idx on bmsql_item
  (cost=0.29..2854.29 rows=100000 width=6)
               Index Cond: (i_price IS NOT NULL)
 (5 rows)
```

3. As we created the index on the column `i_price` in descending order, the index's first value will always be the maximum, and the last value will be the minimum value. This is the reason why the preceding query took `Index Only Scan` as it is needed to fetch only one tuple from the index. Let's change the same query to fetch the minimum price item, and evaluate the execution plan:

```
benchmarksql=# EXPLAIN SELECT min(i_price) FROM bmsql_item;
                                         QUERY PLAN
```

```
--------------------------------------------------------------------
----------------------------------------------------
    Result   (cost=0.32..0.33 rows=1 width=0)
    InitPlan 1 (returns $0)
      -> Limit   (cost=0.29..0.32 rows=1 width=6)
          ->   Index Only Scan Backward using pric_idx on
    bmsql_item   (cost=0.29..2854.29 rows=100000 width=6)
                  Index Cond: (i_price IS NOT NULL)
    (5 rows)
```

4. From the preceding plan, the index scan is performed backwards to fetch the minimum value from the index, since the index is created in descending order. If we run both the max and min operations in a single query, then we will be getting both the forward and backward index scans in a single execution path.

Hash aggregate

1. To demonstrate the hash aggregate behavior, let's query benchmarksql as follows:

```
benchmarksql=# EXPLAIN SELECT COUNT(*), c_zip FROM
    bmsql_customer GROUP BY c_zip;
                                    QUERY PLAN
--------------------------------------------------------------------
-----------
    HashAggregate   (cost=29718.00..29817.39 rows=9939 width=10)
    Group Key: c_zip
      ->   Seq Scan on bmsql_customer   (cost=0.00..28218.00
        rows=300000 width=10)
    (3 rows)
```

2. In the preceding example, we have mentioned the GROUP BY operation in the SQL, which makes the optimizer choose one of the aggregate strategies. In the preceding plan, the optimizer chooses the HashAggregate node type to evaluate the data set. PostgreSQL will also prefer another approach called GroupAggregate, which requires the input data set to be sorted. Let's observe the following SQL statements:

```
benchmarksql=# CREATE INDEX zip_idx ON bmsql_customer(c_zip);
CREATE INDEX
benchmarksql=# EXPLAIN SELECT COUNT(*), c_zip FROM
    bmsql_customer GROUP BY c_zip;
                                    QUERY PLAN
--------------------------------------------------------------------
```

```
-------------------------------
        GroupAggregate   (cost=0.42..10731.97 rows=9955 width=10)
          Group Key: c_zip
           ->  Index Only Scan using zip_idx on bmsql_customer
              (cost=0.42..9132.42 rows=300000 width=10)
          (3 rows)
```

As we created an index on the c_zip column, PostgreSQL prefers the group aggregate over hash aggregates, which only needs the index scan. In hash aggregates, the optimizer is needed to do the full table scan, and memory is also required to build the hash table.

How it works...

Aggregate

In PostgreSQL, aggregates are implemented based on multiple state transition functions. We can fetch these functions for each aggregate operator by querying the pg_aggregate catalog table. As we used MAX aggregate functions in the previous example, let's get the internal transition state functions for this operator:

```
postgres=# SELECT * FROM pg_aggregate WHERE aggfnoid::text ~ 'max'
    LIMIT 1;
-[ RECORD 1 ]----+--------------------
aggfnoid         | pg_catalog.max
aggkind          | n
aggnumdirectargs | 0
aggtransfn       | int8larger
aggfinalfn       | -
aggmtransfn      | -
aggminvtransfn   | -
aggmfinalfn      | -
aggfinalextra    | f
aggmfinalextra   | f
aggsortop        | 413
aggtranstype     | 20
aggtransspace    | 0
aggmtranstype    | 0
aggmtransspace   | 0
agginitval       |
aggminitval      |
```

From the preceding output, the transition function for the MAX aggregate is `int8larger`, and there is no final state transition function for this aggregate.

State transition functions

To perform any aggregate operation, a set of transition state functions is required. Let's discuss the MAX aggregate function behavior. To find the maximum record in this column, PostgreSQL needs to fetch each tuple and it needs to compare it with its previous tuple value. If the recent fetched tuple value is bigger than the previous tuple, then it will change the maximum value with the latest tuple. This process will repeat until there are no more tuples to fetch. On this iteration process, the maximum value state will keep on changing as per the latest maximum value. That's why we call these functions state transition functions. Each aggregate function will have a unique set of state transition functions.

Some aggregate functions need another state transition function called final state function, to complete its aggregate operation. The best example for these kind of aggregates is AVG. Let's get the AVG transition functions from the `pg_aggregate` table:

```
postgres=# SELECT * FROM pg_aggregate WHERE aggfnoid::text ~ 'avg'
   LIMIT 1;
-[ RECORD 1 ]----+--------------------
aggfnoid          | pg_catalog.avg
aggkind           | n
aggnumdirectargs  | 0
aggtransfn        | int8_avg_accum
aggfinalfn        | numeric_poly_avg
aggmtransfn       | int8_avg_accum
aggminvtransfn    | int8_avg_accum_inv
aggmfinalfn       | numeric_poly_avg
aggfinalextra     | f
aggmfinalextra    | f
aggsortop         | 0
aggtranstype      | 2281
aggtransspace     | 48
aggmtranstype     | 2281
aggmtransspace    | 48
agginitval        |
aggminitval       |
```

From the preceding results, the final state transition is associated with the `numeric_poly_avg` internal function. This function will be using the results from the state transition function `int8_avg_accum`, which is implemented as return the sum of all tuple values and the count of tuples it is processed. This sum and count information will be used in the `numeric_poly_avg` function to find the final average value as sum divided by count. These transition functions will also serve for the moving aggregates. Moving aggregates are nothing but aggregate operators using window functions. An example of moving aggregates is as follows:

```
benchmarksql=# EXPLAIN SELECT c_zip, COUNT(*) OVER(PARTITION BY
    c_zip) FROM bmsql_customer;
                                    QUERY PLAN
--------------------------------------------------------------------
----------------------------
    WindowAgg  (cost=0.42..13632.42 rows=300000 width=10)
      ->  Index Only Scan using zip_idx on bmsql_customer
        (cost=0.42..9132.42 rows=300000 width=10)
    (2 rows)
```

The MAX aggregate function does not need the final state transition function, as it is not needed to track the number of tuples it processed. That's why the aggregate functions such as MAX, MIN, SUM, COUNT, and so on will have an `aggfinalfn` column value as empty.

> Refer to the following documentation for more information about aggregate behavior: `https://www.postgresql.org/docs/9.6/static/sql-createaggregate.html`.

Hash aggregates

During hash aggregates, PostgreSQL will build a hash table with the given group key columns list. Once the hash table is prepared, then the state transition functions will be executed for each bucket and they will return all the buckets aggregate information. To build this hash table, PostgreSQL will utilize the `work_mem` memory area. If it does not find enough memory to keep this hash table, then the optimizer prefers the group aggregate node type.

Running CTE scan

In this recipe, we will be discussing **CTE (Common Table Expression)** scans.

Getting ready

CTEs are the named inline queries, which we define using the WITH clause, and they can be used multiple times in the same query. We can also implement recursive/DML queries using CTEs. CTE improves the query readability when compared with inline sub queries. CTE also provide the RECURSIVE option, which takes the usage of CTE to another level. Using recursive CTE statements, we can build hierarchical SQL queries where the SQL execution refers to its own results for further processing.

How to do it...

1. Let's get all the costly products from the sample dataset as follows:

```
benchmarksql=# EXPLAIN WITH costly_products AS (
SELECT i_name FROM bmsql_item WHERE i_price BETWEEN 10 AND 100
) SELECT * FROM costly_products;
                                QUERY PLAN
-----------------------------------------------------------------
------------------
CTE Scan on costly_products   (cost=2799.00..4619.68 rows=91034
   width=40)
CTE costly_products
  ->  Seq Scan on bmsql_item   (cost=0.00..2799.00 rows=91034
    width=26)
          Filter: ((i_price >= '10'::numeric) AND (i_price <=
            '100'::numeric))
(4 rows)
```

2. The preceding sample query actually does not require the CTE usage; however, for demonstration purposes we've divided the SQL query into two subsections, where one section gets all the data from the base tables, and another one just scans and returns the records that it got from the previous node type. We can also create multiple CTE expressions in the same SQL statement as comma separated expressions. We can use all these CTEs as a regular table joins, as shown in the following example:

```
postgres=# WITH costly_products AS (
SELECT i_name FROM bmsql_item WHERE i_price BETWEEN 10 AND 100
  ),
not_costly_products AS (
SELECT i_name FROM bmsql_item WHERE i_price BETWEEN 1 AND 9)
SELECT COUNT(*), 'costly products' FROM costly_products
UNION
```

```
SELECT COUNT(*), 'not costly products' FROM not_costly_products;
count | ?column?
-------+--------------------
8018 | not costly products
90986 | costly products
(2 rows)
```

3. By using CTEs, we can implement recursive queries that keep processing the data recursively, until the given predicate satisfies. Let's see the following sample example, which produces the recursive output:

```
postgres=# WITH RECURSIVE recur(i) AS (SELECT 1 UNION SELECT
  i+1 FROM recur WHERE i<5) SELECT * FROM recur;
t
---
1
2
3
4
5
(5 rows)
```

From the preceding example, we just returned the numbers from 1 to 5 without using the PostgreSQL `generate_series` function.

How it works...

Let us discuss how CTE scan and recursive union works in PostgreSQL:

CTE scan

We can assume that CTEs are like in-memory temporary tables, which will be created based on the given expression. Once this in-memory table is created, it will be scanned multiple times as per their usage in the SQL statement. To create this in-memory table, PostgreSQL uses the `work_mem` area, and the scope of this table is the end of the query execution.

As we discussed previously, CTEs improves the query readability, and at the same time it has its own limitations too. At this moment, CTEs are called optimizer fences. That is, CTEs can't be rewritten as like the inline sub queries. Let's see the following example, where optimizer fails to rewrite the SQL:

```
benchmarksql=# EXPLAIN ANALYZE WITH costly_products AS (
SELECT i_name,i_price FROM bmsql_item
```

```
) SELECT * FROM costly_products WHERE i_price BETWEEN 10 AND 100 ;
                                                     QUERY PLAN
--------------------------------------------------------------------
-----------------------------------------------------
    CTE Scan on costly_products   (cost=2299.00..4799.00 rows=500
      width=40) (actual time=0.026..174.884 rows=90991 loops=1)
       Filter: ((i_price >= '10'::numeric) AND (i_price <=
         '100'::numeric))
      Rows Removed by Filter: 9009
      CTE costly_products
        ->  Seq Scan on bmsql_item   (cost=0.00..2299.00 rows=100000
          width=26) (actual time=0.011..37.172 rows=100000 loops=1)
   Planning time: 0.160 ms
   Execution time: 199.404 ms
  (7 rows)
  Time: 200.127 ms
```

From the preceding plan, the given predicate is applied on the `costy_products` CTE. That is, after populating the whole `bmsql_item` table into the memory, the planner is applying the given predicate. Let's observe the following SQL plan, which is written using the inline query, which produces the same results:

```
benchmarksql=# EXPLAIN ANALYZE SELECT * FROM (SELECT i_name,
   i_price FROM bmsql_item) as costly_products WHERE i_price BETWEEN
     10 AND 100 ;
                                              QUERY PLAN
--------------------------------------------------------------------
-------------------------------------------------
    Seq Scan on bmsql_item   (cost=0.00..2799.00 rows=91177 width=26)
      (actual time=0.011..79.378 rows=90991 loops=1)
         Filter: ((i_price >= '10'::numeric) AND (i_price <=
           '100'::numeric))
      Rows Removed by Filter: 9009
   Planning time: 0.340 ms
   Execution time: 85.402 ms
  (5 rows)
  Time: 86.286 ms
```

From the preceding plan, the same behavior is rewritten by the optimizer as the outer query predicate is moved to its inline subquery. That is, during the tuple fetch operation itself, the planner is filter rows. That's why we got the better query response time for this inline sub query.

Recursive union

This is the node type optimizer that is chosen when dealing with CTE recursive queries. The way we should write the recursive queries is as follows:

```
WITH RECURSIVE recur AS (
    Initial values for the recursive statements
UNION
    Recursive statements which runs until the condition satisfies
)
SELECT * FROM recur;
```

To process this `recursive union` operation, this node type needs two temporary tables. One is an intermediate table, and the other one is a work table. The work table will initially assign with the recursive statements initial values. By using this work table, this node type generates an intermediate table, and appends intermediate table results into the work table again. This process will keep executing until the intermediate table result is empty. Once the intermediate table has no entries to append to the work table, this node type returns the work table as a final result. For example, let's see the following example, which demonstrates the work flow of recursive queries:

```
WITH RECURSIVE recur(i) AS (
SELECT 1
UNION
SELECT i+1 FROM recur WHERE i<5) SELECT * FROM recur;
```

Loop count	Work Table	Intermediate Table
1	i = 1	1 < 5 Condition true i = i + 1 i = 2
	1 2	Append to work table
2	1 2	2 < 5 Condition true i = i + 1 i = 3
	1 2 3	Append to work table
3	1 2 3	3 < 5 Condition true i = i + 1 i = 4
	1 2 3 4	Append to work table
4	1 2 3 4	4 < 5 Condition true i = i +1 i = 5
	1 2 3 4 5	Append to work table
5	1 2 3 4 5	5 < 5 Condition fail

Let's observe the following explain plan for the same query:

```
benchmarksql=# EXPLAIN ANALYZE WITH RECURSIVE recur(i) AS (SELECT 1
UNION SELECT i+1 FROM recur WHERE i<5) SELECT * FROM recur;
                                                        QUERY PLAN
    -----------------------------------------------------------------

    ------------------------------------------------------
    CTE Scan on recur   (cost=2.95..3.57 rows=31 width=4) (actual
time=0.010..0.037 rows=5 loops=1)
        CTE recur
          ->  Recursive Union   (cost=0.00..2.95 rows=31 width=4) (actual
time=0.006..0.031 rows=5 loops=1)
                ->  Result   (cost=0.00..0.01 rows=1 width=0) (actual
time=0.001..0.002 rows=1 loops=1)
                ->  WorkTable Scan on recur recur_1   (cost=0.00..0.23 rows=3
width=4) (actual time=0.002..0.003 rows=1 loops=5)
                      Filter: (i < 5)
                      Rows Removed by Filter: 0
    Planning time: 0.108 ms
    Execution time: 0.088 ms
    (9 rows)
    Time: 0.736 ms
```

From the preceding plan, the `WorkTable Scan` node type went through a five loop count, as shown in the preceding snippet. Like CTE, there are also limitations in recursive queries. Recursive queries do not allow us to use any aggregate functions in the recursive statements.

Nesting loops

In this recipe, we will be discussing the nesting loops mechanism in PostgreSQL.

Getting ready

Nesting loops is one of the table joining mechanisms, in which PostgreSQL prefers to join two different datasets based on a join condition. The name itself describes the nesting loops as a loop inside another loop. The outer loop holds a dataset and compares each tuple with the dataset that holds an inner loop. That is, if the outer loop has N number of tuples and the inner loop has M number of tuples, then the nested loop performs $N * M$ number of comparisons to produce the output.

How to do it...

1. For demonstrating the nesting loops, let's run a join query at `benchmarksql` to retrieve the list of warehouse names along with the customer name that got the product from that warehouse:

```
benchmarksql=# EXPLAIN SELECT w_name, c_first FROM bmsql_warehouse,
    bmsql_customer WHERE w_id=c_w_id;
                                                    QUERY PLAN
---------------------------------------------------------------------
-----------------------------------------------
 Nested Loop  (cost=0.42..13743.32 rows=300000 width=21)
    ->  Seq Scan on bmsql_warehouse  (cost=0.00..1.10 rows=10
       width=12)
    ->  Index Only Scan using bmsql_customer_idx1 on bmsql_customer
       (cost=0.42..1074.22 rows=30000 width=17)
          Index Cond: (c_w_id = bmsql_warehouse.w_id)
 (4 rows)
```

2. It seems that the optimizer chooses the nested loops mechanism to join these two tables based on the available statistics of these two relations. From the preceding explain plan, the `Seq Scan` node type is an outer loop and the Index Only Scan is an inner loop. That is, the inner loop Index Only Scan will be executed for each tuple that it read from the `Seq Scan` node type. From the preceding plan, the estimated number of tuples from `Seq Scan` is `10`. So the Index Only Scan will be executed 10 times. To confirm these loop counts, let's add the `ANALYZE` operation along with `EXPLAIN` as follows:

```
benchmarksql=# EXPLAIN ANALYZE SELECT w_name,c_first FROM
    bmsql_warehouse, bmsql_customer WHERE w_id=c_w_id;

QUERY PLAN
---------------------------------------------------------------------
---------------------------------------------------------------------
-----------------
 Nested Loop  (cost=0.42..13743.32 rows=300000 width=21) (actual
    time=0.039..165.479 rows=300000 loops=1)
    ->  Seq Scan on bmsql_warehouse  (cost=0.00..1.10 rows=10 width=12)
       (actual time=0.004..0.016 rows=10loops=1)
    ->  Index Only Scan using bmsql_customer_idx1 on bmsql_customer
       (cost=0.42..1074.22 rows=30000 width=17) (actual
       time=0.016..10.889 rows=30000loops=10)
          Index Cond: (c_w_id = bmsql_warehouse.w_id)
          Heap Fetches: 0
 Planning time: 0.374 ms
```

```
Execution time: 182.885 ms
(7 rows)
```

From the preceding results, as expected the inner loop Index Only Scan is executed 10 times, as the number of tuples in outer loop is 10. From the preceding results, the `Heap Fetches: 0` defines how many tuples the Index Only Scan needed to fetch data from the relation, when the planner doesn't find enough information from the table's visibility map file.

How it works...

To understand the nested loop behavior, let's divide the work that it is doing in two phases.

Phase I

Let's name this phase as an outer loop phase. From the preceding explain plan, we can find this node type as an immediate follower of the nested loop node type, and from the preceding plan it is Seq Scan. In this section, it reads the `bmsql_warehouse` table using a sequential scan and it fetched 10 rows.

Phase II

Let's name this phase as an inner loop. In the explain plan, we can find this node type as an immediate follower of the outer loop section, and from the preceding plan it is an Index Only Scan. In this section, it will take rows one by one from the outer section and compare it with the `bmsql_customer_idx1` index, and produce the matching rows.

The following is a pictorial representation of these phases:

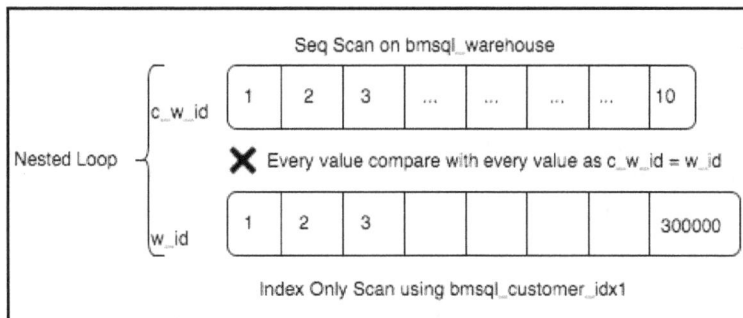

Now you might have a question such as why does the planner choose `bmsql_warehouse` as an outer loop section, and what causes the `bmsql_customer` table to be chosen as an inner loop section? If you are assuming that the reason for this is that `bmsql_warehouse` has fewer rows when compared to the `bmsql_customer` table, then your assumption is not correct. To justify this, let's observe the following example:

```
benchmarksql=# EXPLAIN SELECT * FROM test t1, test2 t2 WHERE t1.t=t2.t;
                                   QUERY PLAN
--------------------------------------------------------------------------------
---------------
   Nested Loop  (cost=0.14..18455.00 rows=109 width=8)
      ->  Seq Scan on test t1  (cost=0.00..1443.00 rows=100000 width=4)
      ->  Index Only Scan using test2_idx on test2 t2  (cost=0.14..0.16
 rows=1 width=4)
            Index Cond: (t = t1.t)
   (4 rows)
```

From the preceding example, the planner chooses the table that has a high estimated number of rows as the outer loop dataset, and the table that has a lower estimated number of rows as the inner loop. The reason behind choosing the `test2` table as the inner loop is the index on that table. PostgreSQL planner always prefers to perform its inner loop section with an index scan if possible; this will improve the data access speed when compared with sequential scans. That is the reason why in the preceding example the planner chose the `bmsql_warehouse` as the outer loop dataset, and `bmsql_customer` as the inner loop section.

Working with hash and merge join

In this recipe, we will be discussing merge and hash join mechanisms in PostgreSQL.

Getting ready

Merge join is another joining approach to perform the join operation between two datasets. PostgreSQL optimizer will generally choose this joining method for an equi joins or for union operations. To perform this join on two datasets, it is required to sort the two join key columns first and then it will run the join condition. The optimizer prefers this node type, while joining huge tables.

Hash join is another joining approach. In general, this approach is pretty fast if and only if the server has enough memory resources. To perform this join, PostgreSQL does not need any sorted results. Rather, it will take one table data to build a hash index, which it will be comparing with the other table tuples. PostgreSQL optimizer will generally choose this joining method for an equi joins or for union operations. The optimizer prefers this node type, while joining the medium size tables.

How to do it...

Let us generate simple hash, merge join plan as demonstrated as follow:

Hash join

To demonstrate the hash join behavior, let's query the benchmarksql to retrieve all the customer IDs along with the amount paid for the all the product deliveries:

```
benchmarksql=# EXPLAIN SELECT SUM(h_amount), c_id FROM bmsql_history,
bmsql_customer WHERE h_c_id = c_id GROUP BY c_id;
                                         QUERY PLAN
    --------------------------------------------------------------------
--------------------------------------------------------------
    HashAggregate  (cost=561095.19..561132.69 rows=3000 width=9)
       Group Key: bmsql_customer.c_id
       ->  Hash Join  (cost=11453.42..411194.93 rows=29980051 width=9)
             Hash Cond: (bmsql_customer.c_id = bmsql_history.h_c_id)
             ->  Index Only Scan using bmsql_customer_pkey on
bmsql_customer  (cost=0.42..9132.42 rows=300000 width=4)
                 ->  Hash  (cost=6238.00..6238.00 rows=300000 width=9)
                     ->  Seq Scan on bmsql_history  (cost=0.00..6238.00
rows=300000 width=9)
    (7 rows)
```

From the preceding example, the optimizer chose the hash join to fetch the matching records from the bmsql_history and bmsql_customer tables. To build the hash table in memory, the optimizer needs to scan the whole table as per the join condition. Once the hash table is built, each row from the bmsql_customer table will probe the hash table with the join condition. Hash join is always preferred by the optimizer, when we are joining two tables where one table is small and the other one is big in size. Also, to build the hash table, the optimizer always prefers the small size table or low cost node type results, since it will reduce the memory usage and also reduces the number of hash buckets.

Merge join

To demonstrate the merge join behavior, let's query the `benchmarksql` to retrieve all the warehouse names that are located in each district as follows:

```
benchmarksql=# EXPLAIN SELECT w_name, d_name FROM bmsql_district,
bmsql_warehouse WHERE w_id = d_w_id;
                                   QUERY PLAN
------------------------------------------------------------------------
------

      Merge Join  (cost=7.59..9.14 rows=100 width=17)
         Merge Cond: (bmsql_warehouse.w_id = bmsql_district.d_w_id)
         -> Sort   (cost=1.27..1.29 rows=10 width=12)
              Sort Key: bmsql_warehouse.w_id
              -> Seq Scan on bmsql_warehouse   (cost=0.00..1.10 rows=10
width=12)
         -> Sort   (cost=6.32..6.57 rows=100 width=13)
              Sort Key: bmsql_district.d_w_id
              -> Seq Scan on bmsql_district   (cost=0.00..3.00 rows=100
width=13)
      (8 rows)
```

For the preceding query, the optimizer actually chose the hash join plan, since the dataset is small. For demonstrating the merge join behavior, I have forced the planner to choose merge join by disabling the optimizer attribute, `enable_hash` join. In general, merge join will come into the picture while joining huge datasets.

As we discussed, merge join needs a sorted dataset as an input, which will produce the matching results. From the preceding plan output, the planner also did the sort operation on both join keys and fed both sorted results to the merge join node type.

How it works...

Let us see how the hash, merge join works in PostgreSQL:

Hash join

Let's divide the hash join internal implementation as two phases. In phase I, it will choose the candidate table to build the hash table and in phase II, it will probe the hash table with the other one.

Phase I

In this phase, PostgreSQL will identify the candidate table to build the hash index. From the preceding example, the optimizer chooses the bmsql_history table as a candidate for the hash index. This is because the table has fewer numbers of relpages when compared to bmsql_customer and that is the reason that the Seq Scan cost on bmsql_history gives a less estimated cost. Let's get a number of relpages of these two tables from the pg_class catalog as follows:

```
benchmarksql=# SELECT relpages, relname FROM pg_class WHERE relname IN
('bmsql_history', 'bmsql_customer');
    relpages |    relname
   ----------+----------------
       3238 | bmsql_history
      25218 | bmsql_customer
(2 rows)
```

Let's try to increase the seq_page_cost to a higher number and see how the optimizer chooses the candidate table for the hash index:

```
benchmarksql=# SET seq_page_cost TO 10;
    SET
    benchmarksql=# EXPLAIN SELECT SUM(h_amount), c_id FROM bmsql_history,
bmsql_customer WHERE h_c_id = c_id GROUP BY c_id;
                                                           QUERY PLAN
    -----------------------------------------------------------------------
----------------------------------------------------------
    HashAggregate  (cost=641453.19..641490.69 rows=3000 width=9)
      Group Key: bmsql_customer.c_id
      ->  Hash Join  (cost=24602.42..491552.93 rows=29980051 width=9)
            Hash Cond: (bmsql_history.h_c_id = bmsql_customer.c_id)
            ->  Seq Scan on bmsql_history  (cost=0.00..35380.00
rows=300000 width=9)
            ->  Hash  (cost=9132.42..9132.42 rows=300000 width=4)
                  ->  Index Only Scan using bmsql_customer_pkey on
bmsql_customer  (cost=0.42..9132.42 rows=300000 width=4)
    (7 rows)
```

From the preceding example, the Index Only Scan on the bmsql_customer table's cost is minimal when compared with Seq Scan on the bmsql_history table. That's why the optimizer choose bmsql_customer as a candidate table to build the hash. To keep this hash table, PostgreSQL uses the configured work_mem memory area. If the hash table size does not fit into the work_mem area then it will process the hash probes using multiple batches, by creating temporary files for each batch.

Phase II

In this phase, PostgreSQL reads the tuples from the other table using the selected node type, and generates a hash value based on a hash function. If the generated hash value matches with any of the hash bucket values, then that tuple will be treated as a matching record. Once it completes probing all the tuple values, then it will return all the matching records. The following is a simple pictorial representation of the hash join:

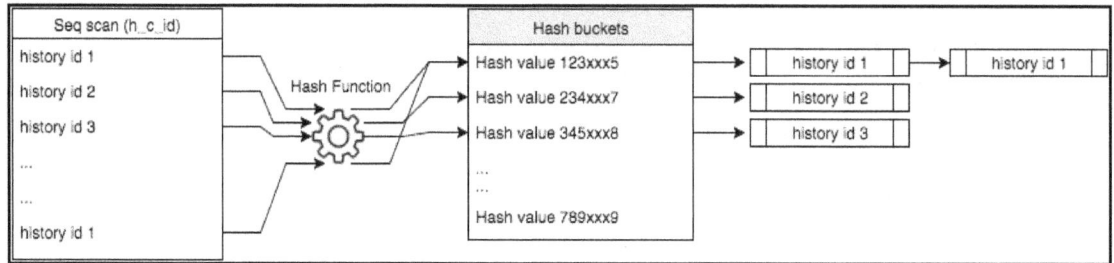

Merge join

Let's divide this merge join operation into two phases. In phase I, PostgreSQL does sort operations on both join key values. In phase II, PostgreSQL compares the two sorted results in parallel.

Phase I

In this phase, PostgreSQL will utilize the work_mem memory area to sort the two join keys one after the other. If any join key column has any sorted index, then the optimizer prefers to choose the index scan over a sequential scan and sort.

Phase II

Once postgres has two sorted results, then it will scan them in parallel, as shown in the following diagram. From the following diagram, **Pointer 1** will only move to its next value if its value is not equal to **Pointer 2**. If the Pointer1 value is equal to the Pointer2 value, then it will produce a matching tuple. Pointer2 will keep moving to its next value if its value is equal to Pointer1. This process will repeat until Pointer1 reaches its end, and returns all the matching records. In this way, it will try to process these sorted results in parallel. The following is a simple pictorial representation of merge join:

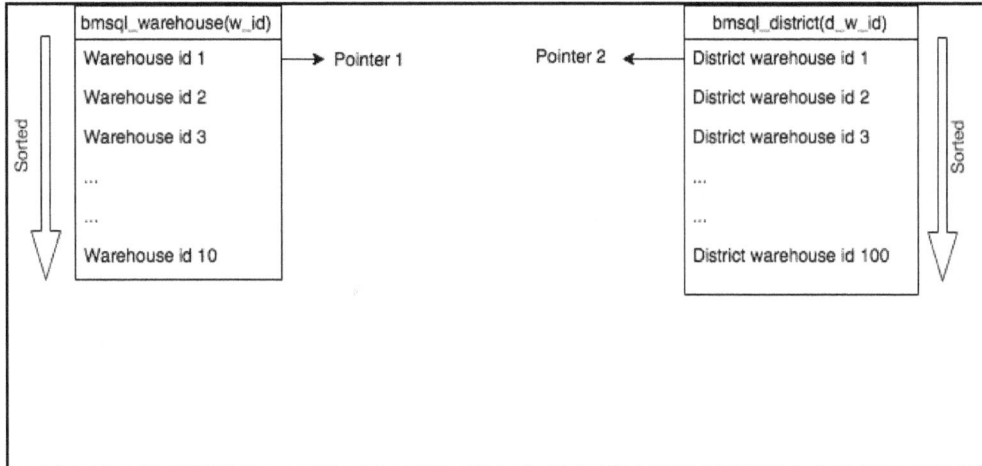

> Merge join always produces the sorted results, whereas hash join does not
> provide the sorted output. This is one major advantage of merge join over
> hash join plan.

Grouping

In this recipe, we will be discussing the optimizer node type, which will be chosen during
the group by operation.

Getting ready

As we discussed group or aggregate operations in the previous recipe, grouping operations
will have performed based on the group key list. The PostgreSQL optimizer chooses hash
aggregate, when it finds enough memory and if not, group aggregate will be the option.
Unlike hash aggregate, the group aggregate operation needs data to be sorted. If the group
columns have a sorted index already, then group aggregate will choose over the hash
aggregate as to reduce the memory usage.

How to do it...

1. To demonstrate group aggregate, let's run the query in the `benchmarksql` database to get the count of customers, grouped by their city:

```
benchmarksql=# EXPLAIN SELECT COUNT(*), c_city FROM
  bmsql_customer GROUP BY c_city;
                                       QUERY PLAN
----------------------------------------------------------------------
----------------------------------------
   GroupAggregate  (cost=0.42..11570.20 rows=33378 width=16)
    Group Key: c_city
    ->  Index Only Scan using city_idx on bmsql_customer
       (cost=0.42..9736.42 rows=300000 width=16)
   (3 rows)
```

2. From the preceding plan, the optimizer chooses the `GroupAggregate` as the `c_city` column is already indexed. Let's run the same query, by dropping the index:

```
benchmarksql=# DROP INDEX city_idx ;
DROP INDEX
benchmarksql=# EXPLAIN SELECT COUNT(*), c_city FROM
  bmsql_customer GROUP BY c_city;
                                    QUERY PLAN
----------------------------------------------------------------------
-------------
   HashAggregate  (cost=29718.00..30053.29 rows=33529 width=15)
   Group Key: c_city
    ->  Seq Scan on bmsql_customer  (cost=0.00..28218.00 rows=300000
      width=15)
   (3 rows)
```

3. As we expected, after dropping the index, the optimizer chooses the `HashAggregate` node type, which will utilize the `work_mem` area to perform the hash aggregate operations. Let's run the same query, by reducing the `work_mem` setting as follows:

```
benchmarksql=# SET work_mem TO '64kB';
SET
benchmarksql=# EXPLAIN SELECT COUNT(*), c_city FROM
  bmsql_customer GROUP BY c_city;
                                   QUERY PLAN
----------------------------------------------------------------------
------------------
   GroupAggregate  (cost=70892.40..73477.69 rows=33529 width=15)
```

```
        Group Key: c_city
     -> Sort  (cost=70892.40..71642.40 rows=300000 width=15)
           Sort Key: c_city
           -> Seq Scan on bmsql_customer  (cost=0.00..28218.00
             rows=300000 width=15)
  (5 rows)
```

From the preceding plan, the optimizer chooses the GroupAggregate as it does not find enough memory areas to build the hash. If GroupAggregate does not find enough work_mem, then it will use the external disk to perform the sort operation.

How it works...

PostgreSQL tries to divide the whole dataset into multiple groups by doing either sort operations, by choosing an order index over the group column, or by creating a hash table for the mention group column list. Once the complete dataset is divided into multiple groups, then the mentioned aggregate function will invoke for each group and will execute the state transition functions, as we discussed in the previous recipe.

Working with set operations

In this recipe, we will be discussing various PostgreSQL set operations.

Getting ready

PostgreSQL provides various set operations, which deal with multiple independent data sets. The supported set operators are UNION/ALL, INTERSECT/ALL, and EXCEPT/ALL. In general, we use the set operations in SQL when we need to either join or merge operations among independent datasets. To process these independent datasets, PostgreSQL will evaluate each dataset operation independently, and then it applies the given set operation on the final datasets.

How to do it...

1. To demonstrate these set operations, let's query the `benchmarsql` to get all the customer IDs, that have not placed any online order:

```
benchmarksql=# EXPLAIN SELECT c_id FROM bmsql_customer
EXCEPT
SELECT h_c_id FROM bmsql_history;
                                                            QUERY PLAN
-------------------------------------------------------------------------------
------------------------------------------------------------
 HashSetOp Except   (cost=0.42..22870.42 rows=3000 width=4)
   -> Append  (cost=0.42..21370.42 rows=600000 width=4)
         -> Subquery Scan on "*SELECT* 1"  (cost=0.42..12132.42
            rows=300000 width=4)
               -> Index Only Scan using bmsql_customer_pkey on
                  bmsql_customer  (cost=0.42..9132.42 rows=300000
                  width=4)
         -> Subquery Scan on "*SELECT* 2"  (cost=0.00..9238.00
            rows=300000 width=4)
               -> Seq Scan on bmsql_history  (cost=0.00..6238.00
                  rows=300000 width=4)
(6 rows)
```

2. To demonstrate the `INTERSECT` behavior, let's run the query to select all customers who have placed any number of orders:

```
benchmarksql=# EXPLAIN SELECT c_id FROM bmsql_customer
   INTERSECT SELECT h_c_id FROM bmsql_history;
                                                          QUERY PLAN
------------------------------------------------------------------------------
----------------------------------------------------------
 HashSetOp Intersect   (cost=0.42..22870.42 rows=3000 width=4)
  -> Append  (cost=0.42..21370.42 rows=600000 width=4)
        -> Subquery Scan on "*SELECT* 1"  (cost=0.42..12132.42
           rows=300000 width=4)
              -> Index Only Scan using bmsql_customer_pkey on
                 bmsql_customer  (cost=0.42..9132.42 rows=300000
                 width=4)
        -> Subquery Scan on "*SELECT* 2"  (cost=0.00..9238.00
           rows=300000 width=4)
              -> Seq Scan on bmsql_history  (cost=0.00..6238.00
                 rows=300000 width=4)
(6 rows)
```

3. From the preceding two examples, the queries took the HashSetOp mechanism to perform the set operations. PostgreSQL also has another set operation mechanism called SetOp, which will be preferred by the optimizer, when it does not find enough memory for the hash table. Let's run the same query by reducing the work_mem area as follows:

```
benchmarksql=# set work_mem to '64kB';
SET
benchmarksql=# EXPLAIN SELECT c_id FROM bmsql_customer
  INTERSECT SELECT h_c_id FROM bmsql_history;
                                                    QUERY
  PLAN
--------------------------------------------------------------------
--------------------------------------------------------------------
 SetOp Intersect  (cost=103566.23..106566.23 rows=3000 width=4)
  ->  Sort  (cost=103566.23..105066.23 rows=600000 width=4)
        Sort Key: "*SELECT* 1".c_id
        ->  Append  (cost=0.42..21370.42 rows=600000 width=4)
              ->  Subquery Scan on "*SELECT* 1"
           (cost=0.42..12132.42 rows=300000 width=4)
                    ->  Index Only Scan using bmsql_customer_pkey
                    on bmsql_customer  (cost=0.42..9132.42
                    rows=300000 width=4)
              ->  Subquery Scan on "*SELECT* 2"
            (cost=0.00..9238.00 rows=300000 width=4)
                    ->  Seq Scan on bmsql_history
                    (cost=0.00..6238.00 rows=300000 width=4)
(8 rows)
```

From the preceding plan, as the optimizer does not find enough work memory to build the hash table, it chooses the SetOp mechanism, which requires the sorted data as an input.

How it works...

In PostgreSQL, the set operations are implemented based on set operations using sort and set operations using hash. One mechanism among these two strategies will be chosen based on the set operation and dataset size. Let's see a few demonstrations of each set operator as follows.

To demonstrate the set operations behavior, let's choose one small (bmsql_warehouse) table and one table that is bigger than the previous one (bmsql_district).

INTERSECT

This operator returns common tuples among two individual datasets. To process these two datasets, PostgreSQL always chooses the smallest table or minimal cost node type (index scan, bitmap heap scan, and so on) to build the hash or sorted data. Let's see the following query plans, where optimize always chooses the small table:

```
benchmarksql=# EXPLAIN SELECT w_state FROM bmsql_warehouse INTERSECT SELECT
d_state FROM bmsql_district ;
QUERY PLAN
-----------------------------------------------------------------------
-------
HashSetOp Intersect (cost=0.00..5.48 rows=10 width=3)
-> Append (cost=0.00..5.20 rows=110 width=3)
-> Subquery Scan on "*SELECT* 1" (cost=0.00..1.20 rows=10 width=3)
-> Seq Scan on bmsql_warehouse (cost=0.00..1.10 rows=10 width=3)
-> Subquery Scan on "*SELECT* 2" (cost=0.00..4.00 rows=100 width=3)
-> Seq Scan on bmsql_district (cost=0.00..3.00 rows=100 width=3)
(6 rows)
```

From the preceding plan, the first child node `Seq Scan on bmsql_warehouse` chooses to build the hash table. Even if we reverse the dataset, the optimizer will not change the plan:

```
benchmarksql=# EXPLAIN SELECT d_state FROM bmsql_district
INTERSECT
SELECT w_state FROM bmsql_warehouse;
                               QUERY PLAN
-----------------------------------------------------------------------
------------
HashSetOp Intersect   (cost=0.00..5.48 rows=10 width=3)
   -> Append   (cost=0.00..5.20 rows=110 width=3)
         -> Subquery Scan on "*SELECT* 2"   (cost=0.00..1.20 rows=10
width=3)
               -> Seq Scan on bmsql_warehouse   (cost=0.00..1.10
rows=10 width=3)
         -> Subquery Scan on "*SELECT* 1"   (cost=0.00..4.00 rows=100
width=3)
               -> Seq Scan on bmsql_district   (cost=0.00..3.00
rows=100 width=3)
   (6 rows)
```

After observing the preceding two plans, you might have a question such as where in the preceding explain plan is it clearly mentioned that the hash table is built based on the `bmsql_warehouse` table, since we are actually seeing the append node as the parent node of Seq Scan on `bmsql_warehouse`? Currently, the planner will internally choose the node that is needed to build hash, by comparing the node cost values. However, this information is clearly visible when the optimizer chooses the set operation sort mechanism. Let's see the following query to explain where it clearly shows the key value it chooses to do the sort operation:

```
benchmarksql=# SET enable_hashagg TO off;
SET
benchmarksql=# EXPLAIN SELECT d_state FROM bmsql_district
INTERSECT
SELECT w_state FROM bmsql_warehouse;
                                    QUERY PLAN
--------------------------------------------------------------------------------
------------------
   SetOp Intersect   (cost=8.93..9.48 rows=10 width=3)
      -> Sort   (cost=8.93..9.20 rows=110 width=3)
       Sort Key: "*SELECT* 2".w_state
            -> Append   (cost=0.00..5.20 rows=110 width=3)
                  -> Subquery Scan on "*SELECT* 2"   (cost=0.00..1.20
rows=10 width=3)
                        -> Seq Scan on bmsql_warehouse   (cost=0.00..1.10
rows=10 width=3)
                  -> Subquery Scan on "*SELECT* 1"   (cost=0.00..4.00
rows=100 width=3)
                        -> Seq Scan on bmsql_district   (cost=0.00..3.00
rows=100 width=3)
     (8 rows)
```

From the preceding plan, as you can see the planner chooses the `bmsql_warehouse` table data to do the sorting operation.

EXCEPT

Unlike INTERSECT, this operator always tries to build the hash table on the first table. Even though the table size is huge in size, it will try to build the hash on that table. Let's see the following example:

```
benchmarksql=# EXPLAIN SELECT d_state FROM bmsql_district
EXCEPT
SELECT w_state FROM bmsql_warehouse;
                              QUERY PLAN
-----------------------------------------------------------------------
-----------
    HashSetOp Except   (cost=0.00..5.48 rows=96 width=3)
      -> Append  (cost=0.00..5.20 rows=110 width=3)
            -> Subquery Scan on "*SELECT* 1"   (cost=0.00..4.00 rows=100
width=3)
                    -> Seq Scan on bmsql_district   (cost=0.00..3.00
rows=100 width=3)
            -> Subquery Scan on "*SELECT* 2"   (cost=0.00..1.20 rows=10
width=3)
                    -> Seq Scan on bmsql_warehouse   (cost=0.00..1.10
rows=10 width=3)
    (6 rows)
```

From the preceding plan, as expected the hash table will choose the bmsql_district table as it is mentioned on the left side of the EXCEPT operator. Let's swap these relations and see the execution plan:

```
benchmarksql=# EXPLAIN SELECT w_state FROM bmsql_warehouse
EXCEPT
SELECT d_state FROM bmsql_district ;
                              QUERY PLAN
-----------------------------------------------------------------------
-----------
    HashSetOp Except   (cost=0.00..5.48 rows=10 width=3)
      -> Append  (cost=0.00..5.20 rows=110 width=3)
            -> Subquery Scan on "*SELECT* 1"   (cost=0.00..1.20 rows=10
width=3)
                    -> Seq Scan on bmsql_warehouse   (cost=0.00..1.10
rows=10 width=3)
            -> Subquery Scan on "*SELECT* 2"   (cost=0.00..4.00 rows=100
width=3)
                    -> Seq Scan on bmsql_district   (cost=0.00..3.00
rows=100 width=3)
    (6 rows)
```

This time, the plan also changed as the optimizer chose the `bmsql_warehouse` table to build the hash.

UNION

For this set operation, PostgreSQL will not use the `HashSetOp/SetOp` node type, as this can easily be performed by using the Unique or `HashAggregate` node types. For demonstration, let's see the following explain plans:

```
benchmarksql=# EXPLAIN SELECT w_state FROM bmsql_warehouse
UNION
SELECT d_state FROM bmsql_district;
                                    QUERY PLAN
---------------------------------------------------------------------------
------
     HashAggregate   (cost=5.48..6.58 rows=110 width=3)
        Group Key: bmsql_warehouse.w_state
         -> Append   (cost=0.00..5.20 rows=110 width=3)
               -> Seq Scan on bmsql_warehouse   (cost=0.00..1.10 rows=10
width=3)
               -> Seq Scan on bmsql_district   (cost=0.00..3.00 rows=100
width=3)
     (5 rows)
```

Let's disable the hash aggregate, and see the plan it chooses for this union operation:

```
benchmarksql=# SET enable_hashagg TO off;
SET
benchmarksql=# EXPLAIN SELECT w_state FROM bmsql_warehouse
UNION
SELECT d_state FROM bmsql_district;
                                    QUERY PLAN
---------------------------------------------------------------------------
------------
     Unique   (cost=8.93..9.48 rows=110 width=3)
        -> Sort   (cost=8.93..9.20 rows=110 width=3)
              Sort Key: bmsql_warehouse.w_state
              -> Append   (cost=0.00..5.20 rows=110 width=3)
                    -> Seq Scan on bmsql_warehouse   (cost=0.00..1.10
rows=10 width=3)
                    -> Seq Scan on bmsql_district   (cost=0.00..3.00
rows=100 width=3)
     (6 rows)
```

Working on semi and anti joins

In this recipe, we will be discussing hash different joining methods.

Getting ready

Semi or anti joins are kind of sub join types to the joining methods such as hash, merge, and nested loop, where the optimizer prefers to use them for EXISTS/IN or NOT EXISTS/NOT IN operators.

Semi join will return a single value for all the matching records from the other table. That is, if the second table has multiple matching entries for the first table's record, then it will return only one copy from the first table. However, a normal join it will return multiple copies from the first table.

Anti-join will return rows, when no matching records are found in the second table. It is quite opposite to the semi join, since it is returning records from the first table, when there is no match in the second table.

How to do it...

Let's run a query in the benchmarksql database to get the list of items that are in stock:

```
benchmarksql=# EXPLAIN SELECT * FROM bmsql_item WHERE EXISTS (SELECT
true FROM bmsql_stock WHERE i_id=s_i_id);
                                             QUERY PLAN
    ----------------------------------------------------------------
    ---------------------------------------------------
    Hash Semi Join  (cost=42387.40..55508.40 rows=100000 width=73)
      Hash Cond: (bmsql_item.i_id = bmsql_stock.s_i_id)
      ->  Seq Scan on bmsql_item  (cost=0.00..2299.00 rows=100000
width=73)
      ->  Hash  (cost=25980.41..25980.41 rows=999999 width=4)
            ->  Index Only Scan using bmsql_stock_pkey on bmsql_stock
(cost=0.42..25980.41 rows=999999 width=4)
      (5 rows)
```

From the preceding plan, the optimizer chooses the Hash Semi Join as it is returning only matching rows from the bmsql_item table. The same plan will be used if we implement the query with the IN operator.

Let's change the same query to fetch the items that are not in stock at this moment using the NOT EXISTS operator and see the execution plan:

```
benchmarksql=# EXPLAIN SELECT * FROM bmsql_item WHERE NOT EXISTS
(SELECT true FROM bmsql_stock WHERE i_id=s_i_id);
                                              QUERY PLAN
------------------------------------------------------------------------
-------------------------------------------
     Hash Anti Join   (cost=38480.40..44154.40 rows=1 width=73)
        Hash Cond: (bmsql_item.i_id = bmsql_stock.s_i_id)
        ->   Seq Scan on bmsql_item   (cost=0.00..2299.00 rows=100000
width=73)
        ->   Hash   (cost=25980.41..25980.41 rows=999999 width=4)
              ->   Index Only Scan using bmsql_stock_pkey on bmsql_stock
(cost=0.42..25980.41 rows=999999 width=4)
     (5 rows)
```

As expected, the optimizer chooses Anti Join as it is fetching the non-matching records from the first table. Optimizer will choose the same plan if we change the query with the NOT IN operator.

How it works...

Semi or anti join are like hints to the joining approaches, on how to behave when any matching tuples are found.

From the preceding example, the optimizer chooses hash semi join. Unlike hash join, which always chooses the low cost node type to build the hash, hash semi join prefers to build the hash table on the sub select table, which is bmsql_stock in the preceding example. Once the hash table is prepared, it will probe the hash with the first table tuples, and return the matching records. Anti-join works in a similar way, as it does return only the non-matching tuples from the first table.

There might be chances for the optimizer to choose the `merge/nested` loop join along with semi or anti join. Let's see the following example where the optimizer chooses the nested loop semi join:

```
benchmarksql=# EXPLAIN SELECT * FROM bmsql_item WHERE i_id = 10 AND
EXISTS (SELECT true FROM bmsql_stock WHERE i_id=s_i_id);
                                                    QUERY PLAN
-------------------------------------------------------------------------
--------------------------------
   Nested Loop Semi Join  (cost=0.72..18488.85 rows=1 width=73)
      ->  Index Scan using bmsql_item_pkey on bmsql_item  (cost=0.29..8.31
rows=1 width=73)
            Index Cond: (i_id = 10)
      ->  Index Only Scan using bmsql_stock_pkey on bmsql_stock
(cost=0.42..18480.52 rows=10 width=4)
            Index Cond: (s_i_id = 10)
   (5 rows)
```

Here, the nested loop semi join works in a different way compared to the plain nested loop join. As like a regular nested loop join, it does not perform the cross number of matches. Once the outer tuple matches with the inner tuple, then it proceeds to match with the next outer tuple. Anti-join also works in a similar way. If any matching tuple is found from the outer loop, then it skips all the remaining comparisons from the inner loop table. During anti join, the resulting set will form when any outer tuple does not match with any inner tuples. Semi join is opposite to anti-join; as the resulting set will only form when any outer tuple matches with any inner tuple.

12
Database Indexing

In this chapter, we will cover the following recipes:

- Measuring query and index block statistics
- Index lookups
- Comparing indexed scans and sequential scans
- Clustering against an index
- Concurrent indexes
- Combined indexes
- Partial indexes
- Finding unused indexes
- Forcing a query to use an index
- Detecting missing indexes
- Concurrent indexes

Introduction

Indexes play a crucial role in a database as they improve the query response time by adding an amount of overhead for each write operation of a table. Creating or dropping an index is an important responsibility for a DBA as they need to make a choice by looking at the read and write ratio of the database tables. A wise move would definitely be to increase the database performance, which needs some investigation into the table growth, along with its access metrics. In some cases, an index may improve the query performance instantly, which may not be useful in future. In this chapter, we are going to learn how to measure the table growth along with its access metrics using catalog tables, by using the BenchmarkSQL database as a sample dataset.

Measuring query and index block statistics

In this recipe, we will be discussing how to measure the index statistics, using various catalog views.

Getting ready

PostgreSQL offers a few catalog views and extensions, which are enough to study the index usage statistics. The catalog views are `pg_stat_user_indexes` and `pg_statio_user_indexes`. These give the index usage statistics, and the extension `pgstattuple` provides insight into the details of the index by reading its physical files.

How to do it...

1. Let's get a sample non-primary key index to measure its statistics, as follows:

   ```
   benchmarksql=# SELECT indexrelid::regclass FROM
   pg_index WHERE indisprimary IS FALSE AND
   indrelid::regclass::text='bmsql_item' LIMIT
   1;
   indexrelid
   ------------
   pric_idx
   (1 row)
   ```

2. Let's reset the statistics using the `pg_stat_reset` function, as follows:

   ```
   benchmarksql=# SELECT pg_stat_reset();
   pg_stat_reset
   ---------------
   (1 row)
   ```

3. Let's run the following sample query on `bmsql_item`, which uses the index `pric_idx` to fetch the heap tuples from the table:

   ```
   benchmarksql=# EXPLAIN ANALYZE SELECT COUNT(*)
   FROM bmsql_item WHERE i_price BETWEEN 1 AND 10;
   QUERY PLAN
   ---------------------------------------------------
   ---------------------------------------------------
   -------------------------------
   Aggregate  (cost=1649.57..1649.58 rows=1 width=8)    (actual
   ```

```
             time=1647.810..1647.810 rows=1 loops=1)
       ->  Bitmap Heap Scan on bmsql_item  (cost=192.74..1627.02
         rows=9019 width=0) (actual time=327.813..1646.526 rows=9021
           loops=1)
       Recheck Cond: ((i_price >= '1'::numeric) AND (i_price <=
         '10'::numeric))
       Heap Blocks: exact=1299
       ->  Bitmap Index Scan on pric_idx  (cost=0.00..190.48 rows=9019
         width=0) (actual time=288.113..288.113 rows=9021 loops=1)
       Index Cond: ((i_price >= '1'::numeric) AND (i_price <=
         '10'::numeric))
       Planning time: 399.779 ms
       Execution time: 1756.573 ms
       (8 rows)
```

4. Let's run the following query, which returns the index usage of the preceding SQL statement:

```
benchmarksql=# SELECT idx_scan, idx_tup_read,     idx_tup_fetch,
   idx_blks_read, idx_blks_hit
FROM pg_stat_user_indexes psui, pg_statio_user_indexes psiui
   WHERE psui.relid=psiui.relid AND
     psui.indexrelid=psiui.indexrelid AND
       psui.indexrelid='pric_idx'::regclass;
-[ RECORD 1 ]-+------
idx_scan      | 2
idx_tup_read  | 9022
idx_tup_fetch | 1
idx_blks_read | 28
idx_blks_hit  | 2
```

How it works...

From the preceding example, we can see that the optimizer preferred to use an index scan to fetch the tuples from the bmsql_item table. Let's get the pric_idx index details by using the pg_class catalog table, as follows:

```
benchmarksql=# SELECT relpages, reltuples FROM pg_class WHERE relname =
'pric_idx';
-[ RECORD 1 ]------
relpages  | 276
reltuples | 100000
```

From the preceding output, the `pric_idx` index has `100000` tuples in `276` pages. Each page is of 8 KB (default block size), in size and the total size of the index would be *276*8*1024 = 2260992* bytes, that is approximately 2 MB. However, we can also get the size of an index using the `\di+` PostgreSQL meta command, as follows:

```
benchmarksql=# \di+ pric_idx
List of relations
-[ RECORD 1 ]-----------
Schema      | public
Name        | pric_idx
Type        | index
Owner       | postgres
Table       | bmsql_item
Size        | 2208 kB
Description |
```

idx_scan

This defines the number of times the index is scanned to fetch the results. According to the preceding index scan metrics, the query took two index scans (`idx_scan`) to fetch the tuples. Now you might ask, "In the preceding plan, I only see one index scan node type; where is the other one?" The answer to your question is that the optimizer performed one additional index scan, for its selectivity. That is, in the preceding SQL statement, we have an inequality predicate, which is an operator. If the optimizer sees any inequality predicate in the SQL query, then it tries to calculate the selectivity of the index with its histogram boundaries. We can find these histogram boundaries of each column in the `pg_stats` view. This index selectivity ratio defines whether the optimizer needs to choose an index scan over the sequential scan. To demonstrate this, let's play around with index selectivity.

Let's get the maximum and minimum values from `i_price`:

```
benchmarksql=# SELECT max(i_price), min(i_price) FROM bmsql_item;
   max    |  min
----------+------
 100.00   | 1.00
(1 row)
```

Let's reset the statistics, using the `pg_stat_reset()` function:

```
benchmarksql=# SELECT pg_stat_reset();
pg_stat_reset
-----------------

(1 row)
```

Let's run the same SQL statement, with the minimum and maximum values of the `i_price` column:

```
benchmarksql=# EXPLAIN ANALYZE SELECT COUNT(*) FROM bmsql_item WHERE
i_price BETWEEN 1 AND 100;
QUERY PLAN
--------------------------------------------------------------------
Aggregate  (cost=3049.00..3049.01 rows=1 width=8) (actual
time=41.861..41.861 rows=1 loops=1)
->  Seq Scan on bmsql_item  (cost=0.00..2799.00 rows=100000 width=0)
(actual time=0.011..34.318 rows=100000 loops=1)
Filter: ((i_price >= '1'::numeric) AND (i_price <= '100'::numeric))
 Planning time: 0.164 ms
 Execution time: 41.885 ms
(5 rows)
```

From the preceding plan, we do not see any index scan node types. But the optimizer decided to go with the sequential scan, by referring its index selectivity. If the given range values try to fetch the whole index, then the optimizer chooses the sequential scan to avoid the index lookup overhead. We can confirm this statement by referring the number of index scans the optimizer performed to the preceding SQL statement, using the following SQL statement:

```
benchmarksql=# SELECT idx_scan
FROM
pg_stat_user_indexes psui, pg_statio_user_indexes psiui
WHERE psui.relid=psiui.relid AND psui.indexrelid=psiui.indexrelid AND
psui.indexrelid = 'pric_idx'::regclass;
-[ RECORD 1 ]-+--
idx_scan      | 2
```

From the preceding results, we can see that the optimizer performed two index scans to find the index selectivity and then chose the sequential scan as the better plan, to execute the given SQL statement. To confirm this index selectivity, the optimizer does not read the whole index; rather, it only fetches a few index blocks.

idx_tup_read

This defines the number of tuples read from the index. From the preceding example, it reads the total tuples as 9022, which includes the number of tuples it read during the index selectivity.

idx_tup_fetch

This defines the number of tuples read from the table with the simple index scan. In the preceding plan, the optimizer chose the bitmap index scan, which is not a regular index scan method. From the preceding results, the value of `idx_tup_fetch` is 1, which is fetched during the optimizer index selectivity.

idx_blks_read

This defines the number of blocks read from the disk. From the preceding results, the value of `idx_blks_read` is 28, and each block is 8 KB in size. This includes the number of blocks read from an index, during the index selectivity.

idx_blks_hit

This defines the number blocks read from the cache. From the preceding results, the value of `idx_blks_hit` is 2, and each block is 8 KB in size. This includes the number of blocks hit from the cache, during the index selectivity.

Index lookup

In this recipe, we will be discussing various index scans, and how they try to fetch matching tuples from tables.

Getting ready

As we all know, an index is a physical object that can help a query retrieve table data much faster than a sequential scan. In the explain plan, we frequently get index scan, bitmap heap scan, or index only scan node types, which works on a particular index. Whenever an index is scanned, then an immediately followed action would be to return the matching tuples from the index, build a bitmap in memory, or fetch the tuples from the base table.

How to do it...

To demonstrate the index scan, let's run the following simple query and see how many tuples it is reading from the base table:

```
benchmarksql=# SELECT pg_stat_reset();
pg_stat_reset
---------------

(1 row)
benchmarksql=# SET enable_bitmapscan TO off;
SET
benchmarksql=# EXPLAIN ANALYZE SELECT * FROM bmsql_item WHERE i_price = 1;
                                                        QUERY PLAN
---------------------------------------------------------------------------
---------------------------------------------------
Index Scan using pric_idx1 on bmsql_item   (cost=0.29..32.41 rows=7
width=72) (actual time=0.019..0.026 rows=7 loops=1)
Index Cond: (i_price = '1'::numeric)
Planning time: 0.650 ms
Execution time: 0.049 ms
(4 rows)
```

In the preceding SQL statements, we have forced the optimizer to choose its behavior by disabling `enable_bitmapscan`. Now let's see how many tuples the index scan read from the `bmsql_item` table using the following SQL statement:

```
benchmarksql=# SELECT idx_scan, idx_tup_fetch FROM pg_stat_user_tables
WHERE relname = 'bmsql_item';
idx_scan | idx_tup_fetch
---------+---------------
       1 |             7
(1 row)
```

To demonstrate the bitmap scan behavior, let's enable `enable_bitmapscan` and then rerun the same statement to see how many tuples it read from the index to build the bitmap, and how many tuples it read from the table using that bitmap index:

```
benchmarksql=# EXPLAIN ANALYZE SELECT * FROM bmsql_item WHERE i_price = 1;
                                                        QUERY PLAN
---------------------------------------------------------------------------
---------------------------------------------------
Bitmap Heap Scan on bmsql_item   (cost=4.35..30.89 rows=7 width=72) (actual
time=18.373..48.416 rows=7 loops=1)
  Recheck Cond: (i_price = '1'::numeric)
  Heap Blocks: exact=7
  -> Bitmap Index Scan on pric_idx1   (cost=0.00..4.35 rows=7 width=0)
```

```
(actual time=0.328..0.328 rows=7 loops=1)
  Index Cond: (i_price = '1'::numeric)
Planning time: 125.660 ms
Execution time: 48.515 ms
(7 rows)
```

Get the number of tuples and queries read from the index by using the following SQL statement:

```
benchmarksql=# SELECT idx_scan, idx_tup_fetch, idx_tup_read
FROM
FROM
pg_stat_user_indexes
WHERE indexrelname = 'pric_idx1';
-[ RECORD 1 ]-+--
idx_scan      | 1
idx_tup_fetch | 0
idx_tup_read  | 7
```

Get the number of tuples that the bitmap index read from the table using the previous SQL, which we executed on pg_stat_user_tables:

```
-[ RECORD 1 ]-+--
idx_scan      | 1
idx_tup_fetch | 7
```

To demonstrate the index only scan behavior, let's modify the SQL statement to only fetch the records from the indexed column by disabling enable_bitmapscan:

```
benchmarksql=# EXPLAIN ANALYZE SELECT i_price FROM bmsql_item WHERE i_price
= 1;
                                                    QUERY PLAN
-----------------------------------------------------------------------
-----------------------------------------------------------
Index only scan using pric_idx1 on bmsql_item  (cost=0.29..32.41 rows=7
width=6) (actual time=0.018..0.025 rows=7 loops=1)
Index Cond: (i_price = '1'::numeric)
Heap Fetches: 7
Planning time: 0.598 ms
Execution time: 0.047 ms
(5 rows)
```

Let's run the previous SQL statements that use pg_stat_user_indexes:

```
-[ RECORD 1 ]-+--
idx_scan      | 1
idx_tup_fetch | 7
idx_tup_read  | 7
```

From the preceding plan, the index only scan performs `Heap Fetches: 7`, which fetches the actual tuple from the base table, to confirm its visibility information. Once the index only scan gets the visibility information, it will return the tuples from the index.

How it works...

Let us discuss about various index scan techniques:

Index scan

In general, an index scan fetches the matching tuples from the index and then immediately hits the table to fetch the heap tuples. An index does not maintain any visibility information, whereas a heap does. This visibility information helps the index scan to return only the committed live rows, rather than returning the uncommitted dirty rows.

Bitmap heap scan

A bitmap heap scan builds the bitmap index with the matching tuples, and then tries to fetch the heap tuples from the table. One advantage that a bitmap heap scan has over an index scan is a sequential order of reading the table pages, rather than doing random reads due to the index scan. We will be discussing this in more detail in further chapters.

Index only scan

An index only scan is the mechanism which PostgreSQL tries to fetch all the required data from the index it self rather fetching it from the table. This index only scan utilizes the visibility map file of the table, to avoid the heap scan. In the preceding demonstration, the index only scan performs seven heap fetches, as it does not find any visibility map file for the `bmsql_item` relation. In this case, the index only scan behaves like a normal index scan. Let's consider the following test case, where the index only scan fetches the tuples from the only index:

```
benchmarksql=# VACUUM bmsql_item;
VACUUM
benchmarksql=# EXPLAIN ANALYZE SELECT i_price FROM bmsql_item WHERE i_price
= 1;
                                             QUERY PLAN
---------------------------------------------------------------------------
------------------------------------------------------------
Index Only Scan using pric_idx1 on bmsql_item  (cost=0.29..4.42 rows=7
```

```
width=6) (actual time=0.017..0.019 rows=7 loops=1)
Index Cond: (i_price = '1'::numeric)
Heap Fetches: 0
Planning time: 0.674 ms
Execution time: 0.040 ms
(5 rows)
```

In the preceding example, we run the VACUUM command on the table, where it generates the visibility map file, which will feed the index only scan operation. In the preceding plan, we can also observe the Heap Fetches: 0, since it utilizes the visibility map file.

> Please refer to the following URL for more information on index only scans: https://www.postgresql.org/docs/9.6/static/indexes-index-only-scans.html.

Comparing indexed scans and sequential scans

In this recipe, let's compare the index and sequential scan behaviors using the inotifywait utility command, which will print a message when the mentioned event occurs on the given files.

Getting ready

inotify tools is a module that we can download using either the apt-get or yum command in the corresponding Linux distribution. This contrib module is developed based on the inotify kernel API, which provides some kind of audit mechanism over the filesystem. To compare the index and sequential scan behavior, let's audit the relation and index physical file while executing the SQL queries.

How to do it...

Let's get the locations of index and relation physical files location using the pg_relation_filepath function, as follows:

```
benchmarksql=# SELECT pg_relation_filepath('pric_idx');
pg_relation_filepath
----------------------
```

```
base/12439/16545
(1 row)

benchmarksql=# SELECT pg_relation_filepath('bmsql_item');
pg_relation_filepath
--------------------
base/12439/16417
(1 row)
```

Let's add these two physical files to the `inoitfywait` command, as shown here, and observe the output after each SQL statement execution:

```
$ inotifywait -m -e access base/12439/16417 base/12439/16545
Setting up watches.
Watches established.
```

Let's run the SQL query, which does the sequential scan over the table, as follows:

```
SELECT * FROM bmsql_item;
Output of inotifywait
base/12439/16545 ACCESS
base/12439/16417 ACCESS
```

Let's run the SQL query, which does the index scan over the table, as follows:

```
SELECT * FROM bmsql_item WHERE i_price = 1;
Output of inotifywait
base/12439/16545 ACCESS
base/12439/16417 ACCESS
```

Let's run the SQL query, which does the index only scan, as follows:

```
SELECT i_price FROM bmsql_item WHERE i_price = 1;
Output of inotifywait
base/12439/16545 ACCESS
base/12439/16417 ACCESS
```

Let's run the same preceding SQL after running the VACUUM operation on the `bmsql_item` table, which prefers index only scans:

```
Output of inotifywait
base/12439/16545 ACCESS
```

Let's enable `enable_bitmapscan`, and then run the following SQL statement:

```
SELECT * FROM bmsql_item WHERE i_price = 1;
Output of inotifywait
base/12439/16545 ACCESS
base/12439/16417 ACCESS
```

While performing the preceding test cases, we needed to restart the Postgres instance multiple times. This is because, if the object file is already cached, then Postgres will return the required tuples from memory.

How it works...

Sequential scan

From looking at the preceding demonstration results, you might wonder why the query accessed the index file to perform the full table scan. As aforementioned, the optimizer tries to generate multiple plans for the submitted SQL statement, even though the SQL does not have any predicate clause in it. In the preceding sequential scan, the optimizer tried to read each index that was created on the bmsql_item table. Let's run the same SQL statement by adding all the indexes of that table to the inotifywait command, as follows:

```
$ inotifywait -m -e access base/12439/16417 base/12439/16545
base/12439/16457 base/12439/24576
Setting up watches.
Watches established.

base/12439/16457 ACCESS
base/12439/16545 ACCESS
base/12439/24576 ACCESS
base/12439/16417 ACCESS
```

Index scan

From the preceding results, as expected, whenever the index scan is performed then an immediate table scan is also performed.

Index only scan

From the preceding results, before performing VACCUM on the table, the result of the inotify output is similar to the index scan's inotify output. Once VACUUM is performed, then inotify only shows the output of the index entry, which is as an expected behavior.

Bitmap heap scan

From the preceding results, as expected, the index and heap file is scanned for the bitmap heap scan node type.

There's more...

The `inotifywait` and `inotifywatch` commands provide multiple audit levels of the given file or directory. That is, whenever the file events are removed, updated, accessed, moved, and so on, then these utility commands print some useful audit information. I would encourage you to go through more details of this command on the man page.

Clustering against an index

In this recipe, we will be discussing a table reordering strategy based on an index, which will improve the query performance for a certain time.

Getting ready

In PostgreSQL, we have a utility command called CLUSTER that is like VACUUM. It will do some kind of table reorganization by acquiring access exclusive locks on the table. The CLUSTER command will create a new physical table by aligning its pages in the order of the mentioned index. An advantage of doing this is to avoid the index lookup overhead during the index scan, since the table itself is in ordered. Another benefit of doing this is removing all dead tuples from the table and index.

> Running the CLUSTER command during the business hours is not recommended as it will acquire the access exclusive lock, which will block the incoming queries on the table. Also, the CLUSTER operation requires an additional amount of disk space for the newly created table and indexes, which will drop the old table and its associated indexes when the operation is successful.

How to do it...

For demonstration, let's do the cluster operation on the bmsql_item table using the pric_idx index:

```
benchmarksql=# CLUSTER bmsql_item USING pric_idx;
CLUSTER
```

Let's perform the ANALYZE operation on the table after the CLUSTER operation:

```
benchmarksql=# ANALYZE bmsql_item;
ANALYZE
```

How it works...

As aforementioned, the CLUSTER operation will acquire an exclusive lock on the table as it needs to rebuild the table. After clustering is complete, we need to perform an ANALYZE operation as to update the statistics about the table ordering. Once the table is ordered, then the further index scan's future required disk reads will be much faster, as the table is already ordered, and we will get better performance.

There's more...

In PostgreSQL, the CLUSTER operation will not keep its table ordering as per the incoming transactions, as we need to execute the same operation frequently to get better performance.

> Please refer to the following URL for more information about CLUSTER behavior: https://www.postgresql.org/docs/9.6/static/sql-cluster.html.

Concurrent indexes

In this recipe, we will be discussing how to create an online index that will not block the base table for the incoming transactions.

Getting ready

In general, while creating/dropping an index, it will block the table to avoid further write operations into the index. Until the index operation is complete, the whole table will be locked for write operations, which will be an outage to the application. To avoid this table lock problem, PostgreSQL provides an option called **concurrent**, which will avoid this blocking behavior. It will also keep this index status as invalid until its creation is successfully completed. Building an index concurrently takes more time, as the operation needs to allow the incoming write operations.

How to do it...

Let's create a regular index on the `bmsql_item` table, and see how many full table scans it performed to build this index:

```
benchmarksql=# CREATE INDEX data_idx ON bmsql_item(i_data);
CREATE INDEX
benchmarksql=# SELECT seq_scan,seq_tup_read FROM pg_stat_user_tables WHERE
relname = 'bmsql_item';
 seq_scan | seq_tup_read
----------+--------------
        1 |       100000
(1 row)
```

Let's drop and re-create the same index using the CONCURRENTLY option, and see the number of full table scans it performed:

```
benchmarksql=# CREATE INDEX CONCURRENTLY data_idx ON bmsql_item(i_data);
CREATE INDEX
benchmarksql=# SELECT seq_scan,seq_tup_read FROM pg_stat_user_tables WHERE
relname = 'bmsql_item';
 seq_scan | seq_tup_read
----------+--------------
        2 |       200000
(1 row)
```

How it works...

While creating a regular index, it only needs to do a full table scan as it is locking the table for write operations, whereas, while building the concurrent index, it needs to do two full table scans over the table, as it is not locking for write operations. If the table size is huge in size, then we can expect that the concurrent index takes more CPU and I/O usage when compared with the regular index creation. These two full table scans will perform in two different transaction snapshots, which will help in building an index concurrently, by waiting for any ongoing write operations on that table.

During the two table scans, if any error occurs then it won't mark the index as valid, and these invalid indexes won't be used for any SQL queries. However, these invalid indexes don't hide from the incoming write operations, which leads to an unnecessary I/O. To repair these invalid indexes to be valid indexes, we have to either reindex the index, or drop the index concurrently and then recreate it again. Use the following query to get the list of invalid indexes:

```
SELECT COUNT(*) FROM pg_index WHERE indisvalid IS FALSE;
```

Combined indexes

In this recipe, we will be discussing how PostgreSQL combines multiple indexes to produce desired results.

Getting ready

When the query has a predicate with multiple columns and each column has associated with an index then the optimizer combines all the index results to fetch the desired results.

How to do it...

For demonstration, let's query the database as follows:

```
benchmarksql=# EXPLAIN SELECT * FROM bmsql_item WHERE i_data = 'Item Name'
OR i_price = 3;
                                  QUERY PLAN
---------------------------------------------------------------------------
----------
 Bitmap Heap Scan on bmsql_item  (cost=8.82..60.67 rows=14 width=71)
   Recheck Cond: (((i_data)::text = 'Item Name'::text) OR (i_price =
```

```
'3'::numeric))
   -> BitmapOr  (cost=8.82..8.82 rows=14 width=0)
   -> Bitmap Index Scan on data_idx  (cost=0.00..4.45 rows=4 width=0)
     Index Cond: ((i_data)::text = 'Item Name'::text)
   -> Bitmap Index Scan on price_idx  (cost=0.00..4.37 rows=10 width=0)
     Index Cond: (i_price = '3'::numeric)
(7 rows)
```

How it works...

In the preceding example, the optimizer performed two bitmap index scans and combined the results with the bitmap OR operator, which finally performed the bitmap heap scan.

> Refer to the following URL for more information about combined indexes: https://www.postgresql.org/docs/9.6/static/indexes-bitmap-scans.html.

Partial indexes

In this recipe, we will be discussing how to create an index for the required data sample set.

Getting ready

Using partial indexes, we can reduce the size of an index by adding a predicate in the index definition. That is, only the entries that match the predicate will only be indexed instead of all of them. This partial index will be utilized when the index predicate satisfies the submitted SQL predicate.

How to do it...

For example, let's say that our application does a frequent query on bmsql_item as to list all the items that have a price between $5 to $10, then it is a candidate predicate to create a partial index as follows:

```
benchmarksql=# CREATE INDEX CONCURRENTLY part_idx ON bmsql_item(i_price)
WHERE i_price BETWEEN 5 AND 10;
CREATE INDEX
```

Let's query the table so as to return the items that have a cost between 5 and 10:

```
benchmarksql=# EXPLAIN SELECT * FROM bmsql_item WHERE i_price BETWEEN 5 AND
10;
                                  QUERY PLAN
-----------------------------------------------------------------------------
-------
Index Scan using part_idx on bmsql_item  (cost=0.28..206.97 rows=4979
width=72)
(1 row)
```

How it works...

As aforementioned, when the submitted SQL predicate matches with the partial index predicate, then that index will be preferred. This might happen during the parameterized SQL too. Parameterized SQL statements will pick the partial index, as per the submitted parameters. Consider the following example, where the parameterized SQL query picks the partial index when the given range falls under the index predicate:

```
benchmarksql=# PREPARE params(int, int) AS SELECT * FROM bmsql_item WHERE
i_price BETWEEN $1 AND $2;
PREPARE
benchmarksql=# EXPLAIN EXECUTE params(4, 6);
                                  QUERY PLAN
-----------------------------------------------------------------------------
Seq Scan on bmsql_item  (cost=0.00..2800.00 rows=2035 width=72)
  Filter: ((i_price >= '4'::numeric) AND (i_price <= '6'::numeric))
(2 rows)

benchmarksql=# EXPLAIN EXECUTE params(5, 6);
                                  QUERY PLAN
-----------------------------------------------------------------------------
-----
Index Scan using part_idx on bmsql_item  (cost=0.28..50.87 rows=1005
width=72)
  Index Cond: (i_price <= '6'::numeric)
(2 rows)
```

Finding unused indexes

In this recipe, we will be discussing how to find the unused indexes from their creation time, which is utilizing the unnecessary I/O.

Getting ready

In a database, unused indexes will cause an unnecessary I/O for each write operation to be written into a table. To find these unused indexes, we have to depend on the number of scans that an index has performed as of that moment. From the time of index creation, if the index scan count is zero and the index is not a primary key index, then we can treat that as an unused index.

> To get the number of index scans of a table, we have to depend on PostgreSQL statistical counters. However, these counters can be reset to zero using `pg_stat_reset()`. It would be wise to check when was the last time the stats were reset, using the `stats_reset` column from the `pg_stat_database` view.

How to do it...

Let's run the following query to get the list of unused indexes from the database:

```
benchmarksql=# SELECT
indrelid::regclass tab_name,pi.indexrelid::regclass
   unused_index
FROM
pg_index pi, pg_stat_user_indexes psui
WHERE pi.indexrelid=psui.indexrelid AND NOT indisunique AND
   0idx_scan=0;
tab_name      |     unused_index
-----------------+----------------------
bmsql_customer | bmsql_customer_idx1
bmsql_district | d_state_idx
bmsql_item     | pric_idx
bmsql_customer | zip_idx
bmsql_item     | pric_idx1
bmsql_item     | data_idx
(6 rows)
```

Rather than dropping these unused indexes immediately, let's make all these indexes as invalid and then observe the application behavior for a certain time and then drop them using the CONCURRENTLY option:

```
UPDATE pg_index SET indisvalid = false
WHERE indexrelid::regclass::text IN ( < Unused indexes > );
```

How it works...

As aforementioned, once the index is marked as invalid, then it won't be used for any queries. If a table is clustered with that index, then it will also ignore the index scan and do the normal sequential scan on the table. After making the unused indexes as invalid, if we do not find any application performance issues, then it is a good sign that we should drop those indexes permanently.

Forcing a query to use an index

In this recipe, we will be discussing how to force a query to pick an index.

Getting ready

As we discussed in the previous chapters, the optimizer generates a set of plans based on the statistics it collected. Among all these plans, whatever plan has the least cost value would be preferred as a final execution plan of that query. Forcing a specific index to the SQL query is not possible in the current release of PostgreSQL; however, you can somehow guide the planner to pick the index scan over the other bitmap and sequential scans by disabling the session level optimizer parameters. Otherwise, you have to change the arbitrary cost value of `random_page_cost` so that it is close to the value of the `seq_page_cost` parameter.

How to do it...

Let's write a sample SQL query that prefers the sequential scan, as follows:

```
benchmarksql=# EXPLAIN ANALYZE SELECT COUNT(*) FROM bmsql_item WHERE
i_price BETWEEN 10 AND 80;
                                                    QUERY PLAN
----------------------------------------------------------------------------
-----------------------------------------------
Aggregate  (cost=2976.67..2976.68 rows=1 width=8) (actual
time=47.900..47.900 rows=1 loops=1)
   -> Seq Scan on bmsql_item  (cost=0.00..2800.00 rows=70669 width=0)
(actual time=3.341..40.537 rows=70947 loops=1)
     Filter: ((i_price >= '10'::numeric) AND (i_price <= '80'::numeric))
     Rows Removed by Filter: 29053
Planning time: 0.168 ms
Execution time: 47.936 ms
```

```
(6 rows)
```

Let's force the index scan for the same query by reducing the `random_page_cost` value so that it is near to 1 (default `seq_page_cost`):

```
benchmarksql=# SET random_page_cost TO 0.9;
SET
benchmarksql=# EXPLAIN ANALYZE SELECT COUNT(*) FROM bmsql_item WHERE
i_price BETWEEN 10 AND 80;
                                                          QUERY PLAN
-------------------------------------------------------------------------
-------------------------------------------------------------
Aggregate  (cost=2685.65..2685.66 rows=1 width=8) (actual
time=34.134..34.134 rows=1 loops=1)
   ->  Index Only Scan using pric_idx1 on bmsql_item  (cost=0.29..2508.97
rows=70669 width=0) (actual time=0.054..27.760 rows=70947 loops=1)
      Index Cond: ((i_price >= '10'::numeric) AND (i_price <= '80'::numeric))
Heap Fetches: 70947
Planning time: 0.187 ms
Execution time: 34.176 ms
(6 rows)
```

We will also get the same behavior if we turn off the `enable_seqscan` parameter.

How it works...

In the preceding example, as we set the `random_page_cost` value to `0.9`, the optimizer got the final cost value of the index only scan as `2685.66`, which is `2976.68` in the sequential scan plan.

Detecting a missing index

In this recipe, we will be discussing how to identify the tables that need to be indexed.

Getting ready

To find the missing indexes in a database is a tricky task. To find the missing indexes on a table, we have to use the sequential, index scan counter values from the catalog tables. In case we see too many sequential scans on a table, then we can't confirm that the table is a candidate for the index. To confirm this, we have to analyze the queries that we execute on that table using hypothetical indexes.

In general, it is always recommended that you create indexes on foreign key columns, as it helps the query to choose an index while joining parent and child tables. The foreign key's index also improves the key validation among child and parent tables. It is also recommended that you create indexes on the child tables, while creating child tables by inheriting from parent tables.

How to do it...

Let's query the database as to whether the delta of `seq_scan`, `idx_scan` is greater than a certain number, as shown here:

```
benchmarksql=# SELECT relname, seq_scan-idx_scan delta FROM
pg_stat_user_tables WHERE seq_scan-idx_scan >0;
   relname   | delta
-------------+-------
 bmsql_item  |     8
(1 row)
```

Now let's get the list of queries that our business logic implemented on the preceding `bmsql_item` table, and then identify the candidate for the index creation.

How it works...

Before creating any index on the table, it would be good to check whether the newly created index will be used in the required SQL statements. To get this confirmation about the indexes, we have to create hypothetical indexes using the HypoPG extension.

> You can find more information about this extension at the following URL: https://github.com/dalibo/hypopg.

Index

C

cache
  clearing 261, 263, 264
checkpoint
  overhead, identifying 50
  URL 51
checksums
  enabling 194
clustering
  against index 321
  reference link 322
cold cache
  about 257, 258
  working 261
combined indexes
  about 324
  reference link 325
Completely Fair Queuing (CFQ) 48
concurrent 323
concurrent indexes
  creating 322
connection pooling
  configuring, with PgBouncer 82
  implementing, with PgBouncer 82
connection-related parameters
  listen_addresses 35
  max_connections 36
  port 36
  superuser_reserved_connections 36
  tuning 35
  unix_socket_directory 36
  unix_socket_permissions 36
CPU bottlenecks
  identifying 62, 63
CPU consuming processes
  tracking 60
CPU load
  monitoring 61
CPU scheduling parameters
  about 46
  kernel.sched_autogroup_enabled 47
  kernel.sched_latency_ns 47
  kernel.sched_migration_cost_ns 48
  kernel.sched_min_granularity_ns 47

  kernel.sched_wakeup_granularity_ns 47
CPU speed
  benchmarking 8
  benchmarking, reference link 8
  benchmarking, with Phoronix 8, 10
  benchmarking, with sysbench 10
CPU usage
  monitoring 56, 57
CREATE AGGREGATE
  URL 284
CTE (Common Table Expression) scans
  about 285
  performing 285
  recursive union 288
  working 286
current running SQL commands
  obtaining 173, 174

D

data replicating
  from Oracle to PostgreSQL, Goldengate used
    236, 238, 240, 241, 242, 246, 248, 249
database corruption 193
database
  monitoring 169
  performance 170
  server, restarting 34
dead tuples
  generation, controlling 227
deadlocks
  troubleshooting 182, 183
  troubleshooting, advisory locks used 184
  troubleshooting, FOR UPDATE used 183
disk growth
  estimating, with pgbench took 22
  estimating, with pgbench tool 21
disk I/O bottlenecks
  identifying 63, 64
disk I/O schedulers
  about 48
  CFQ 49
  deadline 49
  noop 49
disk IOPS
  benchmarking, with open source tools 19, 21

shared_buffers 25
work_mem 25
PostgreSQL server
  memory units 41
  starting, manually 30
  stopping 31, 32
  stopping, in emergency 32
  URL 26, 232
postgresql.conf file, parameters
  archive_command 109
  archive_mode 109
  Listen_Addresse 109
  max_wal_senders 109
  wal_keep_segments 109
  wal_level 109
prepared transaction locks 179

Q

query optimization
  performing 252
query plan node structure
  about 264, 265
  working 265
query-related parameters
  tuning 36, 37, 38, 39
query
  forcing, to use index 328
  measuring 310

R

recovery.conf file, parameters
  primary_conninfo 110
  standby_mode 110
  trigger_file 110
Redundant Array of Interdependent Disks (RAID)
  about 23
  levels 22
  RAID 0 23
  RAID 1 24
  RAID 10 24
  RAID 5 24
  RAID 6 24
  references 24
replica
  creating, with repmgr 163, 165

creating, with Walctl 168
repmgr
  setting up 160
  URL 160
  used, for creating replica 163, 165
repository packages
  URL 124
routine reindexing
  about 197
  performing 198, 200
  working 200

S

sample data sets
  using 252, 254
semi join
  about 306
  performing 306
  working 307
sequential scans
  about 274, 320
  running 273, 274
  versus index scans 318
  working 275
server configuration
  reloading 33
set operations
  about 299
  demonstrating 300, 301
  EXCEPT 304
  INTERSECT 302, 303
  UNION 305
  working with 299, 301
shared buffers 259
SKIP LOCKED usage 181
skytools 3.2
  URL 116
Slony
  URL 111, 115
  used, for replication 111
slow statements
  logging 188
  working 189
statistical information
  URL 203

www.ingramcontent.com/pod-product-compliance
Lightning Source LLC
Chambersburg PA
CBHW080905220326

41598CB00034B/5483